Praise for So...

Sober Living for the Revolution is a ... compilation with passionate manifesto... insightful articles and inspiring stories tha... demonstrate the radical potential of a sober lifestyle. With perspectives from straight edgers involved in various struggles the world over, thi... ok is not just for (sXe) hardcore nerds, bu... yone willing to put aside prejudices and ... out about the impact straight edge has a... n have on radical politics.

Splitz – Projekt X, Vienna, Austria

Wh... nk has become the soundtrack for l... ruises, and most bands think they ... ommercial licensing deals to surv... collection inspires resistance to Co... sm in all its forms. Combining con... al style with rigorous scholarship ... an essential exploration of the exp... ssibilities at the intersection of stra... e, punk rock and political action. You ... have to pour all your booze in the sink ... ou should read this book.

K...s Lefcoe – writer/director of Public Domain and Tiny Riot Project

... is as important for radicals who dri... for those who don't. Its international sco... what makes it so appealing, talking abo... he development of political punk/hard... re throughout much of the world. Plu... here's no way you can put down this boo... nd still believe that all straightedge punks are a bunch of hardline asshole jocks.

Margaret Killjoy – editor of Mythmakers & Lawbreakers: Anarchist Writers on Fiction

...discover something new!

Michael Kirchner – compassion|media, co-director of Edge - Perspectives on Drug Free Culture

At last a book that gives a voice to the "other edge": the edge that searches for a political and social transformation, not only in the U$, but around the world. The value of its well chosen interviews and essays resides in decentralizing straight edge history by exploring its radical politics and its global manifestations.

Diego Paredes – Colectivo Res gestae, Red Libertaria Popular Mateo Kramer, Bogotá, Colombia

This is a great international(ist) sidekick to the recent avalanche of books about American-only hardcore. Instead of just crazy tales and funny characters, the story here is kids, all over the globe, pre-internet, taking the original straightedge idea one step further, adapting it to different realities and trying to empower it by connecting it to a broader political and social context. If you want to know what happened between the early days of hardcore and the nostalgic/fashioncore era of the 00's, look no further.

Pedro Carvalho – Newspeak, I Shot Cyrus, B.U.S.H., São Paulo, Brazil

Many ways of life have revolutionary potential: the lumpenproletariat, the anarcho-syndicalist industrial workforce, the disaffected petty-bourgeoisie, and, of course, punk. Getting pissed as a fart is a typical part of these lifestyles (and I like that!), but it might not always (or ever) contribute to overthrowing social structures of oppression, inside and outside of our scenes. This collection provides crucial and self-critical insights on, well, sober living for the revolution – without just preaching to the already converted. *Highly* recommended!

Peter Seyferth – Pogorausch Beer & Booze, Munich, Germany

No myths, no bummer, no bullshit! At least I can fucking read this sober book.

Johannes Ullmaier – co-editor of Testcard: Beiträge zur Popgeschichte

I remember so well my first Seein Red concert... The anger about issues in society was expressed in this raging, fast and furious music in this really energetic way – which made complete sense to me and which I could completely relate to. This is something I remembered by reading these interviews and articles – and it sparked my enthusiasm once again.

It's always great to read how people are trying to make a radical change by combining personal and social choices with a broader political perspective in a positive sense, with the idea of building up something. These texts are not just about rage and frustration, not just about anger, but also about an effort to create an alternative, more constructive way to deal with life.

Sanne – Het Fort van Sjakoo, Amsterdam, The Netherlands

This clamour of voices, essays, and manifestos shows that there's more to nay-saying the intoxication culture than male posturing and aggressive dogma. With interventions by queers, the sXe sisterhood, and anti-imperialists, alongside many other activist goals and players, *Sober Living for the Revolution* creates a gloriously messy tale of straight edge history and idealism, told with unfailing passion and an eye for challenging the scenes' own myths and shortcomings. Straight up, this book dares to document, talk back, and re-engage the sXe idea of creating community through putting original pleasure, dissent, and care back centre stage.

Red Chidgey – DIY activist historian, www.grassrootsfeminism.net

A refreshing addition to the ongoing documentation of punk and political subculture, this book accomplishes the remarkable task of being highly relevant both as a focused academic resource about political straight edge and as a source of potential inspiration for a broad range of activists who want to change the world. Kuhn captures the visions and ideas of key straight edge figures from various generations and from around the world in order to present a multi-faceted and fascinating read regardless of whether one was previously familiar with straight edge subculture or not. We all face the challenge of seeking change in a world where profit is made by clouding the minds of tired souls. The existence – and prevalence – of a straight edge movement with progressive elements needs to be remembered and examined. If nothing else, this book should help set the record "straight."

Troy Eeyore – Kingdom Scum

Sober Living for the Revolution

Hardcore Punk, Straight Edge, and Radical Politics

Gabriel Kuhn (ed.)

Sober Living for the Revolution: Hardcore Punk, Straight Edge And Radical Politics
Edited by Gabriel Kuhn
ISBN: 978-1-60486-051-1
LCCN: 2009901398
This edition copyright ©2010 PM Press
Copyright for work contained within this book remains with the original writers.
All Rights Reserved

PM Press
PO Box 23912
Oakland, CA 94623
www.pmpress.org

Layout by Daniel Meltzer
Cover art by John Yates
Back Cover Photograph by Nina Hansson (Umeå, Sweden, 2009)

Printed in the USA, on recycled paper

Table of Contents

Timeline 8
Introduction 12

Chapter 1: Bands
- **Minor Threat** - Interview with Ian MacKaye 22
- **ManLiftingBanner** - Interview with Michiel Bakker, Olav van den Berg, and Paul van den Berg 44
- **Refused** - Interview with Dennis Lyxzén 53
  The Shape of Punk to Come 63
- **Point of No Return** - Bending to Stay Straight 67
  Interview with Frederico Freitas 87
- **New Winds** - Interview with Bruno "Break" Teixeira 97

Chapter 2: Scenes
- **Israel** - Interview with Jonathan Pollack 110
- **Sweden** - Interview with Tanja 118
  Interview with Gabriel Cárdenas 128
- **Poland** - Interview with Robert Matusiak 130
- **USA** - Interview with Kurt Schroeder 149

Chapter 3: Manifestos
- **XsaraqaelX** - The Antifa Straight Edge 154
  Interview with XsaraqaelX 160
- **CrimethInc.** - Wasted Indeed: Anarchy and Alcohol . 164
  Interview with CrimethInc. agent Carrie No Nation ... 172
- **Nick Riotfag** - Towards a Less Fucked Up World: Sobriety and Anarchist Struggle 176
  Afterword: Towards a Less Fucked Up World: Five Years and Counting 193

Chapter 4: Reflections

- **Nick Riotfag** - My Edge Is Anything But Straight: Towards a Radical Queer Critique of Intoxication Culture 200
- **Lucas** - "The Only Thing I'm Drunk on is Cock" (Interview)... 213
- **Jenni Ramme** - Emancypunx (Interview) 218
- **Kelly (Brother) Leonard** - xsisterhoodx (Interview) ... 233
- **Bull Gervasi** - When the Edge Turns Crust (Interview) 240
- **Andy Hurley** - Straight Edge, Anarcho-Primitivism, and the Collapse (Interview)................ 247

Chapter 5: Perspectives

- **Federico Gomez** - Hardcore Networks (Interview).... 260
- **Santiago Gomez** - Between Culture and Politics: Straight Edge as Intuitive Resistance 266
- **Laura Synthesis** - Queen of the PC Police 278
- **Ross Haenfler** - Why I'm Still Straight Edge 282
- **Mark Andersen** - Building Bridges, Not Barriers: Positive Force DC, Straight Edge, and Revolution..... 286

Timeline

This timeline is meant to be a reference guide for the readers of this book. It does not claim to offer an exhaustive overview of straight edge history. While one intention was to include "objectively" important periods, bands, and events, another was to focus on aspects of straight edge history that are of particular relevance to this volume.

While there have been straight edge scenes in Australia/New Zealand and several Asian countries since the late 1980s, the lack of international recognition they have received puts them beyond the scope of this project. Their history is for others to write.

Key
- North America
- Europe & Israel
- Latin America

1978 — 1st wave of Washington, DC, hardcore: Bad Brains, Teen Idles, Untouchables, S.O.A., Minor Threat, The Faith

1979

1980 — Dischord Records founded; Lärm (Netherlands) pioneers sXe in Europe

1981 — Early Boston sXe scene: SSD, DYS; 7 Seconds (Reno, NV) becomes defining sXe band

1982

1983

- First Positive Force punk collective founded in Reno, NV
- 2nd wave of Washington, DC, hardcore, often considered the beginning of "emocore": Embrace, Rites of Spring

1984

1985

- "Revolution Summer" in Washington, DC. Positive Force, DC, founded
- 1st strong wave of European hardcore, including some sXe bands, particularly in the Netherlands: Profound, Crivits, Betray
- "Youth crew" (later known as "old school") sXe: Slapshot (Boston), Youth of Today, Gorilla Biscuits, Bold, Judge, Wide Awake (NYC/Connecticut), Uniform Choice, Insted, Chain of Strength (California)

1986

1987

- Revelation Records founded

1988

1989

- First sXe-influenced band forms in Brazil: No Violence
- Crucial Response, defining label for European sXe, founded in Germany

1990

- Beginning of a political sXe scene in São Paulo, Brazil: Clear Heads, Personal Choice, Positive Minds
- Left-wing ("commie") European sXe develops: ManLiftingBanner (Netherlands), Nations on Fire (Belgium)
- Blindfold (Belgium) becomes influential emo sXe band.
- H8000 hardcore scene, including many sXe bands, develops in West Flanders, Belgium

1991

- Politically conscious sXe scenes develop in various countries: Poland (Cymeon X), Portugal (X-Acto), Israel (Nekhei Naatza)
- Vegan Straight Edge develops, centered in Syracuse, NY, around the band Earth Crisis

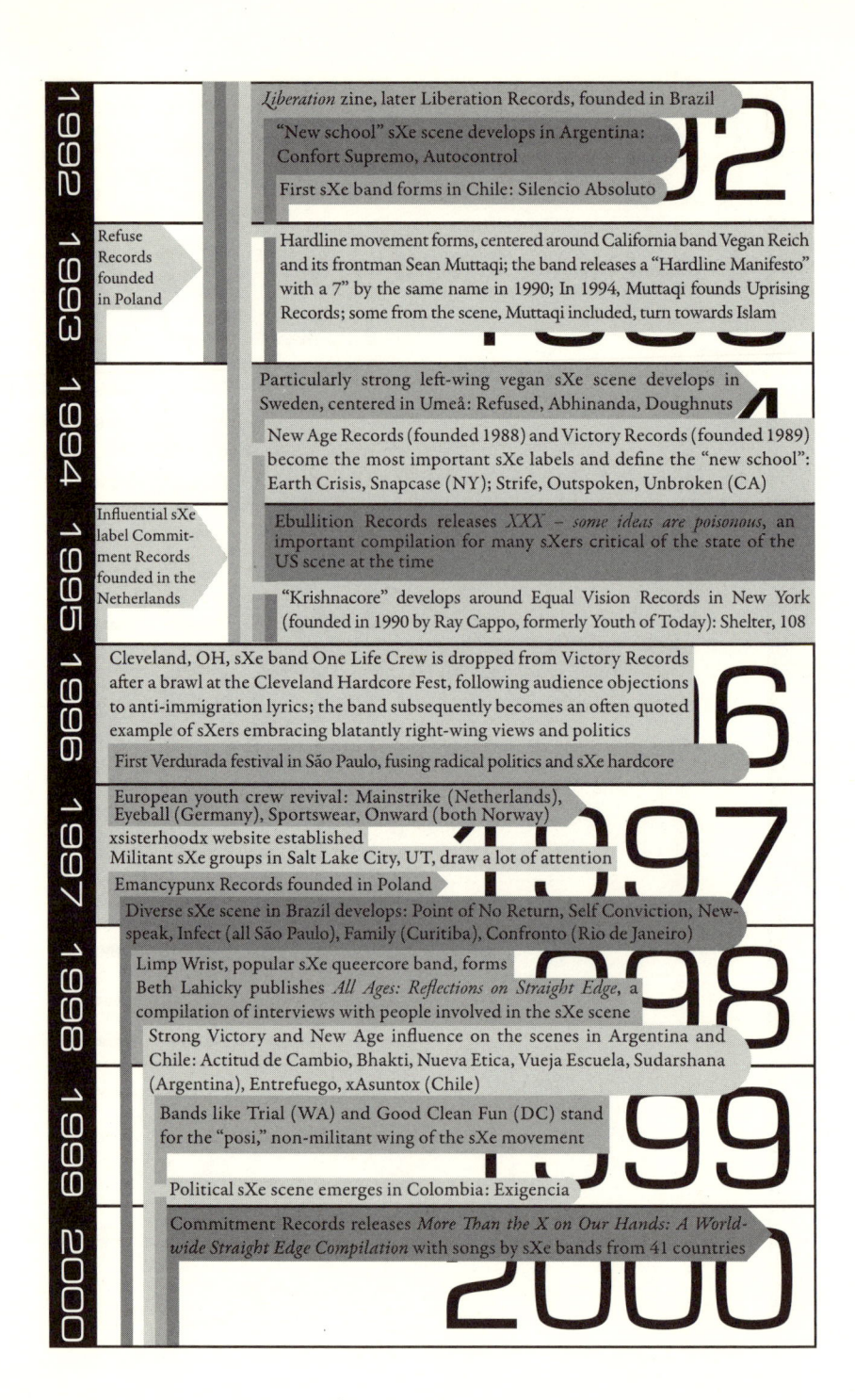

1992
- *Liberation* zine, later Liberation Records, founded in Brazil
- "New school" sXe scene develops in Argentina: Confort Supremo, Autocontrol
- First sXe band forms in Chile: Silencio Absoluto

1993
- Refuse Records founded in Poland
- Hardline movement forms, centered around California band Vegan Reich and its frontman Sean Muttaqi; the band releases a "Hardline Manifesto" with a 7" by the same name in 1990; In 1994, Muttaqi founds Uprising Records; some from the scene, Muttaqi included, turn towards Islam

1994
- Particularly strong left-wing vegan sXe scene develops in Sweden, centered in Umeå: Refused, Abhinanda, Doughnuts
- New Age Records (founded 1988) and Victory Records (founded 1989) become the most important sXe labels and define the "new school": Earth Crisis, Snapcase (NY); Strife, Outspoken, Unbroken (CA)

1995
- Influential sXe label Commitment Records founded in the Netherlands
- Ebullition Records releases *XXX – some ideas are poisonous*, an important compilation for many sXers critical of the state of the US scene at the time
- "Krishnacore" develops around Equal Vision Records in New York (founded in 1990 by Ray Cappo, formerly Youth of Today): Shelter, 108

1996
- Cleveland, OH, sXe band One Life Crew is dropped from Victory Records after a brawl at the Cleveland Hardcore Fest, following audience objections to anti-immigration lyrics; the band subsequently becomes an often quoted example of sXers embracing blatantly right-wing views and politics
- First Verdurada festival in São Paulo, fusing radical politics and sXe hardcore

1997
- European youth crew revival: Mainstrike (Netherlands), Eyeball (Germany), Sportswear, Onward (both Norway)
- xsisterhoodx website established
- Militant sXe groups in Salt Lake City, UT, draw a lot of attention
- Emancypunx Records founded in Poland

1998
- Diverse sXe scene in Brazil develops: Point of No Return, Self Conviction, Newspeak, Infect (all São Paulo), Family (Curitiba), Confronto (Rio de Janeiro)
- Limp Wrist, popular sXe queercore band, forms
- Beth Lahicky publishes *All Ages: Reflections on Straight Edge*, a compilation of interviews with people involved in the sXe scene
- Strong Victory and New Age influence on the scenes in Argentina and Chile: Actitud de Cambio, Bhakti, Nueva Etica, Vueja Escuela, Sudarshana (Argentina), Entrefuego, xAsuntox (Chile)

1999
- Bands like Trial (WA) and Good Clean Fun (DC) stand for the "posi," non-militant wing of the sXe movement
- Political sXe scene emerges in Colombia: Exigencia

2000
- Commitment Records releases *More Than the X on Our Hands: A Worldwide Straight Edge Compilation* with songs by sXe bands from 41 countries

2001
- Strong connection between the political sXe scene and the global justice movement in various Latin American countries
- Catalyst Records (founded 1993) develops into the most important political sXe label in the US: Birthright, Risen (both IN), 7 Generations, Gather (both CA), Point of No Return (Brazil)

2002

2003

2004
- "Total Liberation Tour," blending music and politics at ten events across the US in July, features a number of vegan sXe bands and coincides with a revival of the scene
- Several "old school" sXe reunion tours, e.g. Bold, Youth of Today, Gorilla Biscuits

2005

2006
- New Wave of European sXe, strong emphasis on animal rights: Hoods Up (Germany), Eye of Judgement (Netherlands), True Colors (Belgium)
- Ross Haenfler publishes *Straight Edge: Clean-Living Youth, Hardcore Punk, and Social Change*. Robert T. Wood publishes *Straightedge Youth: Complexity and Contradictions of a Subculture*

2007
- Raymond McCrea Jones publishes the photo book *Faces of Straight Edge*

2008
- The National Geographic documentary *Inside Straight Edge* focuses on the gang classification of sXe in Salt Lake City, UT, and Reno, NV

2009
- Brian Paterson publishes *Burning Fight: The Nineties Hardcore Revolution in Ethics, Politics, Spirits, and Sound*; the book includes many interviews with influential 1990s US sXe bands
- Refuse Records publishes the book *The Past The Present 1982-2007: A History of 25 Years of European Straight Edge* by Marc Hanou and Jean-Paul Frijns, released in connection with a Birds of a Feather album
- German radical media collective compassion|media releases the documentary film *Edge: Perspectives on Drug Free Culture*, based on interviews with US sXe musicians and activists

Hoods Up (Germany), Hengelo/The Netherlands, 2007   Bartosz Skowron (bartskowron.com)

Introduction

Gabriel Kuhn

The history of the term "straight edge" in the hardcore punk community has been much more colorful and long-lasting than Ian MacKaye could have ever imagined. MacKaye, at the time singer in the Washington, DC, band Minor Threat, wrote the lyrics to the song "Straight Edge" in 1981:

I'm a person just like you
But I've got better things to do
Than sit around and fuck my head
Hang out with the living dead
Snort white shit up my nose
Pass out at the shows
I don't even think about speed
That's something I just don't need
I've got the straight edge

I'm a person just like you
But I've got better things to do
Than sit around and smoke dope
Cause I know that I can cope
Laugh at the thought of eating ludes
Laugh at the thought of sniffing glue
Always gonna keep in touch
Never want to use a crutch
I've got the straight edge

Against both expectations and intentions, these lyrics would not only provide a label embraced by scores of drug-free hardcore punk kids, they came to spawn a self-identified straight edge movement spreading around the world and remaining a vital part of the hardcore punk community to this day.

The US history of the movement has recently been traced by Ross Haenfler in the book *Straight Edge: Clean-Living Youth, Hardcore Punk, and Social Change* (2006), a study that is highly recommended to anyone interested in the straight edge phenomenon.

A superb history of straight edge from an international perspective is provided by the Brazilian band Point of No Return in their essay "Bending to Stay Straight," which is included in this volume.

Roughly speaking — numerous exceptions will be encountered throughout the book — straight edge history can be divided into four phases:

1. The early days of Washington, DC, hardcore punk when straight edge ethics became a prominent part of a fledgling and visionary underground scene — roughly 1980 to 1983.

2. The first wave of self-identified straight edge bands across North America, often referred to as the "youth crew movement" — roughly 1984 to 1990.

3. The "new school" straight edge bands of the 1990s, strongly characterized by the increasing significance of animal rights, hence often known as the "vegan straight edge movement," with the so-called "hardline movement" as its most ardent wing — roughly 1991 to 1999.

4. A rather diverse global straight edge movement, including old school revivals as much as vegan straight edge reunion tours, straight edge pop bands as much as straight edge power violence bands, and anti-materialist attitudes as much as a lucrative straight edge merchandise industry — roughly 2000 to present.

A more detailed timeline, intended to help situate the contributions to this book, is included above.

While the core of straight edge identity has always been the abstinence from alcohol, nicotine, and common illegal drugs such as cannabis, amphetamines, LSD etc., there have been considerable variations on how far to take the interpretations of "abstaining from intoxicants" or "living drug-free." Many heated discussions have concerned the consumption of caffeine, the use of animal products, or sexual conduct. Disagreements often relate to the primary reasons for living straight edge. Is it simply to remain "sober"? Is it to "avoid cruelty"? Is it to be "anti-consumerist"? Is it to attain "moral purity"? These questions — and many others — will be discussed in this collection.

Straight edge politics have varied significantly, from the explicitly revolutionary to the outright conservative. It is the latter strain that has dominated — at least in public perception.

The overall impression of straight edge within radical political circles has been negative as well. While the early Washington, DC, hardcore punk underground is usually praised for its commitment to positive social change, both the youth crew movement of the 1980s and the vegan straight edge movement of the 1990s have drawn much criticism. While the critique of the former largely focused on male bonding ("brotherhood," "wolfpack"), martial posturing ("true till death," "nailed to the X"), and the lack of political perspective beyond vague affirmations of "youth" and "unity," the latter was criticized for self-righteous militancy, a reductionist focus on animal rights and environmental issues, and an ethical fundamentalism that, in its worst forms, resembled reactionary Christian doctrines: condemnation of premarital sex, abortion, homosexuality etc.

Both movements have been accused of extreme male dominance, violent behavior, intolerance, and an inability to detach their sober principles from a moralistic puritan tradition. These images seemed further confirmed by severe clashes between straight edge youth and rival groups in Salt Lake City, Utah, and Reno, Nevada, which left people badly injured and even dead. The subsequent classification of straight edge as a "gang" by the cities' police departments was much exploited by the corporate media.

For all these reasons, straight edge has been approached by many radical activists with a strong dose of skepticism, often ridicule, and sometimes unabashed hostility. Despite the ideologically less dogmatic and more multifaceted character of contemporary straight edge, reservations remain strong.

However, there has always been a "different edge": engaged in political struggle and social transformation, but not judgmental, belligerent, or narrow-minded. This is what will be presented in this book. The aim is not to define the "true meaning" of straight edge. There is no intention to engage in pointless definitional battles. The intention is to demonstrate that there has always been a strain of radical, politically conscious straight edge culture that has manifested itself in many different forms.

Needless to say, understandings of "radical" differ. In the context of this book, the attribute refers to people who **a)** actively pursue a fundamental (radical) social change in order to create free and egalitarian communities, and **b)** maintain a clear distance to politically ambiguous ideologies. Hence straight edge activists affiliated to religious groups or belief systems will be as much absent as those representatives of the 1990s vegan straight edge scene whose political legacy remains in doubt. This is neither to deny the progressive potentials of religious movements nor to pass judgment on any particular scene. It is merely an expression of the frame that I, as an editor, felt most comfortable with. I understand and appreciate that other frames could have been used — and hope others understand and appreciate the one I have chosen.

Apart from an involvement in radical politics in its myriad forms, all the contributors to this volume are or have been connected in one way or another to hardcore punk straight edge culture: as artists, organizers, or activists. This is why the book is about straight edge and radical politics, not about sobriety or drug-free living and radical politics. The latter book would be very different, accounting for a wide range of radicals, from Andalusian anarchist teetotalers to American Indian Movement activists advocating abstinence to conscious hip hop artists like Dead Prez. Although I very much hope for such a book to be published, the focus of this volume is more specific.

The volume's contributors represent influential straight edge bands, scenes, and labels as much as radical political projects with straight edge sympathies and leanings. Despite shared convictions, the authors and interviewees cover a range of perspectives: from conceiving straight edge as a "lifestyle" to objecting to such a definition; from questioning the straight edge label to defending it; from describing straight edge as a central part of political activism to declaring it above all a personal choice. The contributors also differ in their interpretations of hardcore punk, the culture that straight edge is rooted in. Many readers will have their own understanding of the term. For those not versed in the culture and its vocabulary, the following very general definitions may serve as guidelines:

Punk: an anti-establishment counterculture, most notably expressed by provocative (anti)fashion and an aggressive minimalist ("three-chord") musical style, most iconically embodied by the British Sex Pistols in 1977.

Hardcore: first used as a synonym to punk in the US, developing into its own genre (often named hardcore punk) in the early to mid-1980s by favoring low-key visual aesthetics over extravagance and breaking with original punk rock song patterns.

DIY: a principle of independence and of retaining control over one's work, DIY (abbreviating *Do It Yourself*) defines original hardcore punk ethics and, to many, remains the decisive criterion for "true" hardcore punk; the most tangible aspects of hardcore punk's DIY culture are self-run record labels, self-organized shows, self-made zines, and non-commercial social networks.

Crew: commonly used in hardcore culture as a reference to a group of hardcore peers; particularly popular within straight edge during the so-called "youth crew" movement of the late 1980s.

To X up: the phrase refers to the most common straight edge symbol, the X painted on the back of your hand; the symbol's origins lie in minors being marked that way at shows so they could not drink; when the mark was turned into a self-affirming indication for drug-free living, it became a positive reference point for sober hardcore punk kids and has appeared in countless variations within straight edge culture since.

Posi: short for "positive," the term has been used to indicate straight edge bands and activists advocating social awareness and rejecting the self-righteous tendencies within the movement.

Hardcore punk eventually split into several sub-genres. Relevant for this volume are mainly the following (descriptions are necessarily simplified and further personal research is strongly recommended):

NYHC: common abbreviation for the hardcore scene that developed in New York City in the 1980s, often associated with aggressiveness and tough-guy bravado.

Grindcore: blends hardcore punk with metal, industrial, and noise, often with extreme speed; primarily used as a musical category.

Power Violence: characterized by distorted sounds, radical tempo changes, and short forceful songs, the genre shares grindcore's main influences.

Crust (or **crust punk**): taking its name from the "crusty" image of its adherents, crust developed its own aesthetic blend of 1977 British punk, roots culture, and black metal; visually, piercings mingle with dreadlocks and black clothing, while musically classic punk riffs meet death metal, grindcore, and power violence elements; generally considered politically conscious, often linked to the "anarcho-punk" movement, and outspokenly DIY and anti-consumerist.

Metalcore: mainly a musical category, it indicates a blend of hardcore and metal elements; popularized in the 1990s vegan straight edge scene, particularly by bands from the Victory and New Age record labels.

Emo (or **emocore**): a conscious attempt to go beyond the hardcore "tough guy" image, musically, lyrically, and image-wise.

Screamo: a variation on emo, considered more experimental and intense musically.

Riot grrrl: a feminist punk hardcore movement that emerged in the early 1990s.

Queercore/homocore: a fusion of hardcore and queer culture/politics.

Important hardcore punk periodicals include:

Maximumrocknroll (MRR) (1982 to present): founded by Tim Yohannan, *MRR* remains the key publication for the international hardcore punk community.

Profane Existence (1989 to present): one of the main voices of the anarcho-punk movement; based in Minneapolis, MN.

HeartattaCk (1994-2006): during its existence rivaled in importance for the hardcore punk underground only by *MRR*, and especially popular with a political and DIY-oriented audience; *HeartattaCk* had a straight edge editor in Ebullition Records founder Kent McClard, but was never run as a straight edge project.

Punk Planet (1994-2007): both in terms of design and contents, *Punk Planet* built important bridges between DIY hardcore punk and a wider audience interested in underground culture.

Hardcore punk scenes, including straight edge scenes, have always been predominantly male. In Western societies they have also remained largely white, despite notable exceptions — see, for example, James Spooner's documentary *Afro-Punk* (2003).

The image of male and white dominance has further been reinforced by the fact that many histories of hardcore punk have solely focused on North America. In this book, a conscious effort has been made to include voices that are often underrepresented. This means a strong international focus as well as a relatively strong presence of routinely overlooked minority groups within the scene. However, there seems little point in denying the demographics of straight edge culture by assembling an overly misrepresentative cast of contributors. Admitting to the culture's problems and engaging in critical debate seems mandatory.

The respective chapters only serve as vague markers. There are plenty of overlaps: the members of former straight edge bands talk about local scenes as much as the "Manifestos" reflect on straight edge culture or the chapter on "Perspectives" adds information to hardcore history. The chapters' main purpose lies in avoiding a completely random order of the volume's complex and rich contributions.

Chapter 1, **Bands**, provides a historical overview of political straight edge culture along the lines of highly influential bands: Ian MacKaye of Minor Threat talks about the origins of straight edge in the early Washington, DC, punk hardcore scene, critically reflects on the development of a "straight edge movement," and offers his own understanding of the term. Michiel Bakker, Olav van den Berg, and Paul van den Berg tell the story of the "original communist straight edge band," ManLiftingBanner, hailing from the Netherlands in the early 1990s. Dennis Lyxzén revisits the exploits of Sweden's unique punk hardcore outfit Refused and the strong impact it had on the Swedish vegan straight edge movement of the

1990s — one of the strongest left-wing straight edge movements in history. The interview is accompanied by the liner notes to the last Refused record, *The Shape of Punk to Come* (1998). Frederico Freitas of São Paulo's celebrated radical vegan straight edge band Point of No Return provides an overview of Latin American straight edge culture with a focus on its political ramifications. The interview is preceded by "Bending to Stay Straight," a Point of No Return essay about the history, values, and politics of the straight edge movement, originally included in the 2002 release *Liberdade Imposta, Liberdade Conquistada / Imposed Freedom, Conquered Freedom*. Bruno "Break" Teixeira, singer of Portugal's main straight edge export, New Winds, talks about the band's history, his personal blend of drug-free living and radical activism, and one of Europe's strongest recent political straight edge scenes.

Chapter 2, **Scenes**, focuses on countries and regions where significant radical straight edge scenes have developed: Jonathan Pollack, co-founder of Anarchists Against the Wall, an Israeli direct action group in support of Palestinian resistance, talks about the intriguing anarchist straight edge scene that appeared in Israel in the 1990s. Tanja, a longtime radical straight edge activist, provides further insight into Sweden's vegan straight edge movement of the same decade, while Gabriel Cárdenas adds an update on political straight edge in Sweden today. Robert Matusiak, founder of Warsaw's Refuse Records, one of the most important international labels for political straight edge, provides a sketch of the Eastern European straight edge scene and its conflicting political orientations reaching from antifascist crews to white power factions, particularly in Russia. Finally, Kurt Schroeder, a veteran of the US vegan straight edge scene of the 1990s and founder of Catalyst Records, globally renowned for its blend of straight edge hardcore and radical politics, reflects on developments in North America.

Chapter 3, **Manifestos**, brings together documents that have drawn explicit links between radical politics and sober living: "The Antifa Straight Edge" was published by Alpine Anarchist Productions in 2001, "Wasted Indeed: Anarchy and Alcohol" by the CrimethInc. Ex-Workers' Collective in 2003, and "Towards a Less Fucked Up World: Sobriety and Anarchist Struggle" by Nick Riotfag in 2005. Current updates by the authors follow the texts.

Chapter 4, **Reflections**, features pieces on often neglected aspects of straight edge culture. Nick Riotfag examines the relations between sobriety and queer culture in "My Edge Is Anything But Straight: Towards a Radical Queer Critique of Intoxication Culture," while the interview with drug-free and radical queer activist Lucas, "The Only Thing I'm Drunk on Is Cock," adds personal tales and thoughts. Jenni Ramme, founder of Poland's Emancypunx Records, home of the seminal 2003 *X The Sisterhood X* compilation, explores queer and feminist themes in her interview, while Kelly (Brother) Leonard shares her experiences of running xsisterhoodx, an online network for straight edge women. Bull Gervasi, bass player in Philadelphia's iconoclastic straight edge band R.A.M.B.O., ponders the difficult relations between straight edge and crust punk, while Andy Hurley, currently drumming for Fall Out Boy, outlines personal politics where veganism and straight edge meet anarcho-primitivist convictions.

Chapter 5, **Perspectives**, offers contemporary ideas on straight edge living and radical politics. Federico Gomez draws on his experience as a straight edge singer and political activist on three continents when stressing the importance of international networking. Santiago Gomez provides an in-depth analysis of both straight edge's radical potentials and conservative pitfalls in "Between Culture and Politics: Straight Edge as Intuitive Resistance." Laura Synthesis, founder of London's Synthesis zine distribution, takes a sharp look at the contemporary straight edge scene in "Queen of the PC Police." Ross Haenfler, author of the above-mentioned *Straight Edge: Clean-Living Youth, Hardcore Punk, and Social Change* explains "Why I'm Still Straight Edge," before Mark Andersen, co-founder of the punk activist collective Positive Force DC, closes the book with a touching appeal for straight edge's place within a broad radical movement in "Building Bridges, Not Barriers: Positive Force DC, Straight Edge, and Revolution."

Unless noted otherwise, the contributions are all original. The five reprints have been included with kind permission of the authors.

All the interviews were conducted between August and December 2008 in person, on the phone, via live chat, or over email; all were updated in June 2009. All the interviews were conducted by Gabriel Kuhn, except for the interview with XsaraqaelX, conducted by Daniel Freund, and the interview with Lucas, conducted by Nick Riotfag.

Since different spellings of "straight edge" have developed over the last twenty-five years — including "Straight Edge," "straightedge" and the abbreviations "sXe" and "SXE" — the choice was left to the authors. US spelling has been used in general, except for Laura Synthesis' essay that is kept in British English.

All photographers are listed. Significant contributions have come from Daigo Oliva and Mateus Mondini, two São Paulo based artists who dedicate a lot of their time to documenting the hardcore punk underground. They also issue a photo zine, *Fodido e Xerocado*. Mateus Mondini founded his own record label, Nada Nada Discos, in 2009.

Working on this volume has been a tremendously encouraging and joyful experience. It has confirmed the perseverance of a vigorous, caring, and inspirational global DIY hardcore movement that retains all of its political promises. The beauty of this movement is, to borrow one of Ian MacKaye's favorite phrases, *no joke*. I am tremendously grateful and indebted to everyone who has been involved in this project. While I had the privilege to put it together, it has truly been a collective effort — any editorial mishaps remain of course entirely my responsibility.

When I first planned this book, the idea was to create a valuable resource for a group of people I considered big enough to make such an effort worthwhile: namely, radical straight edge activists. Once the contributions began to trickle in, I realized that the book's appeal would be much wider and that its audience would extend far beyond this community.

The texts collected here ought to be of interest to anyone fascinated by the history of punk, hardcore, and underground culture; to students of sociology, social movements, and international politics; to seekers, existentialists, and philosophers; to radical activists, no matter their diets or drinking habits, and to sober folks, no matter their cultural adherences.

Bands

- **Minor Threat**
  Interview with Ian MacKaye

- **ManLiftingBanner**
  Interview with Michiel Bakker, Olav van den Berg, and Paul van den Berg

- **Refused**
  Interview with Dennis Lyxzén
  The Shape of Punk to Come

- **Point of No Return**
  Bending to Stay Straight
  Interview with Frederico Freitas

- **New Winds**
  Interview with Bruno "Break" Teixeira

Minor Threat
Interview with Ian MacKaye

Ian MacKaye was a founding member of the early 1980s Washington, DC, punk hardcore bands Teen Idles (1979/80) and Minor Threat (1980-83). He was one of the most important influences on the development of the US hardcore punk underground, and — albeit unwillingly — the instigator of the worldwide straight edge movement. The Minor Threat songs "Straight Edge," "In My Eyes," and "Out Of Step" remain the most referenced songs in straight edge communities. Ian continued his musical career with the bands Embrace (1985/86), Fugazi (1987 to present), and The Evens (2001 to present). He co-founded Dischord Records in 1980 and still runs the label out of "Dischord House" in Washington, DC.

Discography:
- *Minor Threat*, 1981, Dischord Records (EP)
- *In My Eyes*, 1981, Dischord Records (EP)
- *Out of Step*, 1983, Dischord Records
- *Salad Days*, 1985, Dischord Records (EP)
- *Live*, 1988, Dischord Records (DVD)
- *Complete Discography*, 1989, Dischord Records
- *First Demo Tape*, 2001, Dischord Records

Since you asked me about this the last time we spoke: I checked on how many white guys in their thirties and forties we have in the book. It's about twelve out of twenty.

That's not so bad. I mean, it's not that you are doing anything wrong. It's just that there exists a certain kind of people who put a claim on history; and this seems to be a particularly acute pathology amongst aging white dudes. It's like history should somehow be their province. I find this really disturbing. Mostly because I'm a white guy and I'm forty-six and a lot of people ask me about history, and I just don't want to be another one of them dudes, 'cause I don't claim history. That's also why I don't read a lot of punk histories, because, having been there, I started to understand how people who write histories — or about histories — ultimately tend to shape them into manageable narratives, and in doing so they pervert or distort the reality. And since I was there, it'd be difficult for me to read these books without going, "That just did not happen that way!"

Well, this book doesn't focus so much on history, I suppose. I think it's mostly about gathering people's thoughts on all sorts of issues. I mean, sure, I'll ask

Opposite: Ian MacKaye, São Paulo, 2007 Daigo Oliva

people about history too, and I'll probably ask you a couple of questions about DC in the 80s, but I mean, you can dodge those if you don't want to talk about it...

Oh, I don't mind talking about it. It's just that I think of it more in terms of being somebody who's experienced something and is willing to share these experiences. The problem is that within our culture — and when I say our culture, I specifically mean American culture, but I think it extends to Western culture in general — there is a celebrity factor that makes people who are in the public eye appear to be all-important as opposed to those who just do their work and stay on point. There is the classic moment when people say, "Yes, and then punk, or hardcore, or straight edge, or whatever, died." But it always died when they left the picture or when their band split up. It seems that they are talking about an energy that was contained within them — whereas I see an energy that is a constant ever-flowing river. And this river has always been there, and it always will be there. And what this river ultimately stands for is the free space in which unconventional, unorthodox, contesting, and radical ideas can be presented.

When I first approached you concerning this project I sent an email saying that I wanted to talk about the "political dimensions of straight edge." You said that this set off alarm bells for you. Why was that?

I mainly said that because I was born and raised in Washington, DC, and people obviously associate me with the town and its politics. When you wrote that, I felt that you were perhaps trying to appeal to what you might have thought was my political leaning — like you would say, "Look I don't want to ask you about straight edge, I want to know more about the political stuff because you are from Washington, DC." And so I was like, whoa, I don't know what the political dimension would be in that case? I think a lot of people assume that because I live in Washington I'm really caught up in the kind of politicking in a way, because the White House is here, or the Congress.

However, what I really learned from living in a city in which you have an industry like the government was that the way to navigate these institutions is to never engage with them, and to work on the margins instead; to always work around them. There was a saying amongst the young punks here about how if you went to public schools in Washington, DC, you learned two basic things: one, how to wait in line; and two, never ask for permission because the answer is always no. So the thing to do was: just do it, don't ask for permission! At some point the authorities would come along and say, "You can't do that!" but then you just said, "Oh, I didn't know." If you had asked them, they would have just said no right away. Mainly because of the bureaucracy and the sludge of the administration. They just didn't want to do any extra work.

This played a really big part in the development of the punk scene: we didn't ask, we didn't get permission, we didn't get licenses, we didn't get copyrights, we didn't get trademarks, we didn't fill out any forms, we didn't get lawyers... We just rented rooms and put on shows, and we never formalized anything with the government whatsoever. We just put on these shows that were completely illegal, but nobody cared, because, essentially, you didn't give them the opportunity to care.

But taking that initiative without asking for permission is a political statement, right?

There is no doubt about that. See, email is a very stupid form of communication and I balked when the word "political" appeared. I don't know you, I'm not sitting with you, I can't understand you, I don't hear the tone of what you are saying. The word "political" is just a difficult word. Many people ask me whether Fugazi is a political band, or Minor Threat... Well, of course! Every band is political. Everything is political. Every action is political. But I think there are plenty of people who consider themselves political activists and who do not believe that these bands are political because they don't do this or they don't do that; like, they don't go to this particular protest, or they don't sign this particular petition, or on their liner notes they don't list this particular organization.

It just depends on what one's relationship with the word "politics" is. I know that in this country — at least during the last decade, but I would say probably during the last twenty or thirty years — the overarching dominant political party is not the Republican Party or the Democratic Party; it is the "Apathetic Party." For example, there are many bands that do not want to think about where they play, who they play for, how much they charge, what the arrangements and settings of their shows are, etc. These are people who feel like that's just not part of their world. This is an example of the politics of apathy.

When you say that everything is political, is that because everything we do affects others?

I guess I would say yes. I mean obviously everything we do — or don't do — has its effects. There are many ways to illustrate this. For example, for the life of me I cannot understand how bands would submit to playing shows that are limited to people over the age of twenty-one. I find it unconscionable. Today there are a significant number of people playing shows whose love of music goes back to seeing bands like Fugazi when they were fifteen or sixteen years old. However, now that they're in a band themselves this is somehow no longer relevant. And this is a political action on their part, because what they are saying is: we support the status quo, we support the corporations, and we do it because it's easier for us, because it's more convenient for us, and because it's more lucrative for us. So by not doing anything about this, they are making a very political statement — especially in this day and age when politics are governed by business.

Let me ask you about the famous "political" DC hardcore scene in the 80s. I think we've already clarified what you understand as political, so I'm not going to ask whether it was "really" political or not. But let me ask you this: was the involvement in what we might want to call "social struggles" — like anti-racism, gender and sexuality issues, support for the homeless, etc. — really a crucial part of the scene? I'm asking because you always hear conflicting reports. There are some who claim that this was important to the kids in the scene, while others say that it was all just about music and individual rebellion...

Who are all these people?

People who write books about the history of hardcore, for example...

Oh, okay. Well, punk, or underground music, or hardcore, or whatever you want to call it, is not singular. I mean, it is essentially a projection of every person. So, for instance, for people who filter things politically it was one thing, while for people who filter things purely through amusement it was another.

In my estimation, the early punk scene, in the late 70s and early 80s, was going through a birthing process, and every time something new is created you have friction. I think that in the early days much energy was being spent on recognizing that we were part of something new, and a lot of us were trying to get our minds around what the hell it was.

Punk rock in the beginning was so many different people who came from so many different places. They were all these outcasts, all these people who just did not fit in for various different reasons. Some people didn't fit in because they had troubles with their families; some people didn't fit in because of their sexuality; some didn't feel normal psychologically; some didn't feel normal politically. And all these sorts of margin walkers, these people who were outside, joined together and gathered under this new manifestation of the underground. And there was a lot to learn, a lot to take in, and there was also a sense of circling the wagons...

Like defense?

Yes, exactly. You create a position of defense. I think that's where a lot of the really tough guy posturing, the spiky hair, and the leather jackets came from. It was basically circling the wagons.

The activism came in where, coming out of the late 60s as a child, you felt that the government should never be trusted and that authority should always be questioned. In this sense, I was always interested in activism. The problem was that you had people, certain political activists, who only saw music as a way of raising money for their causes. They only had interest in bands when they played for their fundraisers. I reject that. There are probably some people in music who don't take politics seriously, but there are certainly many people in politics who don't take music seriously. But the thing about music and politics is that music was here *before politics*. Music was here *before language*. This is no fucking joke!

I know that the big industries have trivialized music in many ways by turning it into entertainment or amusement, but music as a point of gathering is something that goes back all the way to the beginning. So what I was often dealing with when talking to political people was an attitude like, "Well, we don't really care about your music, as long as you can generate an audience and we can get some money..." I remember with Fugazi, these people would come to us and would want us to play for them, and we'd say, "Okay, we do a $5 door," and they'd say, "Oh no, we should do a $25 door," and we'd say, "No, we do a $5 door." They were unable to appreciate our insistence of having a low door price, but *this is activism*, this is activism in our own life.

So, yes, even in the very beginning of the underground punk scene, in 1979, 1980, there were people who were just political activists, who really didn't give a goddamn about the Teen Idles or about Minor Threat. They were just concerned with their own issues. And some of them were a little obsessive. They were kind of — they were almost like a cult. So I think that, in response to that, we — and I mean Minor Threat, SOA, that era of early hardcore bands — moved away from "Politics with a capital P," like, the *formal* version of politics. We said, "We're not interested in *your* politics, what we are interested in are *personal* politics; we're interested in this music, in this community, in this scene."

At the same time, we did do benefits, but we always demanded that the benefits were actually connected to the shows themselves. Like, we would have a show — and then give away the money we made. For example, we did a number of benefits for the Bad Brains 'cause they were always getting their stuff stolen. We also did benefits for venues that were getting evicted, or for kids who were getting evicted from their house.

HR from the Bad Brains also had the idea to do a "Rock Against Racism." There had been these Rock Against Racism shows in England, where the Clash and Sham

69 and those bands played. But HR just saw those events as rock concerts for a lot of white kids. So he said, "Well, we're gonna do a Rock Against Racism here in DC, but we're gonna go play in a black neighborhood." Washington, DC, especially then, was primarily a black town. The majority of the town was black, like 60-70 percent, and there were neighborhoods that were 100 percent black. It was very polarized. So HR organized a couple of Rock Against Racism shows, including one with the Teen Idles, Untouchables, and the Bad Brains. We just played in a housing project. In my mind that certainly counts as political.

So this was all in the early 80s?

Yes. And then by around 1984 things changed. The elders in the DC punk scene began to drift away for various reasons, and the scene was left to these younger kids. There was a lot of senseless violence going on and it was really off-putting. The problem was not limited to DC. Skinheads seemed to be rampant all over the United States. In other towns, there were kids who were trying to battle with skinheads. They wanted to beat them up and chase them out of town. I thought that was just ridiculous. In DC, we decided to just create a new scene instead. That was certainly a political action, too. Not least because a part of creating a new scene created a situation in which we, being in our early twenties, began thinking about the larger world. I believe there was a very natural evolution, which then led to what became known as "Revolution Summer."

Can you tell us a little more about that? What happened?

I would say that Revolution Summer was an infusion, a moment when the DC punk scene and its personal politics suddenly merged and dovetailed with formal politics. We got involved in political action. Reagan was in office and the apartheid issue was really big. We were discussing gender issues, environmental issues, diet issues, and so on. It was a time of politicization.

Unfortunately, the name Revolution Summer has caused some false interpretations — which is partly our fault because we came up with it. Some people were like, "Oh, look, they think they are being revolutionary!" But that was not actually what we were thinking. We used the word "revolution," and it is a very strong word, but it was not to suggest that we were creating a revolution. For us Revolution Summer was all about our immediate community. It really came out of a loss of direction or emphasis.

How so?

In 1983, a lot of people were very discouraged. A number of bands, most notably Minor Threat, Faith, and Insurrection, had broken up, and even though there were other bands — good bands: Government Issue, Marginal Man, bands like that — the bands that had been crucial for us, the kids I hung out with, were gone. Especially Faith, who were just an enormously important band — I think a lot of people don't realize how significant they were. Anyway, 1984 kind of turned into a dark year, and no bands were really forming. Eventually, everyone was like, "Well, we're gonna do something!"

So we decided to pull something together. First we planned "Good Food October." The idea was that in October 1984 we were all going to eat good food, we were going to make good music, and we were going to be politically active. But then October came and went. So we set a new target date for the summer, and this time it worked.

What kinds of actions did you do?

One of the most successful was the Punk Percussion Protest, something that I remember being hatched at Dischord House. We initially discussed the idea of putting a band on a truck and driving back and forth in front of the South African embassy to protest apartheid. We gave up on that concept because no one we knew had a truck and we figured that the cops would shut us down immediately. So instead we put word out to as many people as we could that they should come join us near the embassy with any sort of percussion item they might be able to find. We got a lot of people out and it was such a baffler for the police — just a really positive experience. We definitely created enough noise that the people in the embassy knew we were out there. There was a series of creative actions along those lines throughout the summer.

You said that your goal at the time was to create a new scene. Did Revolution Summer help with that?

Definitely. It established a new beachhead. A lot of kids at the time felt very discouraged about the violence in the punk scene. There were a lot of kids who felt that they were going to walk away from punk altogether and do something new — goth or heavy metal or whatever the fuck they were going to do. Revolution Summer showed them that there was a possibility to be into punk rock without being into guys stomping on your head. Revolution Summer really showed the possibility of a new underground.

You talked about "personal" and "formal" politics merging at that time. What happened then? Why did that momentum get lost?

I don't agree with that. That kind of momentum might not have been celebrated in the same way afterwards, but I know people who have been involved with this stuff for twenty-five years now. It's true that if you are a collective — even an informal collective like we were — you are able to craft and execute actions that are harder to do once that collective has dissipated. But people continued doing things within Positive Force, for example, which was a sort of confluence of Revolution Summer.

We have Mark Andersen, one of the co-founders of Positive Force, contribute to the book too.

There you go. Many people who came out of that scene went on to do really intense political work.

Did a lot of them — or all of them — stay connected to the hardcore scene?

Well, it depends on what you define as the hardcore scene. Like, whenever Fugazi played throughout the 90s, I would see those people. But if you're talking about seeing every band that called itself "hardcore" or...

...reading *Maximumrocknroll* up and down...

...right, they wouldn't do that. But we didn't even do that in 1985. This is a good example of just having different perceptions of politics. Tim Yohannan had a more squared off idea of politics and of political action. Yohannan was a dear friend of mine, I loved and respected the dude, so I'm not saying that he was wrong. But by the mid-80s, he certainly ridiculed us and thought that we were wimpy. That's how "emo" became a pejorative... Yohannan really loved the term and he used it all the time to dismiss bands. But, that's alright. Yohannan just had more of an orthodox idea of what punk was, an idea that ran really contrary to mine. For me, punk has always been the free space.

What about political action?

I think of political action as an exercise, and people should exercise throughout their entire lives. If you believe that the people who are calling the shots should not be trusted, if you believe that power corrupts, then you should always be prepared to protest and to act against those who get too much power. And you must know that you're not finished even if you put one person out of power or make one aspect of the power structure disappear. You're never finished! I don't have this kind of romantic notion about political activism where it's like, "We go out into the streets and we bring down the government and everything will be fine!" I just don't think about things like that. I think that political action is a lifelong effort that will manifest in specific ways, depending on where you are and whatever it is that you are doing. It's the same with punk: I believe that punk doesn't end with your leather jacket. I imagine my funeral is going to be punk! I'm serious about that.

Because it will be outside of mainstream society's norms?

Let me explain it this way: I'm a parent now. Amy and I had a kid back in May; we have a six-month-old son. When he was first born and I was walking with him, I kept on running into these guys in the neighborhood. Maybe I've seen them before, maybe I haven't, but they are always like, "Hey dude, welcome to the club!" And I'm like, "Wow, what club did I join?" It confused me and I didn't feel comfortable with it at all. How could something so organic — what is more organic than the birth of a human being? — turn into a "club"? But then suddenly it struck me and I was like, "Wait a minute! I'm a fucking punk!" I've always felt like a freak, it's just that I had never been a parent before. And I realized that these were the same dudes who used to say, "What's with your hair? Are you a fag?" I'm not saying they are bad guys — they are just normals, they are regulars, they are straights. Me, whatever I do in my life, I'm interested in creative response — and that's what I call punk. If people don't agree with me, that's fine, I don't care. They can have punk, and they can have it however they want to have it. But I have it my way.

You mentioned Rock Against Racism in DC being organized in a housing project. I'm wondering whether that means that the early DC hardcore scene wasn't as white as the hardcore scene later became.

First off, I think those Rock Against Racism shows were highly entertaining for the kids in the projects because they thought it was the most ridiculous thing they had ever seen.

The scene has always been predominantly white and the whiteness of the scene has been an issue from time to time. People have asked me, "Well, if Washington is 70 percent black, how is it that your shows are 90 percent white?" My response is: apparently that's who wants to come see kids jumping around on stage with a guitar. I don't know what else to say about that. We never turned people away at the door. I mean, we played shows at the Wilson Center with fifteen bands for three dollars. Three dollars! No one has ever been turned away. The Wilson Center was in a neighborhood that was at the time largely African-American. I don't know why they didn't want to come see the shows, probably because they thought it was stupid. For the same reason, a lot of Latino kids don't come. It's just not their music. And I find the notion that you should "reach out" and try to get these people involved not very convincing. Why? It seems disrespectful. I mean, these kids are certainly capable of making up their own minds of whether this is something they want to get involved with or not. Again, I don't think it's a matter of access. I think it's just a matter of taste.

Look at the go-go scene. This is a thriving underground music scene in DC. It is almost entirely black. However, I don't think anybody asks go-go bands, "Well, how come you don't have a 30 percent white audience?" It is because for many varying reasons these are just different cultures; and I'm talking about *real* culture, culture that speaks to a certain part of the population. Don't you think that if culture spoke to everybody, it wouldn't really be culture anymore? It'd be like network television.

Let me also go back to what you said about kids fighting skinheads out on the streets, and your approach of creating a new scene instead...

Let me be more specific: for most of the skinhead kids — and they weren't all skinhead kids, but they were all troubled — the issue was violence. The punk scene was a perfect nest for them. People who have violence and control issues need an environment to exercise these things. The world at large is too scary for them, they need something more immediate and conquerable. Especially since punk had gotten the "nihilistic" and "self-destructive" tag from the media, it drew these people. It made punk perfect for them, and violence was their language. If you spoke to them in violence, then you were only awarding them.

In the early stages of the punk scene I did that. I fought a lot. I operated under a philosophy: *bruise the ego and not the body*. The idea was that I would never back down from a fight, but I would also never take a brick and smash someone's head in after I had knocked them down. All I wanted to do was to repel these kids, to stop them by standing up to them. This was how I thought I could reconcile what was essentially a pacifist mindset with punching people.

This violence seemed necessary because I felt that we are under attack. For example, there was a gang in Washington called the Punk Beaters. They were a bunch of redneck guys, jocks, who would go out looking for punks to beat up. So, then we would go with my brother Alec, who was fourteen years old at the time and a very punk-looking kid, to the area where the Punk Beater guys hang out. We would have Alec walk a block ahead of us, and if these guys came to get him, twelve or fifteen of us would take them out. Our idea was to show them that you can't fuck with the punks like that.

At some point, however, the whole violence thing just turned upon itself. People at shows would get into fights because somebody was wearing a wrong T-shirt or had long hair or just something really absurd like that. This made me realize what a completely pointless, unconstructive activity it was, but, by talking to these kids, I also understood that they had been inspired by my violence. It was like this biblical concept coming true, violence begets violence, and it became very clear to me that this was something I had to stop in my life.

At first it was difficult, and I remember thinking, "How can I stop when I'm always under attack?" I don't know how many times I would have a car go by and someone would scream, "Fuck you, you fucking punk faggot!" But then I realized that if you do not speak that language, you recognize that they are not talking to you. Let's say that I'm in Sweden, and a carload with a bunch of guys goes by and they yell something at me in Swedish. I don't know what they're saying. As far as I know, they are saying, "I love basketball!" Who knows? So when I'm walking along the street here and some guys go by in a car, and they don't know me, I don't know them, but they say, "You're a fucking punk faggot, fuck you!" then it should have the same effect. They are not talking to me, they don't know me, and I'm not what they say I am, so they must have confused me with someone else. In short, if you don't speak the language of violence, you are released from violence. This was a very powerful discovery for me.

The next step was to start bands like Rites of Spring, Embrace, Lunchmeat, Beefeater —bands that were considered very wimpy at the time. We stopped with the aggressive posturing and started playing different kinds of music. This infuriated many kids, because they had no longer a soundtrack for their violence. It was too wimpy for them.

And straight edge was part of that change?

No. Straight edge was already in place in 1979, 1980, it was something that had always been happening and that wasn't particular to that time. The song "Straight Edge" was a song about the way I lived, about who I was, and about living my life however I wanted.

In the 1970s, I was given a lot of grief of my high school peers and my friends for being straight; I was ridiculed. Then when we got into the punk scene, all these punk rockers ridiculed me. And all the time I just felt like, "Hey, I'm just me!" I didn't say to anyone that they were stupid for drinking — still they gave me so much shit. The first sort of straight edge song I wrote was probably "I Drink Milk" by the Teen Idles. This was obviously a joke song — "I drink milk, I drink milk, I drink milk" — but the reaction to it was so visceral, and people were like, "We're gonna tie you up and make you drink a beer!" HR from the Bad Brains always told me that he was going to tie me to a tree and make me smoke pot with him. And I was always struck by this, thinking, "What the fuck is this?" Like, I never said to HR, "I'm gonna tie you to a tree and not let you smoke pot!"

Ultimately, the situation kinda came to a boil in my mind, and I guess eventually I just wrote a more angry song. But I think the beginning of the song is very clear, and I think the first line of the song is the most important: "I'm a person just like you." And then it continues: "I have better things to do." That's the way I looked at it: I had better things to do than just get high, and I was just being straight about it. But it wasn't like I decided, "Oh, I'm going to be straight," or "I'm going to be straight edge." That's just how I was. It's just me.

In life, if you decide to forgo something that everybody else does, it gives you a perspective on society that you couldn't have if you were just engaging. It teaches you a lot about the world. I didn't do these things because I was trying to be different — apparently, I was different. What I learned was that just to be myself meant to be a freak. And so I wrote a song about being a freak. I've said many times before that the biggest influence for the song was the Jimi Hendrix song "If 6 was 9." At the end of the song, Hendrix says, "I'm the one that's gonna die when it's time for me to die / So let me live my life the way I want to." He was singing about being a freak.

Straight edge was just a declaration for the right to live your life the way you want to. I was not interested in trying to tell people how to do that. I mean, obviously things got pretty crazily perverted over the years.

It seems that you were never all that interested in being part of what was later called the "straight edge movement." Was that related to the part of not wanting to tell others what to do? Especially since parts of the straight edge scene started to do exactly that?

Of course! Originally, the declaration was two-fold: one point was to say that this is the way I want to live and that you have to respect my way; the second point was not limited to drinking or to taking drugs — it was about being obsessed. I think some people simply missed that.

The big debates really started when "Out of Step" came out. Specifically, the lyric "don't fuck" seemed to flip people out. You could hear them say, "My god, he's anti-sex!"

I definitely chose those words carefully, and I stand behind them still. But you'll notice for instance that the lyric is "Don't smoke, don't drink, don't fuck, at least I can fucking think." So first off, I use a grammatical trick in there: the fourth line modifies the first three. The first three sound like directives or orders: "Don't do this, don't do this, don't do this." The fourth line says: "But at least I can fucking think!" Which clearly says that I don't do these things — but I can think; I may not be like other people, I may not party — but at least I can think, at least I got that. You can even see on the lyrics sheet that the word "I" is put in parentheses, which was a result of long discussions within the band. Some people in the band were very concerned that kids might read the whole thing as a directive, while I was less concerned about it. But that's part of me, I'm rather unapologetic about stuff. I'm more like, "Fuck it, tough on them!"

Then there is a second thing that's important in those lyrics. If you look at the words "don't smoke," everyone figures I'm talking about smoking cigarettes, or grass, or hash; "don't drink" — everyone figures I'm talking about alcohol; "don't fuck" — everyone figures I'm saying, "No sex!" Think about that! Think about the word "drink": what does "drink" mean? Do you think that people would ever figure, "Oh, he wants people to no longer take any beverages, or any liquids of any sort?" But when the word "fuck" comes on, they cannot understand it the same way. That just blew my mind. What I was clearly discussing was abusive, quest-oriented, manipulative sex. People who were not interested in other people's feelings, but only in getting off. I saw as a teenager that people's energies were so squarely caught up in getting laid that a lot of pain and hurt came with that. People were being hurt and damaged and traumatized by other people's behavior. I knew women who were raped by people who did not care for anything other than getting off. And I just thought that this kind of obsession was not healthy.

So, straight edge, the whole idea, the whole concept was really anti-obsession. If your whole world is committed to this one thing, then clearly it's not a good situation.

Why do you think the sex aspect freaked people out so much?

I think American culture is deeply dysfunctional about sexuality. This is probably true for most cultures, but especially for American culture. Our culture is so fucked up on sex. I mean, you might remember this huge uproar about Janet Jackson's nipple that showed on TV during the Super Bowl some years ago, no matter how imperceptibly. This ridiculous incident caused an unbelievable series of new restrictions. Today, if you have a cussword air on a radio show you might get a half a million dollar fine — for a cussword! What kind of a country are we living in? There is a very dominant right, religious element in this society. You hear people say that America is all about the separation of church and state, the free exercise of religion, etc. That is all bullshit, the conservative component of religion is really powerful. And I think this is why, if you grow up in this culture, there is this idea — also within the punk scene — that sexuality should be transgressive. That's why you have "sex, drugs and rock'n'roll" — the idea that sex is a rebel act. I mean, come on! Sex is the requirement for the perpetuation of the human race. And yet somehow it's been relegated to fucking in the streets.

I think because of all this, sex became this sort of rallying point: if you're rebellious, then you fuck. And I think the problem was that people's sexual behavior, particularly because of the psychological nature of sexual dysfunction, became very abusive, especially towards women. Women were being treated as targets and conquests. Especially in the early L.A. punk scene, there was a lot of emphasis on scamming. It was really a shock to me to meet punk bands who would come to Washington, hit on all the women and say things like, "Hey, will you give me a blowjob in the bathroom of the club?" How is this different than Led Zeppelin or any of these bands? I thought that we rejected groupie culture and rock'n'roll, that we saw it as a bankrupt approach to music, and that we went beyond the idea that rebelliousness can only manifest in either self-destruction or the exploitation of others. So I couldn't understand what was going on, and I thought I'd speak out against it. And I got a rise out of people.

I'm pro-sex, I certainly have no problem with sex between people who want to have sex. But I felt that so much energy in our scene was spent on selfish aims, basically on trying to get laid all the time, to the degree where it really compromised our communities.

I also think that the sexual transgression plays a massive role in the consumption of alcohol. People drink to enter into situations that are not necessarily good for them. I feel that people should always be present.

You said that the song "Straight Edge" was about defending the way you lived your life. Were you the only one who lived that way when the song came out? Or was there already a "straight edge scene"? If not, when did such a scene develop?

When you have a bunch of kids there is always a sense of what's cool and what's not cool. I believe that at the time it wasn't so much about "becoming straight edge," it was more about kids being human beings and making choices.

I think what happened at first was that an alternative had been created — a scene that people could get involved with that wasn't the standard rebel party scene. Of course we were rejected by other kids who thought that we were stupid or made them "feel guilty." But the idea that we were all totalitarian fundamentalists really had more to do with people's own issues than with ours.

There was of course also a pragmatic aspect to this, which was that we were deeply invested in the idea of keeping clubs open to punk bands, and we knew that if kids fucked up by getting drunk and smashing the club or whatever, we would lose our space. So in that sense there certainly was pressure, because we were like, "Hey, we're not fucking around, if you're going to drink, do it after the show, away from the club, don't do it anywhere near here!"

But most of the kids involved with the early DC hardcore scene were drinking. Some of my dearest friends were fuck-ups. It certainly wasn't this weird cult where you'd get slapped if you were seen with a cup of beer in your hand. That is just a fallacy.

When you say "we," who does that include? Minor Threat?

No, it was a larger clique. I guess you could call it the "Dischord scene" — you know, the scene first defined by Minor Threat, Faith etc. and then morphing into Rites of Spring, Embrace, Beefeater, that era.

But not all of these kids were straight edge, right?

No, most of those kids were drinking too, at least sometimes. The kind of strict straight edge thing didn't really show up until SS Decontrol. And the policing aspect of it, that just seemed to come out of New York.

When you say New York, you mean Youth of Today, Bold etc.?

Yes. And there were the Connecticut kids, and it kinda dovetailed, there was Gorilla Biscuits, Crucial Youth. It was a scene that I think was aesthetically to some degree influenced by Dischord, musically very much by SS Decontrol, and attitude-wise mostly by the Boston or New England scene.

Do you have any recollection about first hearing the phrase "straight edge movement" being used?

No. The first time I ever got the idea of a straight edge movement was when I met people who identified as the "bent edge movement." As far as I'm concerned, there was a countermovement before there was a movement. Minor Threat toured in 1982, and kids would show up in Tucson, Arizona, and say that they were "bent edge;" or kids would come up to us in Dallas, Texas, and say that they were "curved edge." These were people who were provocateurs, trying to fuck with us — but they essentially defined the straight edge movement.

Maybe in L.A. or Orange County there were people, like America's Hardcore, who actually identified as such. This would be the origin of a more organic kind of movement: people who say, "Hey, this is weird, there are kids here, and there are kids in Reno, and kids in Boston, and kids in the Midwest, and they are all doing this really cool thing." However, I think it was always more about punk rock than about straight edge. Like, we were the new American hardcore. You had Johnny Thunders and Sid Vicious and these kinds of people, and now you suddenly had these kids who were making this radical music but were not stumbling around like junkies. That was significant.

So in this sense the "we" I used above means all these kids, The Necros and 7 Seconds and others, and I guess it was a kind of a movement, but, again, it was more of a punk rock movement or a hardcore punk rock movement or a kids' movement than a straight edge movement — maybe it was straight edge, but we didn't think of this as a defining element.

There are two different ideas of movements: there is an organic idea of a movement, and then there is a very formal idea of a movement. In the latter case people start to do newsletters and they want you to sign on to something. I've never been interested in that. I'm just not a subscriber.

It's interesting that you stressed the anti-obsession aspect of straight edge. Arguably, it seemed that a lot of straight edge kids became rather obsessive...

No doubt. Even when the second version of "Out of Step," which is on a 12-inch, came out, I put a little thing in there saying, "This is not a set of rules!" So, already in 1983, I'm trying to say, "Look, there is no movement here!"

For me, straight edge was never intended to be a movement and I never saw myself as a part of such a movement. However, I want to be really clear: I think that the vast majority of the people who identify as or with straight edge are human beings who try to do the right thing in their lives. The fact that they are even thinking about their behavior, that they are thinking about the effects of their behavior on the world, is, I believe, positive and good. The problem with movements is that they put humans in something akin to a higher calling and then others have to take the backseat. There's a religious element there. And then you always have people — even if it's only one percent — who have power issues or, more specifically, violence issues. Essentially, what they are wrestling with is not a conflict about intoxication or drug use or sexuality. It is about power and violence. And if people have this inside of them, they have to get it out. So they go around looking for triggers: things that can set off situations in which they can release this energy. This is why these people run to nationalism, religion, or sports, all these really imaginary things. Like, why would people who live in Texas on one side of some imaginary line have an issue with those who live in Mexico on the other side of that imaginary line? It's ridiculous. But if you need a trigger for your violence, you need someone who is "the other" and you need a line on the ground that allows you to say, "Okay, if you step over that line, then we'll beat your ass!" Straight edge was perfect for that if you saw it as a series of directives. And that's how these people started to see it, as very simple rules: "If you do this or that, then you are stepping over that line, and at that point you've waived your rights!" This is something that I saw most clearly articulated in a text handed out by the hardline people.

Didn't hardline activists picket Fugazi shows?

Yes, they would picket us. They were very dogmatic, and their main issue, as far as I could tell, were animal rights. So at one point I received some information from them, a declaration of sorts. It said that all life was precious, and they laid it all out in detail. And then the text said, "We will educate you about this, and if you do not accept the education, then you have waived your status as a living thing." That's basically what it said. I mean it wasn't quite as crude but it was pretty fucking close. Essentially, they were saying, "We will give you a chance; but if you don't agree with us, we're gonna beat your ass!"

I think it's always interesting to look at where these people go. I would meet these hardline kids, and when I came back to their town a couple of years later I would ask, "What happened to this kid?" And often people would be like, "Oh, he's selling crack." They were just gangsters, and if you think about gangsters — gang guys — it's all about turf; which goes back to the example of the line. I remember once visiting this stupid high school and there was a mural of an eagle on the ground in tile, and I walked across it — I mean, it was on the fucking floor — and I got jacked up by these dudes for stepping on their eagle. That's what I mean. These are all triggers.

But you think that, overall, the violence aspect in straight edge was overrated?

The reason why the people who had issues with violence managed to dominate the whole idea of straight edge was that our cultures are obsessed with violence. The media will always talk about violence. If there is a party — and I use this analogy a lot — and there are thirty people talking, twenty-eight having really fascinating, incredibly illuminating conversations, and two ending up punching each other, all that people will talk about the next day is the fight. I don't know why. This is just the way we process things. Violent people end up getting an enormous amount of attention. And then kids who have never heard about straight edge will hear about it in the context of violence, and some will be like, "That sounds cool, you punch people out — I'm in!"

The whole idea of straight edge was incredibly maligned by a small amount of people. It became vulnerable because everyone gathered under one tree. This means instant death for everybody when the lightning strike comes. By referring to straight edge as a movement and by identifying with it and by adopting rules or whatever, people allowed themselves to be put into trouble. Because when things start to go wrong, you need to react, and once these guys started beating everybody up, a lot of kids were like, "This is stupid, I need to get out of this situation, I don't wanna be identified with that!" So then they "stopped being straight edge," whatever the fuck that means. And then in turn you have internet sites where people out those who "broke their edge." It's so ridiculous! This is why I cannot understand that people would want to huddle under the same tree.

When hardline people picketed your shows, what exactly was their problem? That you weren't outspoken enough?

I think that there were two reasons why we were picketed. Actually, picketed might be too strong of a word, they came "to talk to us" and give us "a chance to explain ourselves." One of the reasons was that we were pro-choice. This was a big issue for them. The other one was that we were not more outspoken about our diets. I mean, I've been a vegan for twenty-two years now, Joe was a vegan for almost the entire time in Fugazi, and we were all vegetarians. But I guess the hardline people wanted us to make this some kind of an issue. I remember this one time in Memphis a hardline activist confronted us in front of the local health food store. He asked us why we didn't have any vegan songs. We just totally couldn't believe the question. Guy finally said, "Well, considering that none of our songs eat meat or dairy or any animal products, I guess they're all vegan." It's just so absurd! I also remember the kid wearing fake leather DocMartens. I always felt that this was absurd too. I mean, I don't wear leather. But I would never wear anything that looks like leather either. It seems to be completely counterproductive 'cause the main issue with the leather industry is that it's fashionable. So if you wear something that looks like leather, what's the statement that you're making? (your NOT WEARING LEATHER so where's the problem)

Anyway, I think that a lot of hardline kids felt that there was a war happening. So they were militant, and they felt that we should also be militant. You gotta remember that in the punk scene, or the underground community, the self-cleaning oven is always in place. People's power is limited to their scope, and it's like that saying goes: "The people who get hit are the people within arm's reach." So, instead of them picketing Aerosmith or whoever, they go to some little punk show and are rough on the people there.

What about those rumors of you...

...slapping a beer out of somebody's hands?

For example.

That's one of the most annoying fucking things. I've been told so many times that I slapped a beer out of somebody's hands. I don't think I ever did that, not once, and yet it has become part of my legacy. Then there is also the story about me hitting someone with a hammer for blowing pot smoke in my face. This is actually true, but the story is never told correctly: When I was in high school, I was part of a community theater group. We had this club house within the school that was completely underground. People were drinking and getting high, but it was our club house, and so I hung out there too. They always called me "the group conscience." One day this kid from my school — who was a stoner and a kind of bully — was getting high, while I was building flats. We were teasing each other, we did that a lot. At one point he came over, tapped me on the shoulder, and gave me this look, like, "You got a problem or something?" So I stood up holding the hammer, he blew pot smoke in my face, ran away, and I threw the hammer and it hit him in the leg. So, yes, I literally hit someone with a hammer for blowing pot smoke in my face. However, it's really different from the idea that most people have. They always see me attacking somebody and putting a hole in their head.

This is precisely the kind of thing that my life is filled with: people have this perception of me that is so inaccurate. It has largely to do with other people's projections of what my work has been about. But my work has basically always been about peace and love, that's it. It's not true when people say, "Ian, you never wrote any love songs." My songs are all love songs, ultimately. Think about a song like "Filler." I'm talking about one of my best friends there, and about what he's been doing to himself and why he got so fucked up. Songs like that are all songs about my passion for connection, and my agony over disconnection.

I heard you make a really interesting distinction between straight edge as a "lifestyle" and, as you put it, straight edge as "life." Can you explain this?

When I wrote the song "Straight Edge" I wasn't writing about something new. I wasn't saying, "Hey, here is a new way to live!" I was talking about the way that people live to begin with. Later I read so much about the "straight edge lifestyle," and I was confronted with it all the time. There have been so many times when I would read something like, "Ian MacKaye is a practitioner of the straight edge lifestyle." A few years ago it finally hit me what was so annoying about it: it's no fucking lifestyle! A lifestyle is something that one chooses. Like, if you choose to live on a beach and go surfing all day, that's a lifestyle. But being straight is the base, that's what's underneath all of this! We're born that way!

I've always thought about life as a straight line, a simple, straight line, on which we are all equal and identical. Everything added to that — like our surroundings, our culture, all these things — that's what makes us different. But as far as the essence of life goes, we are identical, we are the same thing, all of us. And so, in my mind, when someone starts saying, "So, you live the straight edge lifestyle," I say, "No. *I live life.*" And last time I checked, there are three or four necessary components to life: air, water, food, and sex. The sex is there because we must procreate since otherwise we're out of luck. So, as far as I am concerned, straight edge is just life. I don't choose to be straight, I *choose not to be the other thing.* It's the semantic subtlety that matters here.

Another problem I see associated with the "straight edge lifestyle" is that it becomes a framework for merchandise. "Okay, now I decide to live the straight edge lifestyle. What do I need to buy?" People look for things to signify their lifestyle choices. I cannot believe it when I see straight edge merchandise! It's just mind-boggling.

So being straight edge means to follow that straight line of life without adding anything that we don't really need; things that mainly serve the interests of corporations?

Well, I mean, if you want to take it extremely literally, yes. However, obviously I think that there is some merit in talking to you on the telephone, otherwise I wouldn't do it. I mean, any literal interpretation of what I just said could ask, "So, why are you wearing shoes?" I understand that. But I just want to stress the problems associated with the word "lifestyle." I think that people use the word for two reasons: either they use it to dismiss something; or they use it to suggest that there is a certain way to be. But what's the blueprint of the straight edge lifestyle? How do you live that lifestyle? Do you have to go to a particular website? Do you need any particular clothing? I don't know.

My point is: to live simply and not to buy into any such demands, *that is normal*. What is perverted is the mainstream understanding of living.

You've said something — and I don't remember the exact quote — but you've said something to the extent that the only thing you really want is people to be well.

Of course! There was a certain period in my life when I was very angry, when I was really agonizing over things. It made me feel miserable, and I began to question everything: What is the point of all this punk rock? What is the point of me singing? What am I trying to do? Eventually, I realized that the reason I was so angry was because I want people in the world to be well. And I realized that it was a worthwhile project to pursue in my lifetime. But I also understood that I myself needed to be well to do that. So I figured that I would do my best to live a life of wellness. This doesn't mean that I'm trying to bask in my riches. It means that I'm trying to release myself from the anger and agony. Remember what I said earlier about someone going by in a car and calling me "a fucking asshole"? They are not talking to me — 'cause I'm not a fucking asshole.

There are a lot of things happening in this world that are horrific. But I have no control over this. The day them fucking planes crashed into the buildings here in 2001, I was in Dischord House, right here. People called me to tell me what had happened, so I turned on the TV, I saw the planes crash and immediately turned the TV off, and returned to the book I was reading — a Kurt Vonnegut book, which in fact was a perfect book for that moment. While I sat there reading, I looked out the window, and it was an absolutely crystal clear, gorgeous day. I saw the trees and thought, "These trees don't give a fuck about what just happened. They don't care. And they're going to be here after all this shit is over."

Humans have been brutalizing each other since the beginning of time. I don't know why. But there is a certain point where one has to accept that this is a little bit like the weather. You cannot control it, and you cannot understand it. What happened that day was incomprehensible. No matter who did it. Whether it was Al-Qaeda or the US government or someone else. And it will remain incomprehensible, no matter how often you look at it. The only result of looking at something that's incomprehensibly brutal over and over again is detachment. If you take your hand and you start slapping yourself as hard as you can, it's going to hurt — but after a while you'll feel nothing 'cause that's the way we survive. We become numb. I don't think that helps anybody.

So on September 11, after I had finished the book, I sat down and I answered all the mail. Everything was fucked up here — all the bridges were closed, the phones were down, etc. — and it seemed like answering the mail was the best thing to do. I looked at it as a vote for the future. Because I believed that someone would read it — that there would be a September 12.

I guess that's an illustration of putting into action a philosophy of *Live as you desire the world to be*! It doesn't mean to be unaware and not to care. It means to love and to be well and to wish for others to be well too.

ManLiftingBanner

Interview with Michiel Bakker, Olav van den Berg, and Paul van den Berg

ManLiftingBanner was a Dutch hardcore band from 1990 to 1993. It had developed out of the band Profound, founded in 1988. The brothers Paul van den Berg (guitar) and Olav van den Berg (drums) had already played in the pioneering European straight edge band Lärm (1980-85). The ManLiftingBanner lineup equaled that of Profound except for the addition of another guitarist, Lord Bigma. The band combined a commitment to sobriety with communist politics and soon defined what became known as "communist straight edge." It has served a source of inspiration for left-wing straight edge bands to this day. The records *Myth of Freedom* (1991) and *Ten Inches That Shook the World* (1992) came equipped with quotes from Lenin to Trotsky to Rosa Luxemburg.

Discography:
- *Myth of Freedom*, 1991, Crucial Response Records (EP)
- *Ten Inches That Shook the World*, 1992, Crucial Response Records (10-inch)
- *We Will Not Rest (Complete Discography)*, 1995, Crucial Response Records

Michiel Bakker was ManLiftingBanner's frontman. Today he sings for the band Veins, teaches history and social science at an Amsterdam high school, is a member of the International Socialists, and co-runs New Radical Chic, a street wear outfit whose profits support political struggles in the Netherlands. Paul and Olav van den Berg continue playing in Seein Red, a mainstay of politically conscious European hardcore since 1988. Each year, they join the former members of Lärm for an annual reunion show in Amsterdam. Paul works as a garbage man, Olav as a printer.

Since some of the readers of this book were probably not even born at the time — can you give us a quick summary of ManLiftingBanner's history?

Michiel: ManLiftingBanner started in 1990 on the ashes of Profound, which I think was one of the first sXe bands in Europe of the wave that started in '87 and '88. With ManLiftingBanner we recorded an EP and a 10", did some small tours in Germany, one in Italy, and called it quits in 1993. We did a reunion in 1998 and one more in 2008, so we could share the stage with Negative Approach, hardcore gods we grew up on.

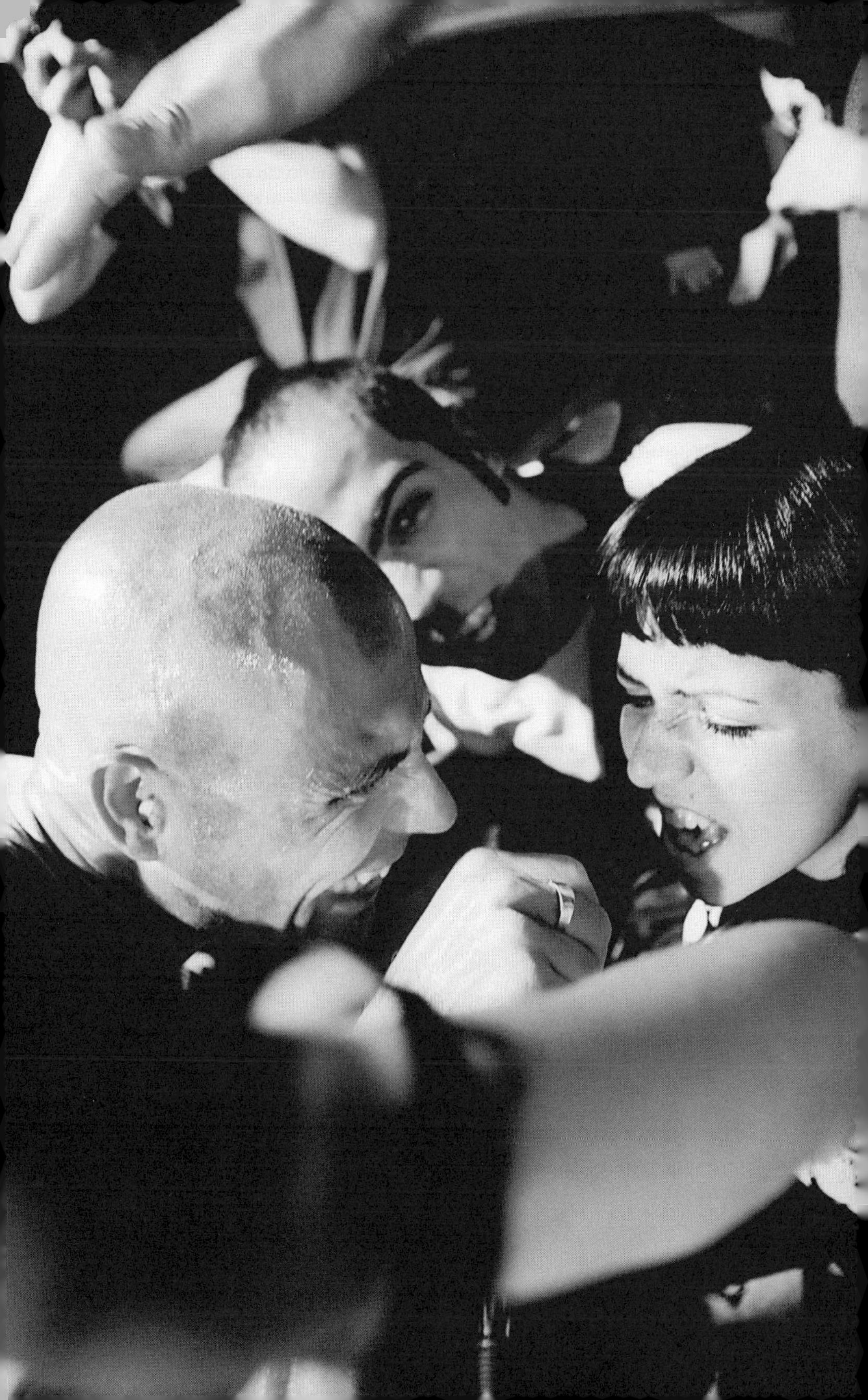

ManLiftingBanner is known as the most prominent communist straight edge band and many folks still refer to it as a very unique phenomenon in the history of hardcore. How big was the impact you had?

Michiel: Actually, I think the mix of sXe and communism, and its impact, was not that big. We had bands like Colt Turkey and Feeding The Fire in Holland. There was the Last Struggle Crew which was a group of diehard sXe communists from Holland and Germany who were also involved in the *Counter Clockwise* zine. Our label, Crucial Response Records also backed us up politically. Then you had the bands Comrade in Rome or Manifesto in Spain, but they came out when we were already gone; the same goes for Sober Response in Holland, who were partly communist as well. What happened after that I'm not so sure. Were Miozän and Refused commies? sXe?

Olav: There is truth in what Michiel says, but at the same time let's see it in some perspective: the early 90s were a pretty bad time for hardcore in general, especially after the glorious decade of 80s hardcore. If there were thirty-fifty people at a concert in the early 90s, you would be happy. If you look at the small output of ManLiftingBanner, just one 7" EP and a 10", and the amount of concerts and tours we did, then I would say that our impact was pretty big.

Seein Red is still alive and kicking, we play a lot of shows and did several tours around Europe, the USA, and Japan. Everywhere we go, we meet people who tell us that they were influenced by ManLiftingBanner. For example, when we toured the US, we met a group of Mexican punks after a gig in L.A. and they told us how Lärm, Profound, and ManLiftingBanner had changed their lives. When they were fourteen, they had listened to tapes of our bands, and some showed us their Profound and ManLiftingBanner tattoos. I thought that was fucking awesome. In Japan, we played "Myth of Freedom" as an encore and every time people would come up to us to testify how much ManLiftingBanner changed and rocked their lives.

I know that bands in numerous countries are covering ManLiftingBanner songs. I still get emails from people from all over the world telling me how much they love ManLiftingBanner and/or how much the band influenced them. A lot of them became politically active in the socialist/communist movement and such. And this because of a band that called it quits fifteen years ago… That's pretty amazing!

How did straight edge and communism — an unusual combination, at the time of ManLiftingBanner as much as today — come together? Was one more important than the other? Did you see it as a "natural" union?

Michiel: For me sXe came first. But the change from Profound to ManLiftingBanner consciously happened to give more space to political and overtly communist ideas. So in 1990 politics took over, and by 1993 we stopped calling ourselves a sXe band. Burt, our bassist, stopped being sXe as well.

What was very influential was a workshop on the "War on Drugs" and the socialist stance on drugs that Burt and I attended in 1993 at Marxism in London, the yearly discussion forum organized by the Socialist Workers Party, the sister organization of Holland's International Socialists. I remember the workshop vividly. There was a talk by Jonathan Neale, I think it's on mp3 on the net somewhere. Both Burt and I figured by the end of it: that's the final blow we needed, that's the end for us propagating the sXe lifestyle. That's the end of the lifestylism period. I, and later Burt too, joined the International Socialists, who we are still members of.

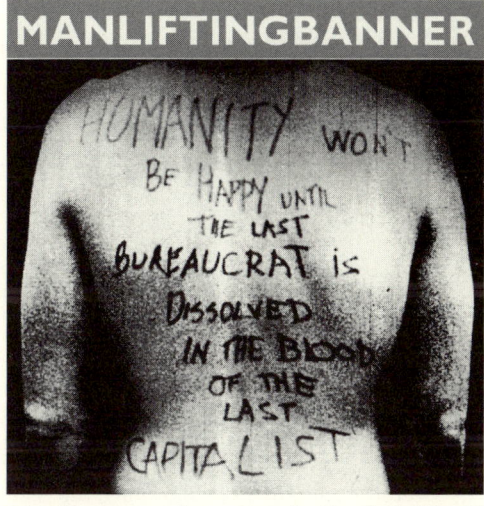

ManLiftingBanner 10" cover: Ten Inches That Shook the World

I think one of the main problems is that moralism and materialism just don't mix. So I would say that straight edge and communism was never a natural union. It was more like coming to terms with what we considered most important in our lives. For some time, sXe and communism coexisted next to each other and there was a marriage of convenience, a sXe commie image that appealed to quite a lot of people — but by 1993, our communist ideas and sXe went separate ways.

Paul: Well to me and my brother Olav those two strains already came together long before we got involved with Profound and ManLiftingBanner. With Lärm, a project that existed from 1980 to 1985, we were probably the first band that mixed punk with (anarcho-)communist ideas and straight edge ethics.

In those days, these two strains came together because one of our biggest influences was the Dutch punk band Rondos from Rotterdam, who mixed punk with communism. They also put DIY on the Dutch punk map by recording and releasing their own records on the King Kong label, making a fanzine called *Raket*, starting the four-band "Red Rock Collective" in which they shared practice hours and backline, and maintaining their own space, De Raket Basis, with an office, record/book shop, printing facilities, etc. We were very inspired by them, and this was reflected in our growing interest in communist ideas.

When Minor Threat hit the punk scene and sXe was introduced, we embraced it because we already were more or less "straight edge": we didn't drink or smoke and we didn't do drugs and fuck around. But another reason to embrace sXe was the fact that in the Dutch punk scene a lot of people were into drugs and alcohol, and we saw how destructive it was to so many of them — particularly young kids. This hit very close to home when Alex, the bassist of our very first band The Sextons, and later on Berletta, one of the vocalists of Total Chaoz, another pre-Lärm band, both got addicted to hard drugs. We could see how much damage these drugs caused to our friends. We also saw how local punks would end up in the gutter because of drug and alcohol abuse. We felt that we had to take a stand and that's what we did with Lärm. So to some extent our leanings toward communism and straight edge melted together naturally at that time — although Lärm was never really a straight edge band in terms of all members being sXe.

When Olav and me joined Profound, the concept of a communist straight edge band became more or less a fact, or, as Michiel put it right: we were coming to terms with what we all considered to be most important in our lives. And when Profound turned into ManLiftingBanner, the whole concept was to give more space to the political ideas — hence the name of the band — while keeping sXe more in the background. We were not that keen anymore on mixing sXe with communism. Although we were sXe, we didn't feel the need to be vocal about it, especially because in our eyes a large percentage of the sXe movement had turned into a mockery of itself, a fucking set of rules which, originally, sXe never intended to be. It became a pretty reactionary scene where jock culture, hardline bullshit, and religions could flourish. We couldn't really identify with most of the new sXe generation, and the pressing question became: around what goals and values do we unite in difficult political times like these? Maybe unlike Michiel and Burt, we never separated the sXe lifestyle from our revolutionary sympathies. But our communist ideals had become far more important.

Michiel, you said before that "moralism and materialism just don't mix" — can you explain that?

Michiel: Within the International Socialists we had a lot of discussions about animal rights and the moralism that came with sXe. These discussions basically revolved around what side you were on: middle class moralism or genuine revolutionary politics. In the case of our 10", for example, a lot of the sXe quotes from Lenin were taken out of context. In a revolutionary organization or situation it's important to keep a clear head, but that doesn't mean you have to refrain from drugs or alcohol at all times if you feel like you wanna use them. It's utterly impossible to lead a pure life, whatever that may be, while living under capitalism. You are a part of the system that you hate and wish to destroy, and you can't be a revolutionary on guard 24/7. I know a lot of revolutionaries who drink or do drugs and have contributed more to changing the world in a positive way than like forty sXe jocks put together. The lifestyle alone doesn't lead to any sort of change.

Paul: I think it is most important that all people make up their own mind, live the life they want to live, and make the choices that suit them best. To quote Lärm, "It's up to you what to do!" Straight edge is there for those who want it and it can be a step in the right direction, but you still need to keep on walking!

However, I do not fully agree with Michiel and Burt on this issue. Of course there have been great revolutionaries who did drink, smoke, and do drugs, bless 'em all! But there is also the other side of the coin, where revolutionaries and potential revolutionaries ended up in the gutter because of alcohol and/or drugs. For example: it's known that the US government was eventually able to destroy the Black Panther/Black Power movement by bringing dope into the black communities. And there are other examples of struggles lost because of alcohol and/or drugs. And let's face it: in a lot of working class and poor communities all around the world, alcohol and drugs do more damage than good.

I also wanna say that, even though we are critical towards the sXe movement ourselves, it's silly to associate sXe only with fucking jocks, because there are a lot of people out there who live the sXe lifestyle and who have their heart and mind in the right place, making a contribution to changing the world.

The sXe lifestyle alone doesn't lead to any sort of profound social change — but there is also no reason to see sXe and profound social changes as contradictions.

I'm curious about the anti-alcohol campaigns that were implemented in the Soviet Union after the Bolshevik Revolution. It seems that they only had limited success, and in the 1930s they were scrapped altogether. What are your thoughts on this?

Michiel: I think the reason why anti-alcohol policies in the early years of the revolution worked was because people had a reason to stay sober. Trotsky sent anti-alcohol militias made up of local people and workers/soldiers to smash alcohol stores and illegal cafés because alcoholism was undermining the discipline needed to win the revolution. People had new hopes to cling on! But with the deepening of the civil war and the policies of Stalin, alcohol consumption rose (limited only by the laws) because there was enough misery to drink away. Alcohol was again both joy and hell. Hence Trotsky's policies only worked for a short period of time. The story just goes to show that any law or policy backed by force is in the end doomed to fail. The only policies that work are policies based on mutual understanding and conviction.

Paul and Olav, some people see your long-standing and still continuing band project Seein Red as a continuation of the communist straight edge theme. Is that a correct perception? I think the two of you, as well as Michiel, are also contributing to the book about the history of straight edge in Europe that will be

released by Refuse Records with the Birds of a Feather album *The Past The Present*...

Olav: Seein Red — just like Lärm — was and is not a sXe band in terms of all band members being sXe. Jos, the bassist of Seein Red, does drink and smoke. This has *never* been an issue within Seein Red or Lärm. We did embrace sXe with Lärm for the reasons mentioned before, but we were never preachy or militant about it. Hence the lyrics of "Up to you": "Smoke, get cancer / Drink, destroy your brains / One night stands, get herpes / Straight edge, die in a car accident!" Basically we were saying: it's o.k. to be sXe, but don't ever think that you are better than anyone who is not.

We do believe that sXe provides possibilities to address the horrendous conditions and the monotony of the capitalist system in ways that differ from trying to escape through alcohol and/or drug use. But these possibilities can never come from a standpoint of superiority; only from one of unity and solidarity. In our eyes, sXe should have been part of the punk movement (and more!) instead of a reason to split and start a separate sXe scene.

As far as the book goes, we are involved in it because we were part of the history of sXe in Europe and probably still are — but in our own stubborn and non-conformist way.

Going back to the unusualness of communist straight edge: most people would say that it was no coincidence that this union was formed in Europe rather than in North America...

Michiel: I'm not sure. I got quite a lot of mail from the US by people who dug the concept. I think what became a problem of sorts in Europe was that, with the end of Stalinism, the difference between our idea of socialism and Stalinism wasn't clear anymore to a lot of people. Stalinism was something Burt and I vehemently resisted, but there was a strong overall anti-communist, even anti-social democratic sentiment in the wake of the Berlin Wall coming down — an event that we welcomed just like any genuine revolutionary! I remember our local Social Democratic Party apologizing for ever having been socialist, and we started to be confronted with anti-Russia slurs when selling papers and handing out flyers. It wasn't until the huge 1995 strike wave in France that people in Europe opened up to radical socialist ideas on a mass basis again.

Olav: America does not really have the socialist/communist history and traditions that we've had in Europe, so maybe that explains the reason why this union was formed in Europe. Let us also not forget the political climate of the Red Scare, which is very pronounced in the US and which does not really welcome radical socialist ideas. But as Michiel says, people in the USA did dig the concept, and it wasn't like we had it easy in Europe with commie sXe either. A band like ManLiftingBanner was not really welcomed in the punk/hardcore scene with open arms. We were going against the grain and had to fight for our own platform or soapbox, if you will.

I assume this was true for the straight edge scene as well?

Michiel: Since sXe is a somewhat more organic expression of sport jock redneck culture where it's popular to suggest that it's your own fault to be a "loser" in capitalist society, of course we did get a lot of negative feedback — which we also got from anarchists who thought that we propagated a new form of evil communist dictatorship. However, we got a lot of positive feedback and support from people who were genuinely interested in learning about the real revolutionary socialist tradition, and from people who thought that it was a great way of being non-conventional.

Paul: I would say that it was a bit tough because at that time a large percentage of the people involved in the sXe scene were nothing *but* sXe. In many ways they were indeed nothing more than sobered-up youth culture jocks, while to us it seemed kind of self-explanatory that, after you've taken the blindfold of intoxication off, your interests would venture towards examining the oppressive conditions of capitalism, the fucked-up gender dynamics, consumerism, class, race, etc. So when ManLifting-Banner hit the sXe scene with this revolutionary message, we experienced a lot of rejection, especially from the jocks who were the majority within the sXe scene at the time. However, our politics certainly did have an impact on some people, and the so-called "sXe commie movement" flourished for a while. As we said earlier, how big its impact was is another question...

What is your relation to straight edge today?

Paul: Me and Olav are still living straight edge, but our interest in the straight edge movement has surely faded over the years. However, we do pick up on the more interesting stuff coming out of the sXe movement. We are still huge fans of the punk and hardcore movement, and if there's a great new sXe band out there, we'll certainly get their records and go see them play.

Michiel: As far as the straight edge "movement" goes, I'm no longer related to that at all. I never got into sXe bands like Unbroken. My taste for hardcore is very old school. Some sXe bands that appeared later were okay musically, but lyrically they didn't touch me. I still follow what's going on in hardcore, but I only really like stuff from 1981 to 1983.

On a personal level, I still don't do drugs and alcohol and smokes. I never did. I also still hate being in a room where people smoke, it gives me headaches. Neither do I like the way people act when they're drunk, but as long as they don't bother me I'm okay with it.

I don't think that peer pressure to drink or smoke is good, but neither is peer pressure that tells you not to. People should make up their own minds about it and not bother others with their choices. As a high school teacher, I see there's a lot of peer pressure to drink, so every once in a while I state my opinion and tell students that you can be cool without doing it. But the older I get, the more they frown upon that...

Paul: In this context, I really want to mention Ian MacKaye as a fucking great example of how you can take sXe to other levels without being vocal about it. His bands, music, words, attitude, etc. still amaze me.

Are you — as well as the other members of ManLiftingBanner — still involved in political activism?

Michiel: As I said earlier, I'm a member of the International Socialists. I write for their publication, *De Socialist*, and I'm a union activist of sorts in the teachers union. The stuff we focus on as an organization is: opposition to the war, the struggle against the rising tide of racism and islamophobia, and the attempt to establish an alternative for a capitalist system in crisis. Burt's on the Central Committee of the IS and revolution is his daily business. Big — or Lord Bigma — is still active as a Krishna and follows his own passions: reptiles, for example...

Olav: It might sound a bit corny but I still see our band Seein Red as a political project. We are not just making a lot of fucking noise with a political message, but we still do many benefit projects and concerts and contribute to many political organizations and causes.

Apart from the activities with the band, we take part in demonstrations and actions that appeal to us. We are committed antifascists and we support the squatters' movement. At the moment we are not aligned to any political party, although we used to be members both in the Communist Party and the New Communist Party here in Holland. But whenever we can, we support organizations fighting for communism.

Dennis Lyxzén, Umeå, 2007 Mateus Mondini

Refused

Interview with Dennis Lyxzén

Refused was founded in 1991 in Umeå, a college town on Sweden's east coast, 650 kilometers north of Stockholm. The band became the flagship of a remarkably strong vegan straight edge movement that engulfed Sweden throughout the 1990s, although it always remained centered in the country's north. The early stages of the movement are reflected in the compilations *Straight Edge as Fuck* (3 volumes, 1994-97).

Refused soon pushed the boundaries of the traditional hardcore genre. Albums were released with witty manifestos and the band's performances challenged many of the scene's standards. The liner notes to their final album, *The Shape of Punk to Come* (1998), are reprinted in this chapter. More Refused texts can be found at www.burningheart.com/refused. The film *Refused Are Fucking Dead* (2006), produced by guitarist

Kristofer Steen, documents the history of the band, especially its final years.

Dennis Lyxzén has been a co-founder, singer, and songwriter for Refused. After the band dissolved in 1998, he initiated The (International) Noise Conspiracy, a favorite among political hardcore fans to this day. Dennis remains involved in a number of other musical projects (see the interview for more details) and still lives in Umeå.

Discography:
- *This Just Might Be… The Truth*, 1994, Startrec (reissued by Burning Hearts 1997)
- *Songs to Fan the Flames of Discontent*, 1996, Burning Heart Records / Victory
- *The EP Compilation*, 1997, Burning Heart Records (reissued by Epitaph in 2002)
- *The Demo Compilation*, 1997, Burning Heart Records
- *The Shape of Punk to Come: A Chimerical Bombination in 12 Bursts*, 1998, Burning Heart Records, (DVD audio version in 2004)

When I first heard about Refused there was a clear association with straight edge. It must have been in about 1994 and I was living in the States. The first *Straight Edge as Fuck* compilation had come out and all this news was coming in about Refused and the intriguingly big straight edge scene in this somewhat obscure northern Swedish town of Umeå. Soon, however, it seemed that Refused dropped the straight edge label, or at least didn't propagate it anymore… What exactly happened?

Well, first of all I think you have to realize that when we started Refused and got into the whole straight edge thing it was very, very different from what was known as straight edge at the time. Also, we always regarded ourselves much more as a political band than as a straight edge band. So I think straight edge was always a minor part of what we were about.

However, in the 1990s, there was a lot of press coverage in Sweden about us, and it only dealt with the fact that we were vegans — not with our politics. Looking back at our catalog, I think we wrote one song about animal rights, and maybe like half a song about straight edge, but it's always easy for people to find labels they wanna throw onto you.

When we first started playing with Refused in Umeå, there were literally three straight edge kids. Then after a while, there were like eight of us, then twelve, then there was Abhinanda, etc. Still, on the *Straight Edge as Fuck* compilations, I don't think all the bands even were straight edge. At the same time, the label unified people and gave people something that they could get behind. The 90s were very different from now.

Refused was a straight edge, vegan, socialist, anarchist sort of band. We were that all along, until we broke up. At the last Refused show, I'm X-ed up, actually.

I don't know if you can see that. I saw footage of that show, but maybe I have to look more carefully...

No, I think you can't see that, but I did actually X up. It was kind of a fun thing to do, but it was also, you know, a statement.

Anyway, I think what happened was that when we got into straight edge — I got into straight edge before Refused, playing in other bands — we were into Youth of Today, Gorilla Biscuits, Minor Threat, and other US bands, but among our biggest inspirations were bands like Seein Red or ManLiftingBanner. These were bands that talked about politics, about communism/socialism *and* straight edge, and they interlinked the two. This appealed to us since we were into politics and kinda used straight edge as a base for our political ideas.

However, coming from Sweden, you always look at the American scene too, and when we were playing with Refused, there were all these straight edge bands coming out in the mid-90s, you know, like Strife, Snapcase, the whole Victory scene. So, in 1996 we went to the States to tour with Snapcase. On that tour, which lasted for a month, all the straight edge kids we met were complete idiots, while the people we could identify and hang out with were the political punk kids. It was frustrating for us, because now we were one of those Victory bands and were lumped in with the whole macho hardcore scene, while we felt much closer to the more PC, you know, mid-90s emo thing. Our politics were definitely closer to that. I always had a weak spot for *HeartattaCk* and its audience, and I remember writing letters to Kent McClard, trying to explain that we felt like we had a lot in common with them.

Part of the whole problem was that we had bar codes on our Victory Records and so zines like *HeartattaCk* would not write about us. So we were basically stuck in a scene that didn't seem like ours at all. I mean, these kids would come up to us and say, "Yeah, I'm straight edge, bro!" and they were all just jocks. All they were interested in was the "hardcore scene" and their politics went no further than demanding that "everyone should get along." Their goals in life were not a world revolution or to create a better life for everyone; their goals in life were to play hardcore for a couple of years, get a decent job, and settle down with a white picket fence. This was really a weird experience for us.

It's interesting that you mentioned Snapcase. Arguably, that was one of the more conscious US straight edge bands at the time...

The Snapcase guys were really nice. We got along well with them, we toured with them twice. They are really cool people. But they were not into politics, they were not radical people, they were like, you know, "yeah, we are sort of straight edge kids, vegetarian guys..." and that was it. I mean, we got into fights with them during the tour 'cause they thought we talked way too much about politics and got upset that we were so radical. Besides, even if the guys in Snapcase were nice and mellow and had a certain understanding of things, their crowd was not always like that. It's funny too, but if you look at footage from that 1996 US tour, we look like crust punks: everyone's wearing Profane Existence and Exploited shirts.

So that was the beginning of straight edge crust? Just kidding...

Well, we weren't crusties by any means. Our two favorite bands were ManLiftingBanner and Born Against — and then Slayer of course. But we clearly defined ourselves as a punk/hardcore band. I mean, there was a metal edge to our music, for sure, but in the attitude, in what we did, in how we did it, in the politics we had, and in the life we led, we definitely identified as a punk band.

I don't know, it was just kind of a weird culture clash when we came to the States. Out of the straight edge kids we knew in Europe, okay, maybe not everyone was a radical revolutionary, but people were interested and had at least a vague idea of our politics. When we played in the States, we constantly had to defend ourselves 'cause we talked about equality and feminism and gay rights. People were just like, "What's your problem?"

So, to sum this all up, coming back from that tour it seemed like we were caught between the PC punk scene that wouldn't accept us 'cause we played metal hardcore and were on Victory, and the Victory crowd itself that we felt we had nothing in common with. It was alienating, and I guess as a consequence, we were like, "Well, fuck all of them, we just do our own thing!" And consequently, we didn't pay much attention to labels anymore, including straight edge.

The differences between the scenes in Europe and in the States have come up in other conversations I've had. Would you say that in Sweden, for example, there was a stronger connection between identifying as straight edge and being a political activist, or at least being politically aware?

Oh, for sure. It's all a bit strange 'cause the 90s were politically a very inept period. The political landscape of the 90s was very individualistic. Many forms of politics mainly concerned yourself as an individual. I think this is also the reason why straight edge was so big in the 90s: it was a way to be political as an individual. At least in Sweden, being straight edge was seen as a political choice, even though in itself straight edge is not all that political. I think this suited a lot of people who saw politics as a smorgasbord of neat ideas: vegetarianism, gay rights, straight edge... Not many talked about the basis of capitalism or about how the world really worked.

What's interesting to see are the ripple effects that this had. Like, a lot of people in Sweden were really into animal rights, and eventually a lot were really into straight edge too, and even if the political landscape we have in Sweden today is maybe not a direct effect of the whole 1990s straight edge scene, that scene has definitely affected everything we have now.

It's interesting you say that, because for me, someone who has moved to Sweden recently, it doesn't seem like there's a huge self-identified straight edge scene within radical circles on the one hand...

Oh no...

...but on the other hand it seems, for example, pretty common to have radical events that are alcohol-free — more so than in other countries, I think — and I've always wondered if that's one of the effects of the 90s straight edge scene.

I think so, and then there's the whole animal rights thing which was very closely connected to straight edge during the 90s. As a consequence, if you're a political activist in Sweden today and you're not into animal rights, then basically, there's something wrong with you. When I became a vegetarian, I was the only vegetarian I knew. Period. No one was vegetarian. Now it's completely different.

Let me say another thing about the differences between America and Europe, though: America is a country that's based on the idea of a utopia. When The Bill of Rights was written, it was like: *This is as good as it gets. This is the ultimate country.* Meanwhile, in Europe, you talked about class differences, there were two World Wars in the last 100 years, we had countries changing names overnight, we had borders being redefined and redrawn... So I think for people in Europe politics is something that's much closer to the heart. Politics is not something that you get "interested in;" politics is something that you live.

Now with Noise Conspiracy, for example, we still have to defend our politics every time we got to America. When we go to Italy, to Spain, to France, to Germany, we don't have to say shit about our politics 'cause people know. People are down when you talk about the class struggle, about the rise of fascism, about capitalism. People are like, "Yes, we know what you're talking about!" In America, we always have to explain. Politics seems very separated from the people. I think this is another explanation for why the straight edge scene in Europe has been so much more political.

Yet another factor is that in Europe we have squats with very political people, and these are the places where you will play as a straight edge kid — okay, maybe not in Sweden 'cause we don't have any squats, but, in general, if you tour in Europe, that's where you'll play, in the political squats, even as a straight edge band. So of course that makes you politically more aware.

I assume this also means that you had better experiences with straight edge kids in Europe than in the States?

I guess so. However, as I said before, just because you are straight edge doesn't mean that you're automatically my friend or that I agree with your overall view on life. Touring with Refused, we did make a lot of friends and had good times. Not because all the people we hang out with were straight edge though — just because they were cool people.

Nowadays, I can't really say 'cause Noise Conspiracy doesn't exactly attract the youth crew posse... The same goes for my other bands, so I mean, I don't know so much about the straight edge scene anymore. But it is definitely different in Europe than it is in America.

You said that there was a point with Refused where you were like *well, fuck y'all*, because there didn't seem to be a real place for the band in the punk/hardcore scene. I think that's interesting, because Refused seemed to become more and more a very unique and ambitious project. There were manifestos, there was a certain existential philosophy around the band, there was curious artwork, and there was the strong political agenda. Especially since watching the *Refused Are Fucking Dead* documentary, I've always been wondering whether these ambitions led — at least in the case of some members of the band — to an eventual frustration because what the band had set out to do seemed unachievable. Is this a completely wrong perception, or...?

No, no, that's completely accurate. I mean, Refused started off as a band that wanted to release a seven inch — which we never did, which is fucking hilarious. Maybe we wanted to play some shows. I think what happened then was kinda like: you look at the rest of the world, you see all these other bands, you start playing shows with these bands, and suddenly you think, "We are better than most of them! Plus, we're a bunch of smart kids and we have cool ideas!" So, yes, quite early on we became very ambitious — and very pretentious. Which has its good and its bad sides: sometimes being pretentious makes you do really cool things, and sometimes, well, it just makes you an asshole. In any case, we realized that music was something that we could use to define who we were *and* to change our surroundings.

However, this also created problems. When we released *Songs to Fan the Flames of Discontent*, we added a kind of fanzine to the record that explained all the lyrics and was very political. The media focused a lot on this and wrote much more about our politics, or even our diet, than about our music. For those in the band whose focus lay more on music than on politics this was frustrating because our music was very ambitious too! And even for those of us who were very much into the politics, it wasn't easy when we felt that we weren't able to instigate the change that we had wished for. Basically, it's just hard to play in a band with the goal to change the world and turn everyone into a revolutionary... It's a pretty big goal and it can lead to exhaustion.

Speaking of bringing different aspects together, your political influences seem rather varied: we've already talked about vegan straight edge; but there are also pretty clear situationist, poststructuralist, and Marxist notions. Do you see all this naturally connected, or did you simply go through different political developments?

Well, I mean, obviously you develop and learn. I was never interested in forming opinions that I would hold for the rest of my life. I find it inspiring to look at things from new angles. Especially since this is what other people do as well. Whatever the core of one's politics, specific views are dependent on personal and cultural backgrounds, on specific times, places, and settings. So what we wanted to do with Refused as much as with Noise Conspiracy was to provide people with a variety of radical ideas. I mean, I sometimes look at the Noise Conspiracy records which have all these books listed as reading recommendations, you know, and a lot of these books totally contradict each other. You read one book, then you read the next, and you're like, "What the fuck is going on?" But I think if you wanna inspire people, you have to give them a bunch of different alternatives. I never wanted to go out and tell people, "This is what you should think! This is the right way!" This is why our politics have always been very loose. Which I think is a good thing.

Personally, I like to mix different sources and hope that something cool will come out of it. Anarchism and socialism I've always been into. Situationism — which is as much an art movement as it is a political movement with an amazing critique of capitalist society, right at the breaking point of modernism and postmodernism — is just really well suited for lyrics, especially if you look at Raoul Vaneigem. And poststructuralism helps you understand how the world works today. Then you throw in some surrealism and some dada, and everything becomes even more interesting. To me it's about the whole history of revolution and radical resistance — this is something that I've been obsessed with for the last fifteen years.

In connection with The (International) Noise Conspiracy, one aspect that I think fascinated not only me but a lot of people were

the band's aesthetics. I mean, if you think of traditional punk/hardcore bands and you go to an (International) Noise Conspiracy show, it isn't exactly what you'd expect: from the fashion to the choreography. And I mean this in a very positive way. What were your inspirations there?

Something that interests me as much as radical politics and great music is pop culture. All the different eras of pop culture that we've gone through. Now with Noise Conspiracy, this interest generated the idea to do a band that was not only politics, not only music, not only stage presence, but that would focus on all the details: the videos we were making, the way we looked, the layout on our records. We wanted to make use of everything we had and not leave anything up to chance. You know, we didn't wanna be like, "Oh, we didn't really think about that!" We wanted to think about every aspect of the band. We wanted to use everything we could to make the band as cool as possible.

Must be a lot of fun, just the experimenting...

Yes, for sure. I mean, we've been playing for ten years now with Noise Conspiracy, and you can look at our outfits throughout the years, and they've changed a lot, and so did the whole aesthetics. With every new record, we try something new — not only with the aesthetics, but with the politics and the music too. We maintain our ideas and our musical foundation, but we kind of switch and twist them a little bit every time and try to spice them up with something new.

You know, a lot of people try to decide what exactly it is that people should like about their band. We just figure that people can dig the politics, they can dig the snazzy outfits, they can dig the music, they can dig whatever — it's up to them to decide what to take with them when they leave our show or listen to our record. So while many bands are like, "This is what we are and this is what you should like about us," we just say, "Whatever you like is cool with us. If you don't like the politics, we're sure you find something else that you like."

I was always into this concept, so with Noise Conspiracy I got a chance to realize it. Actually, when we did the last batch of touring with Refused, I tried to get the band to wear matching outfits, but the guitar players just happened to "lose" them. After a week of shows they were just like, "Eh, these jackets that we had tailor-made are gone..."

I saw The (International) Noise Conspiracy with matching outfits though — so no one there "lost" them...

Oh, no! You know, I think with Refused we were a band that got together and we gradually became what we became. In the middle of all this I was like, "Oh, let's do matching outfits!" and some of the band members were just like, "Come on, I wanna play music!" But with Noise Conspiracy, we had this idea from our very first practice. So it was easier to make it happen 'cause everyone was on the same page. It was not like six years into the band I was like, "Okay, I got some new ideas for you guys!"

Tell us what you are doing now, Dennis. It seems like you are involved in some new musical projects, besides from The (International) Noise Conspiracy. You are even playing with David Sandström again, the only other permanent Refused member...

That's right. Actually, I got a couple of different projects. I'll run it down for you real fast:

I used to be in a band called The Lost Patrol Band, and now we are called Invasionen. We sing in Swedish and we will soon be recording a record.

Then me and David started a band called AC4. The interesting thing is that a lot of people get kind of excited that me and David, the guys from Refused, are doing a band together again — however, me and the drummer, a guy called Jens, started playing music together in 1988. We played in a punk rock band, and in 1989 we started what was probably Sweden's first straight edge band. So me and Jens have known each other for a long time, and now we're back playing together and it's a lot of fun.

Let us return to straight once more. I mean, I don't know how explicit the politics will be in your new projects, but given that The (International) Noise Conspiracy is still running, I assume that politics remain a big part of your art and your life. Does straight edge also remain a part of this, even if you are not exactly advertising it? Is it fair to say that?

Yes, I would say that's true. I mean, it's one of those things where you feel that when you're young — or younger? okay, let's say young — you have maybe a stronger need to define what you are and what you are against. In that sense straight edge was probably a good way to get into politics. But as far as the whole straight edge scene goes, I'm not involved in that today. It seems more like a youth cultural kind of thing, and I don't really feel any connection to it anymore. So, I don't X up, I don't call myself straight edge — but I'm still drug-free, and that's still a part of me that I'm very comfortable with.

Would you still see this connected to your politics on a personal level, though?

I think everything you are, and the way you live your life, is connected to your politics, and there are definitely still political reasons why I don't drink, but, I mean, in broad terms, I'm just very comfortable with the way I am as a person.

I always felt that it was strange to be part of a youth culture where people define you as straight edge and have certain expectations, even if you never wanted to be a spokesperson. I think for a lot of people who were part of the straight edge scene, or that particular 90s scene, it was hard for them when they decided to move on in life. It caused them a lot of anxiety 'cause many others were looking at them as role models. I always felt that if I really wanted to get drunk tomorrow, then I should get drunk.

In short, where I'm at in my life right now, straight edge is not something that defines me all that much. I'm still comfortable with not drinking, but if I had this sudden urge to get hammered, I just might get hammered, you know...

And you wouldn't make the revolution dependent on being straight edge either?

Exactly. But, as I said, I'm comfortable with how I am, and I connect a lot of my drug-freeness to political ideas. I think that's still important. In general, though, as long as you are comfortable with the way you are, I think that's how you should live your life.

The Shape of Punk To Come

Liner notes to the Refused album *The Shape of Punk to Come* (1998)

The worms of the senses ponder quickly towards destruction. Winning is not everything but in our elitist competitive society it is all that matters. Rice cakes for the people and caviar for the leaders who built our world around machines, money and matter. We were left out of the plan and our destination is set by the used car dealer or the factory boss. Bored we walk home with our heads hanging and our creativity stolen as an effect of capitalist gain. In a dream state there is nothing more than simple abstraction of the mind from the matter and the belief that work will somehow "macht frei." The theory that Marx recognised from Feuerbach, and now we, the people, need to see the spectacle that binds us to our "destiny." Alienation is not commodity, figures, statistics or make believe but very much a real tool of oppression and seclusion. If we can't take our part then we must not take part. The faculties of the skull are another dimension of that which is sucking us dry. The imperialisation of the third world is dominant even in our taste for soft drinks and afternoon snacks. With dry wits and knuckles dragging the ground co-operations claim that profit is rightfully theirs and that the blood squeezed out of Africa, South America, Burma, The Baltic states and South Asia is nothing but market interest and public craving. Their products are death and they are salesmen of corruption and power abuse. They are the slave dealers of our time. They are the inquisition. They are the machine that must be stopped.

Turn the knob and wait for the liberating sound of ecstasy and revolution. Who pays the newsman and who owns the radio stations and who runs the record label? Who benefits from the de-politicizing in art and music and who benefits from the clean sound of the next pop wonder? Who runs the game show and who pays the salaries to the reporters? Here and now we offer you a taste of our *liberation frequency*, provided by us for your satisfaction and excitement. This is radio clash, 33 Revolutions Per Minute, our haven of thoughts and ideas. It could be yours too, if only you'd let yourself go and turn the knob and listen and love and sing and think.

Stuck by *the deadly rhythm* of the production line. Stuck by the conditions set by the capitalist market. Stuck by the necessities of living and forced to take part. If we are tired it is because we are supposed to be and if we are hungry it is because we have to be and if we are bored it is because it is expected of us. Bored and chained and stuck and dead. New forms of work camps are arranged and new ways of hiding the monotonous beat of slavery are being presented. The preliminary condition required for propelling the workers to the status of "free" producers and consumers of commodity was the violent expropriation of their own time. The spectacular return of time was made possible only after this dispossession of power. Urbanism is capitalism's seizure of the natural and human environment; developing logically into absolute domination, capitalism can and must now remake the totality of space into its own setting. Time, work, environment and joy all have their norms set by modern ways of production.

The awkward youngster touches his poster and glances upon the stars and the heavens. The day seems never-ending and there is a certain notion of innocence and childhood play. The mantra will be repeated and we will learn to obey and love and cherish the chosen few. Manners inconceivable and then we have to live. Ideals corrupted and echoes from the past about ideas once held true are shining like untouchable constellations. But we are all stars, shining and burning, cruising down the highway looking for the next stop and the next break from capitalised boredom and slavery. Then there is the option of *summer holidays vs. punk routine*. Then there is greed and money and fallen heroes. "We are all tired of dying." So why not try and live for a change and turn that glimmering into bright shining creation through the realisation that you know everything and that you are you?

Must I paint you a picture about the way that I feel? This situation of Art vs. Life and the present elitism within the bourgeoisie and upper-class. The critics hold their heads high cause they know about the real suffering and the real work while we get the easy accessible forms of communication and entertainment, pinned down simple for us to comprehend. The lack of stimulants within art, politics and life lowers our standards, which is why we settle for talk shows and MTV. We are not stupid, but if we are treated like ingrates we will start to act like children. The lack of challenging forms of expression and thoughts of fire and self-confidence gives us a passive and hollow nature. So reclaim art, take back the fine culture for the people, the working people, the living people and burn down their art galleries and destroy their fancy constructions and buildings. Cause we, unlike the bourgeoisie, have nothing to lose and therefore our expression will be the only honest one, our words will be the only challenging ones and our art will be the one revolutionary expression. We need new noise and new voices and new canvases to become something more than the last poets of a useless generation.

The credentials with which we call upon you are simple linguistics thrown and tossed liked flaming songs of discontent. *The Refused party programme* screams out not one, not two, not three, not four, not five but six opinions and six structures of change and six levels of liberation. All in all not mystical but direct and attractive and as we shout "Yeah" you'll feel the same sensation best described by Thomas Paine: "Let them call me rebel and welcome, I feel no concern from it; but I should suffer the misery of devils, were I to make a whore of my soul..." Here and now and all the time the mythical touch and the obvious message. Behold the wisdom of the party programme.

Pro (in favour) — attest (testify for).

The time is now and still we sit and wait for it to become the now that we think we need. The movement of protest has strong traditions and we are far from the first to recognise and use the power of the song and the words from the young poets. We are trembling from the taste of days gone to waste and there is inspiration and there is clarity. Phil Ochs stated firmly "If I have something to say I'm going to say it now" and still *protest song 68* is nothing more than a pastiche, a blueprint of seduction of the echoes that once filled the corridors of dorms and boys'/girls' rooms in an era where rebellion and revolt was present in art and music. From the first until the last, from the taste of longing freedom to the shackles of oppression, the weapon of the artist has always been used.

Refused are fuckin dead that's what the answering machine said, looks like this is it!!! They talked one too many shit about the upper-class and the government, did you hear what those faggots said in some fanzine someone else read. I heard they are a bunch of spoiled little rich kids who need to get their asses kicked. Fuckin ingrates! Fuckin pussies!! Refused are fuckin dead guaw huydsas kjhds aowedde (fighting sequence). Refused are fuckin dead by order of the postmaster general just like the panthers only this time for real because SAPO have tapped their telephones and the Umeå police raided their homes and they must have been killed.

Are you ready baby? For *the shape of punk to come*. Get the equipment together and we'll meet at the show. It's gruesome that someone so handsome should care. We all recognise the hint of the programme screaming at the top of his lungs that "We're all dressed up and we got somewhere to go." Like the rebellious swing kids of the 40's or the crazy jazz heads of the 50's to the stylish mods of the 60's we all need to recognise that style in contradiction to fashion is necessary to challenge the conservatism of the youth cultures placed upon us. Strict in our style but with a touch of elegance and freedom and individualism. The uniform and the production of constructive challenges comes in the most unexpected of shapes, Ornette Coleman reinvented jazz altogether

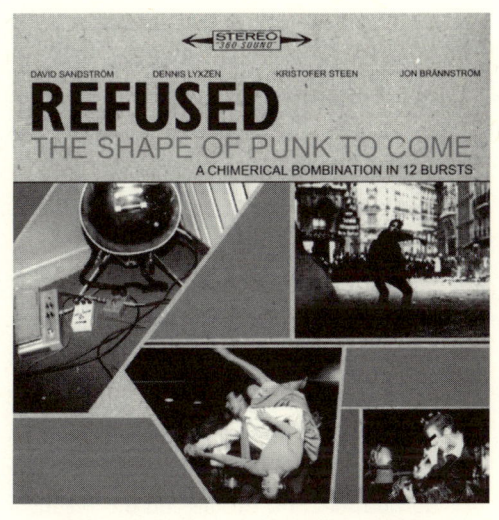

Refused album cover: The Shape of Punk to Come

and we need a new beat to move to so grab your partner and ask: Do you want to go out with me, watch me get on my knees and bleed? This blind date might take you to places unknown and it will be new and scary and vital. But nonetheless there is no danger in exploration and searching. It never tasted this great to scream "yes" and you never had more enticing cavalier to hold hands with. The new teen hysteria of noise and kisses and politics and crazy entertainment and naked fun and beats and books and poetry and travelling and style. It's never been safe to live in a world that teaches us to respect property and disregard human life. So drop your belongings and get on this soul train, dig the static sound and think that maybe this once there is just us, the kids, playing the day away, it's just us kicking over statues and smashing windows of houses of parliaments, just to show them who has the real power. This blind date will take us anywhere we want.

A dream only lasts so long. Imagine the pyramids inhabited by aliens and the dark corridors and the dreams and the longing for better financial conditions. The sweat pours down your neck and you run and you run, heart beating, head pounding, alive tonight. The streets never sleep, they are glowing, vibrating with the echoes of laughter and joy, screams and curses. We just need to take the time and see what it can offer us and how we can break free from this boredom that the capitalist reign has forced upon us. Tonight we can be as mighty as *Tannhäuser* and we can tumble excitedly down the labyrinths and the turns knowing that *derive* is potent. So where do we go from here?

The Apollo programme was a hoax or so we say. The biggest lie was market economy that blinded us with the glory of prosperity and freedom. The deck was dealt and we all lost, on our knees in the dirt hoping for salvation and then we look and there are golden drops of dawn functioning as oral sagas, keeping us shackled, making glory of the lies that the spectacle provides us with. So as we sit tight and enjoy the soap operas that are designed to keep us bleeding out of our eyes and keeps us nodding and sighing, there is still hope in the petrol bomb and in it, the revolution. For in the destruction and the overthrowing there is a certainty of salvation. We need to destroy the museum and its old artefacts, we need to tear down the power structures that enslave and then in revolution we can live and be alive. Yes, this is our hymn and our praise to the brave and bold stranger in the night, to the fed up worker and the angry wife. Hope, revolution and dedication. Fight fire with fire and everything will burn. Yeah.

This manifesto is very much for real.

Point of No Return
Bending to Stay Straight

Point of No Return was a Brazilian vegan straight edge band that proved highly influential for the development of political straight edge hardcore in Brazil, Latin America, and beyond. The band was active from 1996 to 2006. Their album *Liberdade Imposta, Liberdade Conquistada / Imposed Freedom, Conquered Freedom* (2002) was released with an essay sketching the history of straight edge and articulating a political approach to sobriety. The essay, "Bending to Stay Straight," is reprinted here. It is followed by an interview with Frederico Freitas, one of the band's two vocalists. Frederico still lives in São Paulo where he works on motion graphics and pursues a graduate degree in Latin American History.

Discography:
- *Voices*, 1997, Liberation Records
- *What Was Done*, 1999, Catalyst Records
- *Centelha*, 2000, Liberation Records (US release: Sparks, 2001, Catalyst Records)
- *Liberdade Imposta, Liberdade Conquistada*, 2002, Liberation Records (European release: Imposed Freedom, Conquered Freedom, Scorched Earth Policy, 2002)

I. crisis

It's weird, but since that conversation the question would turn into a sort of obsession to her. It's true that the matter had been raised, there in that particular place, in a casual way, amidst a muddle of tables, friends, juices, and all the fun that such circumstances involve. But already in that moment it was evident that the discussion had affected her in a peculiar manner, far deeper than it had affected the others. While all of her friends were speaking, signaling, yelling and laughing, there she stood — grave, incapable of a single movement, obsessively staring at some fixed point and at the same time she stared at nothing — an exterior inertia intensely contrasting with the deluge of ideas and reflections that permeated her thoughts on the occasion. In the others' eyes it might even be that the conversation was nothing but incidental. But to her, that discussion had amounted to a number of concerns that had disturbed her for a long time.

No doubt she had taken that matter quite seriously. It had now been a considerable number of years since she had begun to confine herself behind a flag that would always present, identifying and defining her before anyone even knew her. As if she were claiming something like, "Can you see that? 'Cos that's the way I am and will be." Or, considering the enormity of the mark on her hands, she seemed to be much more emphatic indeed: "Did you get it? That's my essence! And I'm proud of it!" — an ostentation which now, honestly speaking, sounded (why not to admit it?) quite pointless to her.

Not because those labels would somehow distress her — she had never shared such naïve anguish, so proudly re-asserted by those self-proclaimed "original people" or "masters of their own fate," apparently unaware of the obvious yet paradoxical truth that, by denying their participation in any group, they were already affiliating with at least one: the "groupless" group. Nor because she would prefer to run away from discussions and avoid conflicts — to evade life's polemics had not been part of her temperament at all since her earliest adolescent years — a period in which, along with some friends, she started becoming conscious that the world was filled with injustice, and that her role should be to take a resolute stance against this situation. In fact, that ostentation sounded excessive to her because after many years, with all the countless good times and a few (albeit remarkable) deceptions, her experience would end up revealing that pride did not, as she had expected, emerge from the group's ideas but from the group itself: the collectivity that constantly reaffirms its values to its members in jokes, conversations and arguments; in the fanzines that kids read, in the songs to which they sing along, in the eternal tattooed messages through which they more and more attest their loyalty to one another.

It is true that every flock has its evading sheep and she was familiar with these exceptions. To a few people, joining the crew did not imply the adoption of a new stance determined by the group, but only the consolidation of a way of life, which to them was already old and habitual. Even then — she was convinced of it — the evasion of rule in this case could only be partial, since, once protected by the mask of collectivity, the group would always become, on one hand, a major constraint over each individual's role in the play and, on the other hand, a major incentive for the pride everyone felt when enacting it.

That is how she also came to realize that when the group thus vanishes, so does pride — if not immediately and without conflict, then slowly and progressively, over time. She had been a living witness to this truth and, if she had not given up that flag yet, she understood that it was only because that these things worked out more or less like weddings do: people consent to a particular role for such a long time that, after so many years, they would rather remain crawling, on and on, less for satisfaction than for mere convenience. After all she went through, she could now acknowledge that her inspiration was not the same as it had been in earlier years, when she seemed to have found the ultimate answer to all dilemmas of her Earthly existence.

Thus, the crisis.

But time moves on, and backwards, and people along with it. One day, she was confident that she would overcome that near-anomic condition — that common yet perplexing feeling of displacement, of not belonging, which despite being so confusing constitutes such an essential stage of our lives, for that is exactly when people grow more critically toward themselves. One day she would overcome that near-anomic condition to assert that she had finally recovered a solid ground to fix herself with renewed motivation and conviction. At that time, however, overcoming that state was still pretty distant — it was nothing but an aspiration, or, perhaps, a positive obsession.

What was in fact the basis that sustained her? Was this basis the same to her and to other people? Was it the same in her country and in other places? Was it the same in that time as in other times? Those were the questions, which, after that unpretentious conversation among friends, would refuse to leave the mind of this young woman.

ii. definition

It is curious but as soon as she got home the first thing that would occur to her was to check out a dictionary. Initially she had not been considering whether such an idea would be good or not, useful or not — she was just curious to know what it was that the dictionary would have to say about the term employed to define her identity. That would be the second step in her investigation: to explore all possibilities of significance of that word — that which conveyed who she was. In a way it might be said that it was a question for herself that was taking place right there in the middle of that immense mass of letters. Would she really be able to find herself in it?

"To begin with, the 's'..."

She wanted to know whether the dictionary would confirm what the *inquisitive-one* had remarked in that conversation. It was he who had started the whole polemic — though she could not actually remember why — by claiming that straightedge, in many North American bands, was a quite puritan attitude, and that even the very name, *straightedge*, could be considered to hold some conservative connotations.

"Then comes the 't'..."

The *distracted-one* suddenly realized that there was a sort of debate taking place and argued that this conservatism was, in fact, very real — not a trivial point at all. One just needed to observe how kids would come up and categorically claim, "I'll be the same 'til the day I die," or even hypocritically declare, "Watching you fall only makes me stronger," referring in this case to those who, at some point in their lives, decide to embrace life's contingency and change the way they are.

"Now, the 'r'..."

With a subtle smile in her face, she now recalled the way the *short-tempered-one*, already in the early moments of discussion, would manifest a clear irritation, arguing how unfair it was to claim that those people there, in that conversation, discriminated against those who broke the edge. Well, maybe not, she wondered. But that did not mean that the group would deal with changes in a positive way, most of the time.

"Next letter is 'a'..."

Hey! She could remember now. The polemic was actually raised when the *skeptical-one* stood up and proposed, with his unyieldingly sarcastic tone, that they should come up with another movement to follow, since what straightedge meant to most of the North American and European kids had nothing to do with what it meant to those in that place.

"After the 'a' comes the 'i'..."

The *sympathetic-one* laughed as she recalled a stupid term that had in fact already been proposed as a potential new label to replace the old one — the one that some North American youngster had once come up with in a song of his punk band, without his knowing that, from those unpretentious verses on, a whole movement was going to emerge.

"With 'g,' it is near the end..."

As she recalled that conversation, she just started regretting that the *optimistic-one* was not there on that particular day. If he had been, he would surely have enjoyed the *skeptical-one's* proposition, claiming loud and clear to everyone what he always used to say: that the reality of most kids in his neighborhood was far from those experienced by high school teens from Boston.

"Now, the 't': is it before or after the 'h'..."

Straight was the word she was looking for: a sequence of sounds somewhat strange to the Portuguese phonologic system — the reason why all of them held their own proper way of pronouncing it. She was not looking for the whole expression, straightedge, because she knew it would not appear in a dictionary. 'Straight' was enough and after a while she finally reached her point. The aim was to see what the *Cambridge International Dictionary of English* — chosen accidentally, with no particular reason, except that it was a good English dictionary at hand — would have to say about that term. Or, in other words, she wanted to see what the *Cambridge International Dictionary of English* would have to say about who she was and who she had been in the last ten years.

"Here it is..."

straight /streit /
1. NOT CURVING [adj./adv.] continuing in one direction without bending or curving.
2. LEVEL [adj.] not sloping to either side.
3. IMMEDIATELY [adv.] without pausing or delaying.
4. TIDY [adj.] arranged in order.
5. PLAIN [adj.] plain and basic; without anything added.
6. HONEST [adj.] truthful.
7. SERIOUS [adj.] not laughing.
8. CLEAR [adj.] simple or clear; not complicated.
9. FOLLOWING EACH OTHER [adj.] following one after another without an interruption. Consecutive.
10. TRADITIONAL [adj.] conventional or serious.
11. SEXUALITY [adj.] *slang* not homosexual.
12. NO DRUGS [adj.] *slang* not using illegal drugs or alcohol.

Thus, the definition.

What is it that even a brief analysis of this information might reveal? In concrete terms, she reckoned, *straight* was used to describe the mark of the shortest path that could possibly exist between two distinct points in space: a perfectly straight line. When the word referred to the surface of a figure, it would describe the least possible area within three or more points in space: a perfectly flat surface. Despite the fact that the spatial concept related to this word seemed somehow suggestive, she knew that it was its social connotation that would prove most revealing. What did that word come to mean when it was appropriated by a native English speaker to designate some kind of people or to define a certain standard in one's attitudes and behavior? While she examined the definitions provided by the dictionary one by one, the young woman started developing her own conclusions, many quite discouraging: to be *straight* would mean 1) never changing one's philosophy — the always straight path; 2) not having any flaws in one's basis of thinking — the totally flat surface; 3) to be organized; 4) not to be of much complexity; 5) to be honest; 6) to be serious; 7) to take a clear stand; 8) to be traditional; 9) to be a heterosexual; 10) to abstain from drugs and alcohol.

But what is amazing is that many of those meanings, some of them truly repulsive, seemed to reflect, sometimes directly, all of her anxieties raised up in that discussion — the puritanism, conservatism, and fear of change. Her impression was that, if she was to interpret the *Cambridge International Dictionary of English* literally, it would be better for her to quit hardcore as quickly as possible and just go join the Moral Majority. But the young woman was not stupid and she knew how to make this problem relevant. Thank god (or devil, or, most probably, an ideological divergence) there was no need for her to accept such definitions as being in any way representative of her own way of being, as well as of those friends with whom she was affiliated, even if these definitions actually portrayed the way many kids around the world, under the same label, saw themselves.

Indeed ideological as any discourse, the dictionary should be nothing but a preliminary and cautious step in her question — a beginning, but never an end. After all, would it be reasonable for her to limit such an important reflection on (and for) her life to what a group of lexicologists say in a dictionary — people who do not even know the hardcore scene and the specific meanings of the term that it held? That is why this first moment in the investigation sounded to her like a provoking, and even comic, preamble within a rather serious critical process whose satisfactory answer she still hoped to achieve.

If, in the truth that she knew, word meanings did not lie within words, but outside them, in the rather unstable and arbitrary common sense, a more interesting and decisive investigation would be a reflection on some of the most influential meanings that, until then, had been attributed to the term straightedge (SXE) by different groups of people in different times and places. Therefore it would be such consideration that would become her concern from then on.

iii. history

It is interesting, but a fact from which this woman could not hide, that although the power of the group seemed to be a fundamental point as far as SXE was concerned, the motives for each person to become straight were frequently diverse; sometimes, even antagonistic. She had already grasped the truth that, once within the group, people would end up assuming its values in one way or another — some to a higher and others to a lower degree; some more critically, others more blindly. However, what seemed to draw her attention at that second and more reasonable moment of reflection, was that the SXE, according to its place and time, would always assume distinct forms and values. Elaborating a little bit more on the *inquisitive-one's* comments in the earlier conversation, SXE and puritanism might even have had hands defining the perspective of many hardcore kids today, but the fact was that the puritan image did not fit perfectly, or even grossly, into each and every scene, including those in North America.

One had but to consider the great differences that could be seen among the various perspectives on SXE that had arisen in the history of the North American hardcore scene. This seemed to be an interesting point from which to start her reflection, since the USA held the position as the greatest imperialist power, the reason why it came to be the place from which the main SXE models would arise — those that influenced the worldwide hardcore scene in the most impressive way. At that point

Ratos de Porão (Brazil), São Paulo, 2009   Mateus Mondini

she would start recalling, with an amazing clarity, a weekend she had spent debating exactly this topic with her best friend; a discussion in which three main perspectives had caught each one's attention because of the large impact that these perspectives had on the Brazilian SXE scene.

The first important perspective held a strong me-alone-against-the-world idea. Represented by bands like *7 Seconds, Minor Threat* and many other bands primarily from Washington DC, SXE in this trend was quite individualistic — a value which, she had already observed in other occasions, seemed to heavily pervade most of North Americans' views and stances, structuring from progressive to conservative lines of thought. Hardcore itself was also a continuation of a healthful and positive individualism that grounded the basis of the punk attitude, but SXE from that generation would take all this to an extreme: they were the opposition to the opposition, the utmost expression of this individualism.

"I don't smoke, I don't drink, I don't fuck. At least I can fuckin' think," said its maxim — that she held at the tip of her tongue. The principle was for everyone to do whatever they wanted with their lives; to be out of step with society; to give no account for one's actions; or as the great metaphor would synthesize, to be the black sheep. Sustaining such a stance, there lay a firm belief — the product of this same kind of individualism, that each person is the absolute master of his or her own fate — perhaps neglecting that in order for a dissident black sheep to escape, the participation of other cooperative sheep distracting the shepherd's attention was absolutely crucial.

In this model she saw, despite the individualistic façade that had never pleased her, one of the most interesting conceptions of SXE in the North American hardcore scene: an intelligent way of keeping the punk attitude of protest without buying the whole thing and embracing that nihilistic self-destructive lifestyle that — except in the very inception of those restructuring times which marked the beginning of the punk movement — made no sense at all for a youth eager to fight for social change.

As she thought about the portrait that she was sketching little by little, the traces that composed it, and the relationships they established among each other, it became more and more transparent to her. She now turned her focus to a second model, which certainly differed in many respects from the first one. Represented by bands like *Youth of Today* and other bands hailing mainly from New York, this tendency was much less into individualism than into a spirit-of-youth-against-the-world idea.

This was not surprising, since for this trend to appear, two sources seemed to be a decisive influence: firstly, bands such as *Agnostic Front* and the *Cro-Mags* from the old New York hardcore scene, all of them markedly defined by a sort of street-gang culture — characteristic of the place where they came from — that was firmly reflected in their lyrics. Secondly, and more obviously, bands such as *DYS* and *SSD* from the old Boston hardcore scene, where the power of thirty or forty strong guys seemed to render enough security for the crew to survive in a society in which they could not fit. The '88 SXE hardcore, as it would be known later, was the heir to these two scenes and thus it seemed inevitable that it would end up placing value on the role of the group.

"Me, you, youth crew," said its maxim — to which she used to sing along so passionately. The principle was to deny one's heart to a hostile and decaying world, to then devote it to the group of friends; to take a clear stance, "us versus them;" or as the great metaphor would synthesize, to be one more member of the wolfpack. Sustaining such a stance, there lay the NY sentiment of pride of the family, added to the Bostonian sensation of power of the crew — perhaps ignoring the stupid waste of force and cohesion manifested in a wolfpack which is united to fight against another and not to struggle against its real predators.

For the young woman, although sympathetic to that emphasis on the construction of a non-individualistic resistance, the criticism she held for this trend would be one of the gravest: that was, with rare exception, the generation that produced the most futile bands of the SXE history. Through a powerful, energetic music — though excessively tough in her eyes — sterile lyrics, without any critical stance, were articulated. The identity of the group and the aggressiveness that it encompassed lost the relevant significance of opposing a world of absurd values, and turned into mere empty symbols to be perpetually evoked and glorified at the shows — rituals of mental masturbation that came to nothing. Pride, for pride's sake, and that's it. Today, with a more critical perspective, that is how she saw the '88 generation: in the music, greatly powerful, in the ideas, sadly mediocre.

The third and last model had been special — she'd had the opportunity to watch its development at each new step. This was the model which had prevailed in the North American SXE scene since the beginning of the 90's, and whose main representative was *Earth Crisis* from Syracuse. There she could see the fostering of a fairly new concept in SXE, which would give rise to an important trend in the movement: VeganStraightEdge (VSXE). The refusal to inebriate oneself, now added to a vegetarian ideology, ceased to be an individual stance (as in the first model), or a group stance (as in the second model), to then become a political cause for which the militant SXE would feel compelled to fight. At the same time, the trend seemed strongly grounded in a Christian extremist ideology that, as reflected in the lyrics, was used to symbolize the struggle for justice through a vegan-straight-edge-crusade-against-the-evil idea.

"Perpetrators of this madness, your right to live is gone. Your burning bodies shall light the path to a glorious new dawn," said its maxim — in one of the songs that most impressed her. The principle was to become a VSXE warrior; to be the owner and defender of justice; to give oneself to martyrdom; to retaliate all evil perpetrated by those demons who destroy our planet; or as the great metaphor would synthesize, to bring the firestorm to purify. Following this view, many bands who later adopted this trend made a mix of several types of fundamentalism, including, and principally, Islamic. The metaphor, in this case, shifted its form, but not its meaning: the Christian sacred war (the crusade) was gone, only to make room for the Muslim sacred war (the jihad) — perhaps ignoring the fact that the firestorm would inevitably provoke an uncontrollable blaze, burning both the rotten and the healthy trees without discrimination, destroying that which was originally supposed to be preserved.

On the one hand, a specific aspect of this generation grasped the young woman's sympathy as no other trend had been able to do: the power and determination that the SXE would attain when it was seen as a cause for militant politics — the kind of politics which actually transcended the parameters of hardcore. On the other hand, there was another aspect in this trend which, unlike that which had occurred with the other models, contributed to keep her almost totally away from it: the sad contradiction between methods and aims, reflected in the discourse of bands that preached the end of tyranny through fundamentally tyrannical words.

All these SXE models had an undeniable relevance, but the young woman knew that in her country the sources of influence went far beyond them — beyond Uncle Sam's land. Europe, also, because of the same imperialist forces that would uphold the USA as a cultural paradigm to the world, would produce some very influential SXE models — though notably distinct from the North American ones. Among these models, one in particular grasped her — one that had reached its highest intensity in the beginning of the 90's, represented by bands like *Nations on Fire* from Belgium, and *Manliftingbanner* from Holland. Whereas in the USA, the heirs of the vegan jihad were moving towards more and more conservative as well as extremist stances, people with a leftist-struggle-against-capitalism idea would revitalize the SXE at the other side of the Atlantic — following the trail already blazed by bands such as Lärm in the 80s — with a critical and progressive, intelligent and incisive critique.

"When man is free, when there is no more need. I will rest my soul in peace," said its maxim — with which this woman would identify more than any other. The principle was to place social, political and economic matters as top priorities; to propose alternatives of social organization for an unacceptable capitalist system; or as the great metaphor would synthesize, to be positive, political, powerful. Sustaining such concepts, there lay two main lines of leftist thought: communism and anarchism — perhaps defying, through an unbreakable faith, their own historical time, marked by the recent Soviet collapse and the then drowsy international anarchist movement.

Undoubtedly, the European SXE model seemed to her a much more interesting approach than any of the North American ones. Not only because it moved completely away from the right-wing perspective of the purifier firestorm, but also because it denied the political emptiness of the '88 wolfpack and extended the leftist notion of the black sheep, transcending its well-intentioned reformist individualism in order to definitely adopt a radical political and economic critical perspective. Besides, it was in this European model that could be finally seen an explicit concern in extending the idea of the brotherhood to that of the sisterhood, something which had often passed unnoticed through the North American trends.

There was only one problem in this perspective that she could not help but to point out: probably in an unconscious attempt to distance itself from the fundamentalists that liked to impose the drug-free lifestyle upon others by force — something that was in conflict with its progressive stance of respect for individual liberties — the bands in this generation relegated SXE to the personal realm, dissociating the problem of drug consumption from its deep political and economic implications on which drug refusal, and thus traffic refusal, should be based. The model seemed limited, therefore, precisely because it failed to incorporate the very SXE attitude within this larger political perspective of a radical left.

Thus, the history.

Moving toward the end of this second interesting step in her process of reflection on SXE, there was a hesitation that simply refused to abandon her mind: the way she was thinking of those different social movements could barely reflect the way they actually existed. In truth, all that description was nothing but a scheme — something which she had already criticized in other people's discourse as well. History, she thought, did not develop in a linear process, within which different movements simply follow one another — least of all through a discontinuous process within which one movement always rises up from another's demise. On the contrary, experience shows that social movements develop in a mutually dependent and simultaneous manner, in such a way that in each movement it is always possible to identify — through affirmation, negation, or yet ironic references — those signs that constitute the others.

Another aspect to be considered was that the very content attributed to those four categories seemed not to completely reproduce reality: in truth, all that description was nothing but a stereotype. Presumably, for those who have actually experienced some of those trends, her analysis would certainly appear as an unfortunate reduction: a simplification of forms and meanings that, in the everyday life, are mixed and confused in a much more complex and indeterminate way. Besides, for those who had not directly taken part in those trends, but who had experienced other ones which were (to them) equally, if not more, important, the choice of these specific trends could only represent a distortion: an arbitrary selection whose inevitable result would be the depiction of a grotesque caricature of what (to them) SXE was actually about.

But even in the face of all these considerations, something was telling her that the enterprise was still valid. Maybe because her aim had never been to elaborate a detailed or true reconstruction of SXE history, for in her eyes true reconstructions were not something possible to attain. All she wanted to do was to rethink the main lines of thought that, with their values and aesthetics, had remarkably influenced the scene in which she had been initiated and grown. So if her analysis was nothing but a scheme, it was because that analysis was a vulgar exercise, not a scientific research. And if it was nothing but a caricature, it was because her emphasis in some specific aspects of SXE history — and it just could not be otherwise — resulted from her own subjective perspective: the way she — a young, white, middle class woman, involved in hardcore since the 90s, in a third world metropolis — had grasped North American and European SXE hardcore.

Finally, she knew that this small historical reflection, as her search through the dictionary, was not her final goal, but a means through which that journey into herself continued to advance. Indeed, it was precisely this process of investigation that had opened the way for her to then start looking for her own definition of the term straightedge — the possibility of finding out a ground where she could find her feet. At least, the political purpose of these final steps seemed to be pretty clear in her mind: there was a need to achieve an actual re-definition — a definition which could point out the particularities or the new meanings which her group's view on SXE carried on. It was only by attaining such singularity that her definition would be able to subvert the (almost) crystallized flux of cultural colonialism: not only from the center to the margins, but also from the margins to the center.

"Ladies and gentlemen", she thought aloud, as if addressing an audience full of interested people: "Here comes our local definition."

iv. redefinition

It's funny, but as her investigation went on, the somehow excessive reluctance that had characterized her initial moment of crisis — in which her only certainty was her total uncertainty about everything — would now start showing some signs of weakening, giving way to a growing feeling of relief and safety. The initial point of this change had undoubtedly been the retrospection that she had just carried out: it was only by reflecting on each of those SXE models that she could more clearly realize how much of her own conception was borrowed from them, how much she had actually rejected, and how everything that had been appropriated all now seemed to acquire new meanings.

Her perspective on SXE held, as it was with the black sheep model, the conviction that it was important to not blindly follow the stream. It was such conviction that had motivated those kids in the early 80s to intelligently dislocate some elements with no apparent connection in the tradition and then combine them in a defying and interesting manner: the way the straight-punks would bring polemic to a scene in which, ironically, the deviation from rule was acquiring the rigidity of another rule. This new perspective was in defiance because it combined, in a single idea, concepts apparently antagonistic to each other: the straight and the tortuous; and it was interesting because the new meaning thus derived pointed precisely to a more critical way of looking at both: we've got to reclaim freedom, but with responsibility.

While distancing herself from this model, the idea that the young woman just could not buy was the emphasis on individualism. That might have been interesting in the time and place where it had been born, but twenty years later and some thousands of miles to the south, it seemed to her definitely inappropriate. Once and for all, she did not believe in the possibility of a society in which each individual would possess some sort of a purely individual motivation, detached both from the cultural weight into which all human beings are born and grow, and from the material weight that grounds this basis. For this reason attitudes that defended the inviolable right for every person to do whatever he or she wanted as the highest value that there could possibly be, always resulted, in her opinion, in a quite superficial and myopic view of reality.

An almost immediate consequence of this short-sightedness could be seen in the way many remarkably individualistic social movements ended up involved in mere day-to-day politics, with no concern of extending their criticism to a larger economic scale. That is exactly the criticism that one of her favorite writers had addressed to the Civil Rights Movement — of which the writer herself had taken part — during the 60s in the USA. In that time, the struggle against racism and sexism was based on the celebration of diversity and through demands of equal ethnic participation in the media. Deprived of a deep economic critique, those demands for a just representation were quickly accommodated by the market, which then started to incorporate diversity as a key-term in propaganda. The world of consumption opened its doors to the individuals from different minorities, but only those who could afford such expensive integration. The poor black, the poor woman, the poor homosexual, were still equally segregated.

This type of individualism was therefore the product of a society, or a class, that benefited from capitalism. People would arm themselves with a sort of humility which allowed them to wash their hands as far as larger and deeper critiques were concerned — a position which might even be interesting to a group of middle class kids living in a developed country, but which was in no way interesting to those who most suffered the consequences of capitalism. The bands from this first model did not see a terrible urgency in criticizing and trying to change society in a more radical way. However, this young woman, living in a country that occupied the position of eighth largest economy in the world, and yet remained the fourth worst in terms of distribution of wealth, certainly felt that urgency. And that is why, in a sense, this model always seemed to be too small for her.

Her perspective on SXE held, as it had with the '88 wolfpack, a collectivist ideal. She always believed that humans were essentially social beings, and that the individual depended on the group as much as the group depended on the individual to exist and to survive, both symbolically and materially. The thoughts filling our minds were social; the feelings inhabiting our hearts were social; and even human language, which acted as a catalyst for both, was intrinsically social. Besides, it had always seemed clear to the young woman that, politically, the individual would only become an agent of his or her own history as an active member of a group: after all, it was the organized collectivity which had mobilized the great transformations in society. Therefore if the idea of a group was still frightening in the eyes of some people, then she attributed this to a (reasonable) fear that one's subordination to the collectivity would somehow imply the negation of the individual potential for action. But that was not a matter of being in a group: the problem was the kind of principles around which one's group was organized.

It was at this point that her perspective conflicted with this second SXE model: the collectivity to her had a much higher price to be paid: the building of a community, not the cheapening involved in the idea of the crew of the '88 wolfpack. To her, joining the group meant to value the collectivity because it congregates different people in support of a common political goal: to resist a society that worked only for a few of its members and to fight for a society that, once and for all, might work either for everyone or for no one! The way to reach this goal was by incorporating it into the very form of the group's organization: participating means to speak, but also to listen; debating means to confront, but through dialogue; deciding means, thus, to reach consensus. It was in that sense that the group seemed to her not an option, but an absolutely necessary learning exercise.

Another aspect that she had appropriated from this model was its positive outlook on life — something which had certainly arisen before, but which that generation had raised to a higher potency; an optimism reflected in the certainty that things can still be changed for the better. It was the kind of outlook that in a less naïve and a more politicized form could also be seen in the discourse of different social movements. It was important to fight the bitter cynicism of those who only opened their eyes to see problems in everything, who only opened their mouths to say that there was no future at all, and who, making a victim out of themselves as solitary romantics in a sea of stupidity, were more concerned with assuring their place in the line of never-ending-critics than with transforming the scene in something better for everyone.

Working to transform the scene, by the way, was something that the '88 generation especially seemed to deny for women like her. Not that there was any kind of deliberate scheme of feminine exclusion from participation (which certainly did not exist) in this model, but the fact was that the form of SXE embraced by this generation was too "masculine" — an excess reflected in hymns and sing-alongs which reminded her of a bunch of tough football fans, in the pictures of muscular boys with no shirts, stretching in formidable martial arts kicks; and in lyrics about fights, pride and loyalty that pointed to the crew of friends as the most important value in life — what, in one way or another, closed any possibility for a deeper identification as well as a willingness to participation for women like her.

She did not mean to say that in her conception of SXE there was no room for aggressiveness. On the contrary, she saw aggressiveness as something which was absolutely necessary to the construction of a struggle which intended nothing more and nothing less than bringing down a whole system of political and economic power firmly established as a perpetuator of social misery and inequity. In fact she thought there must be a definitive end to the idea that women were destined to privilege sensibility, and men, aggressiveness — which, in her eyes, was a great misunderstanding of sexual (biological) differences and gender (cultural) differences. Aggressiveness and sensibility were symbolic values attributed to social roles that were built by each society and though they could not be totally independent of biological factors, they certainly went beyond its determination. The problem with the '88 wolfpack was that it simply reinforced, implicitly, the idea that aggressiveness was for "boys," its aesthetics associated only to (futile) clichés of masculinity.

Her perspective on SXE held, as it was with the purifying firestorm, the incorporation of veganism as an obvious moral extension of the SXE position. Meat, egg and dairy industries constituted an extremely powerful economic enterprise that placed profits above any consideration for the death and suffering of millions and millions of animals, nor for the destruction — as a result of the enormous waste of natural resources and the devastating pollution of air, soil and water on a frightening scale — of the environment which sustains all forms of life in this planet. The vivisection industry was undoubtedly one of the most cruel human actions against non-humans, disguised by the mask of "Knowledge" and legitimated through the authority of scientists that worked with one eye on the microscope and the other on the research funds that allow them to comfortably persist in their bloody career as executioners. The entertainment industry, in turn, was responsible for jeopardizing the beauty and enchantment of such important cultural manifestations as circuses by condemning animals, whose instincts demand freedom and socialization, to lives of confinement and isolation. The act of ceasing to consume the products of all this misery was a simple gesture that represented a very significant self-exclusion from systematic processes of exploitation.

At the same time, distancing herself from this model, what the young woman could not possibly admit was the fundamentalist stance that characterized its basis for vindication of change. A stance that implied, firstly, a simplistic appropriation of religion, in which the only aspects to be adhered were exactly the most sensationalist ones, such as manichaeism, punishment and martyrdom, all synthesized in the idea of the holy war that seeks to literally eliminate the enemy from the Earth. A position that implied an absolutist viewpoint that transformed conventional principles into dogmas by determining that they must be applied anywhere, at anytime, over anyone, under any circumstances. A stance that implied, finally, a purist notion that would draw an arbitrary moral line, nevertheless rendering it of natural or religious status, so that one could clearly identify purity and impurity, saints and sinners, angels and demons, and in the most extreme cases, those who deserved to die or not. Simplism, absolutism, purism: how could she possibly identify with a philosophy sustained by pillars of such nature?

The answer provided by the purifying firestorm also upset her because of another type of individualistic attitude in which the struggle for social change was seen as a struggle of solitary warriors that find out through their vain search for allies (with a totally senseless pride!) that they can only trust themselves. This option for a lonely path might even be justifiable as a strategy within some branches of the animal liberation struggle, but it was certainly the most counterproductive choice in regard to the necessity of building a new society based upon cooperative values. And within this option it was so because there was no need for the militant to make concessions to or negotiate with, whoever it may be. By ignoring the necessity of an organized and decentralized collective resistance, the fundamental practice that it enables becomes thus underestimated: the immensely difficult effort of looking at the world from the other's eyes. Lacking such effort, one notices that most of the time VSXE warriors' discourse ended up following the most dangerous path: of pure intolerance.

Her perspective on SXE held, as it had with the positive-political-powerful model, an anti-capitalist agenda committed to the end of class struggle — through abolition of private property, socialization of the means of production and decentralization of decision-making processes. But, differing from this same model, to be SXE in her eyes had nothing to do with a personal decision: being straight was deeply embedded in a way of living that was compatible with the revulsion she felt against capitalism. Everyone knew that drug use, be it legal or not, comprised astronomic amounts of money. Stimuli for consuming it were found everywhere, and the consumption was never presented as something which people might do (eventually and with due caution) in search for new sensorial experiences. People, especially young, were deliberately driven to drug use in order to acquire social and sexual status in the eyes of others. And such consumption was satisfactory for the elite because drugs were an efficient mechanism for State control, convenient for sending the criminal, those who threaten the system, to jail — or cemetery.

When the Soviet Union collapsed, narco-trafficking came to be, along with Islamic fundamentalism, the great new subterfuge for the USA to intervene in the Third World as they wished. In the young woman's view, it was clear how the US government, using entirely capricious criteria, classified two kinds of drug dealers: First, those who served their interests — as Noriega in Panama of the 80s, the Afghan warriors against the Soviet invasion, the CIA in the Vietnam War, and so forth — were encouraged and even financed by Washington. Second, those who, on the other side, repudiated US politics for whatever reason — as the FARC in Colombia, other third world popular movements and guerrillas — were stigmatized with the charge of drug dealing. Thus the empire would open the perfect moral scenery for interventions that were not intended to stop the traffic, but rather to eliminate opposition.

Enemies of capitalism were everywhere, not just outside US borders, and they needed to be systematically fought within the limits of their country as well. In the USA, for example, a very well known case was the role of the government in the dissolution of the Black Panthers Party for Self Defense, undermined through drug dissemination by government agents in the poor black ghettos of Oakland — a sad history already told and re-told dozens of times. And in Brazil, the country where the young woman lived, perhaps in a more explicit way than anywhere else, one might clearly see that rich dealers would never go to jail while poor dealers went all the time. Rio's favelas were fed by a mafia of politicians, executives and policemen who provided not only money and access for drugs, but also the armed arsenal that guaranteed the operation of the drug dealing system.

To be drug-free was, as in any massive boycott, more symbolic than practical. But was not this condition a necessary step in the very logic of boycotts? Because what the young woman had observed was that time passed by, and from an initial insignificant state the boycott had started growing, its influence spreading, its implications multiplying, the poles of balance gradually stabilizing, until the practical and the symbolic dimensions acquire equivalent weights. That was the point when both dimensions started feeding each other through a dialectical movement that, in the end, would make the cessation of the boycotted object a simple matter of time. It was in this optimistic perspective that she wanted to reflect: the power of today's elite partially consists of convincing a great number of people to consume drugs; if this consumption is not met, an important power-sustaining mechanism would be lost.

SXE in the perspective that the young woman had built with her group of friends was, in total, the person who would stand for the end of all forms of oppression and discrimination. It was the person who defended the inalienable right for self-determination of peoples that still undergo the humiliation of political intervention and that often find themselves in the difficult position of having to fight tanks with stones, missiles with shotguns. It was the person who fought to overthrow all fences that had privatized property of the few out of that which had once existed for everyone. It was the person committed to recall our collective memory, as a frightening denunciation that the problem was still not overcome, the singular experience of suffering of those who felt the weight of whips in the sadistic game of torture. It was the person who strived for seeing, through critical eyes, the subtle screens, masked by the seduction of entertainment, that bring the necessary ideological charge to assure the perpetuation of the imperialist hegemony. It was the person who felt revolted by the sad irony of a suicidal capitalist society that, as if voluntarily placing its neck in the gallows, first produces the victims of its system through its insatiable greed for wealth, only to be later unforgivably victimized by these very victims. It was the person who regretted the bloody history of our colonial past, in which the price paid for the futile silver mirrors, brought by the white people to be traded, represented an irreparable loss of millions of lives from thousands of nations. It was the person that believed in the structuring of a system of flexible creeds and stances as a fundamental principle for the organization of a collective resistance, the only bridge capable of guiding us to a world of more cooperative and just values. Some positions, reflected the young woman, among hundreds of others…

It therefore seemed clearer to her now that SXE did not belong to North Americans, nor to Europeans, and not even to Brazilians — at least not exclusively. It belonged to everyone and for this reason it belonged to no one. It was also hers to make whatever she wanted of it. Few things distressed her so much as that old mania of always seeing punk, rock, or whatever cultural manifestation coming from the metropolis, as something that the empire invents and the rest of the world merely copies. Why is it that the same analogy was not made, for example, for soccer and carnival in her country? There had been hardcore bands in Brazil since 1978. People there conducted things their own way, a particular way, and they felt inspired by what the metropolis, or wherever, produced in certain aspects, but not all; in certain cases, but not all.

In the perspective of her group of friends, the wish to keep oneself updated on the latest trend in the North American and European hardcore scenes simply made no sense. There was an emergent need to definitely replace the web nature which characterized the traditional cultural relations, inside and outside hardcore, by a net nature: one relationship in which the flux of political and aesthetic ideas would be defined by a different form of dissemination, not plunging from a center to the margins, but circulating from one center to another. In order for this one-way relationship to be finally shifted by a reciprocal relation, it was necessary to use the instrument at hand, that which she was most identified: the international SXE scene.

Faithful as she was, the young woman hoped for the possibility of, in ten years, being able to reflect on the North American and European trends as much as on Latin American, Asian and African trends. And she dreamed of a day when her investigations would be focused on the way different places in the third world would appropriate the SXE models coming from the metropolis, to then re-signify them according to their local particularities, offering new and instigating perspectives about how the SXE international scene can become a cell of real resistance to imperialism.

Thus, the redefinition.

Approaching the end of that long, disturbing, and at the same time fascinating period of doubt, search, analysis and interpretation, the only parts of the young woman that seemed unmodified were her legs — as in the most confusing initial moments of that process, they insisted on defying the smoothing commands of her brain, perpetuating a slight and incessant trembling. But after conflict nothing remains unscathed, and a few minutes were enough for her to realize even that had been changed! Her legs were trembling no longer due to the insecurity of not finding a fixed structure where she could fix her feet, but due to the excitement of realizing that such structure is never fixed; least inexistent; only adjustable. Her legs, she began to understand, seemed, by their own human nature, to prefer the dynamics of dance to the rigidity of absolute inertia. Guided by the rhythm of the music, constrained by the borders of the stage, allocating old steps into new positions, relating her mere two feet in a number of unexpected arrangements, combining movement and stillness, and expanding the very limits of the available stage through the exploration of air space as a basis for new motions, they rendered her body the support it needed not to tumble down — even in the face of the most difficult improvisation, in which every cadence of the song will always reveal itself as the unexpected.

v. synthesis

It is lamentable, but after so much reflection she only now realized the great stupidity that she had just committed by not registering, as she used to, any of those thoughts in her diary. She did not even have an exact notion of how long that investigation had absorbed her. Had she taken proper care to take notes, she might perfectly organize those ideas in a single text and try to publish it later. It could be a sort of essay, that is, a text that presented, though in simple terms, a discussion about her conception of straightedge. It might even be, she reckoned, a sort of manifesto: "In our understanding, SXE is like this, not like that!" But... who knows... is it possible that there was still time for preparing it?

So interesting an idea appeared to her in that moment, that right away she went looking for pen and paper. She sat in front of a desk; rested head on hands; thought for a few minutes; and, raising eyes toward paper, wrote with a delicate calligraphy: "We have no principles. Our principle is made out of one's adaptability to different contexts."

It seemed to be a nice idea: a sort of synthesis of the critique that she would like to propose in her text. But the sentence was not hers; she had taken it from some place, though she could not remember exactly where. Besides, it was too objective, too cold. It was not the kind of sentence with which she wished to finish off her text. She had to find another way of saying the same thing — to find a sharper metaphor. She had to take advantage of that time in which all those ideas were still fresh on her mind.

Closing her eyes, the young woman rested her head on her hands again; reckoned for a few minutes; bit her fingernails as more time passed by; and then, turning her eyes little by little to the paper, wrote — now more convinced that she was almost meeting her expectations:

"The straightedge might even not be god, but they also know that, in certain contexts, they have to write straight with crooked lines."

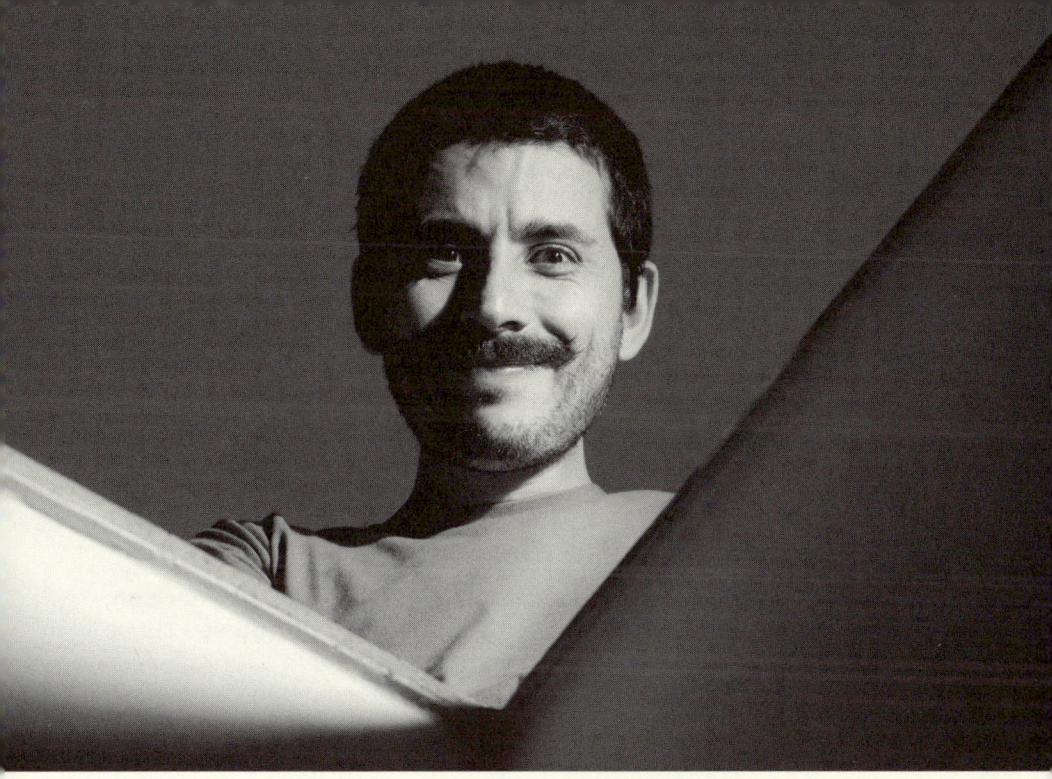

Frederico Freitas, São Paulo, 2009   Daigo Oliva

Interview with Frederico Freitas

"Bending to Stay Straight" talks a lot about different stages in the development of straight edge. The text was published in 2002. What — if anything — would have to be added today?

I was thinking about this when I woke up this morning. We did this kind of analysis of what sXe was in 2002 in Brazil, based on our own history, on having been sXe for a decade back then, and on our perceptions of what sXe was in the US and in Europe. So the essay was heavily based on the circumstances of that time, the beginning of the 2000s. It was also written in Portuguese first, primarily for Brazilian readers. It was translated into English later. So maybe some stuff in the text is kind of hard to relate to if you aren't Brazilian.

If it was written today, some points of the analysis would be different, of course, because the scene is different and we are different too. One thing that totally escaped our critique was how sXe, and punk in general, is youth-oriented. This is something that is easier to notice when you get older (I'm thirty-three now). Straight edge revolves around a lot of concerns that are typical for young people. And in its social events, like at shows, it has a youth dynamic. This isn't necessarily bad, but it can make older people feel alienated.

In my opinion, this all relates to the fact that sXe (as punk in general) is primarily a cultural movement (or scene); the social movement factor is weaker — if it is there at all. At least we did stress this aspect in our essay: that sXe should be a social movement; or at least open to social movements.

The text emphasizes differences between the North American, European, and Latin American scenes. How do you see these relations today? And how did you perceive them touring? Also with respect to the reception of your band's politics?

When we wrote the text we already had first-hand experiences with the scenes in the US and Europe. Some of us had already gone to the US, we had toured Europe once, and in São Paulo we had received people from abroad. Actually, it was the cultural differences we perceived when we had some friends from the US visiting that gave us the idea to write the essay.

A key element was that people from the US seemed so individualistic to us. Today I would say that this was a bias we developed based on the experiences with the people we were hosting. Later I had the opportunity to meet a lot of different people from the US, people with different backgrounds, and not all of them fit so easily into the ultra-individualistic category. But cultural differences always exist.

What was eye-opening to us was to see how much our identity as sXe was tied to US cultural hegemony. This is what we tried to deal with by writing this essay — recalling how we became sXe, but also pointing out how different and particular the sXe history was in São Paulo. We wanted to stress the strong element of politics in our "formation" as sXe, especially because we felt that for the younger sXe kids in Brazil the differences between the scenes in the US and in Brazil became increasingly unclear. We wanted to reinforce the political drive we had, and we wanted to discuss our own understanding of sXe with people in Brazil and abroad.

How do I see the relations between the different scenes today? I'm not so involved with sXe and hardcore as I used to be. My last experience with the European scene was the Point of No Return tour we did in Europe in 2002. Since then I've been back to Europe once, and I've been to the US too. But both times I hung out primarily with political activists and militants, so I can't really say much about the hardcore scenes. Well, I have a kind of preconception, but as I'm not so involved anymore, I prefer not to say anything about this publicly.

I actually found the critique of individualism in your text particularly interesting — also the commitment to a political activity that is both collectively driven and collectively oriented. You've already mentioned cultural differences. Do you think that this generally shows in how people in Latin America approach politics when compared to people in North America, and maybe also in Europe? What were your experiences with the activists and militants who you hung out with?

I think that the individualism has to do both with general cultural aspects and with the political tradition one is connected to. In a general way we can say that North Americans — and maybe that goes for the whole Anglophone world — are very individualistic. Their culture is very individual-oriented, and this has good and bad aspects. A good aspect is that it makes you think for yourself — like being sXe. A bad aspect is that it makes you think you think for yourself — like being sXe because everyone around you is sXe while you think it was your individual choice. Another good aspect is that being individualistic can make you feel powerful enough to start political struggles and take stands without depending on anyone else. Then again, this can also make you think that the only and primary liberation that matters is your own, which can make you forget about solidarity and about connecting your own struggle with those of other people. This kind of reflects the general attitude of people in capitalist societies.

What seems clear to me is that changing society isn't only a matter of individual change. There are some levels of society that depend on bigger structures, and they can only be dealt with collectively. Otherwise nothing will change. Capitalist liberal society has its place for individual outcasts like us.

It is also important to understand that individualism is the foundation of the society we live in today. If we want a different society, we need a different foundation. Again, otherwise nothing will change. Visions and utopias are still important for our thinking.

I think that, in terms of different political traditions in the US and Latin America, a lot has to do with the difference between being "radical" in the US, and being "left-wing" in Latin America. Marxism, socialism, class struggle are big things for the left here, even if you're an anarchist. It used to be like that in the US too, but this tradition kind of died before WWII. I have the impression that the other tradition, the one of being "radical," is more linked to the tradition of fighting for personal freedoms and rights against "big" capitalism etc. I have the impression that Europe, at least continental Europe, has a political left-wing tradition more similar to the one in Latin America, am I right?

> Yes, I would definitely agree with that. Within European anarchism for example it's sometimes really hard for groups like CrimethInc. to even be taken seriously. It is still very important to have class analysis etc. In the States on the other hand, "leftist" has become a bad word in many radical circles — like the left is your worst enemy.

> Let's go back to the Brazilian scene. You said that when you wrote "Bending to Stay Straight," the younger sXe kids didn't see the same differences between the US scene and the Brazilian scene that you saw. Does this mean that they were "less political"?

Back then, in 2002, we had the beginning of a trend. People in hardcore have since become less and less political. I think 2000 was the apex of political activism in the Brazilian sXe scene. Everything was connected to bigger struggles: the so-called days of global action against the big targets (WTO, IMF, G8, etc.), the World Social Forums in Porto Alegre, the Landless Workers Movement, the ties to the Zapatistas in Mexico. That was the atmosphere of the times. But then there was 9/11 and the specific target of that era, neo-liberalism, started to decline as a hegemonic idea and praxis. Security became the main agenda. At the same time, in Brazil, the Workers Party elected a president for the first time and this made all the social movements take a step back in order to give him some time to see what would happen.

> Can you take us back to how the straight edge scene in Brazil first started out? Strongly influenced by the US? Or was there always a stronger, let's call it, "social movement" aspect to it?

Some kids started identifying as sXe in Brazil, more specifically in São Paulo, in the late 1980s: there was Arilson, who later played in this crust band Abuso Sonoro; Ruy Fernando, singer of a band called No Violence; and Marcos Suarez, later in Point of No Return. But there wasn't a scene, or even a group of people being sXe. The ones who were barely knew each other. Back then the punk scene from the 80s was dead, it used to be too gang-oriented and all the violence killed it.

The sXe scene in São Paulo really started in 91/92, when some kids who were involved with anarchism started a group called "Libertarian Youth." It wasn't originally a sXe group, but after a couple of years it became a de facto sXe group — and vegan too. Most of the older people involved with sXe have their origins in that group, like five of the seven Point of No Return members. As we were all anarchists back then, we were much more influenced by political hardcore, from crust bands to political sXe bands like Nations on Fire and Lärm. By the middle of the 90s, the scene got bigger, but our anarchist group broke up. People became less politically motivated and more musically oriented. Then we did Point of No Return in 96 to counter this development. In the end of the decade, the scene was more politically motivated again, filled with the "anti-globalization" spirit that I mentioned above.

How would you compare these developments to other Latin American countries? Did you have many connections outside of Brazil, both in the early 90s and then with Point of No Return? Or was what happened in São Paulo pretty unique even within Brazil?

As Brazil is — compared to Europe — big, I think I should talk about other cities in Brazil first. In the beginning of the 1990s, there was only the sXe scene in São Paulo. We had a big punk scene here in the 80s, and we have this tradition of being a really cosmopolitan place (contrary to Rio, the second biggest city in Brazil, which symbolizes everything stereotypically Brazilian, like carnival, beaches, etc.). So, São Paulo has this tradition of being the place in Brazil where the cultural movements of the "First World" first appear and are then reshaped in our own image and reality. Besides São Paulo, there were some kids in the smaller cities of the State (the city of São Paulo is the capital of São Paulo State, which is the richest and most industrialized state in the country, for better or worse).

As I said before, by '97 sXe became less political — but it also got really huge. There was the whole Victory thing, the "new school," "old school" revivals, and also the 90s emo stuff. Bands started to appear in other States, a "neo-old school" scene appeared in Curitiba, some emo bands in Belo Horizonte, and some mosh-NYHC influenced bands in Rio de Janeiro (which is odd, given the feel of the city). In São Paulo State, there were some bands appearing on the coast, in Santos and São Vicente, which is located an hour's drive from São Paulo City. Even though it was a time when politics weren't as much on people's minds as in the beginning of the 1990s, the bands were mostly political; at least more than the average US band. In 1999, we started to do these big hardcore festivals in São Paulo, and people and bands from other cities started to come. Then some bands started to tour more frequently and all that. All of this was related to sXe.

By the beginning of this decade (the 2000s), bands from other parts than southern Brazil (where São Paulo, Rio, Curitiba, and Belo Horizonte are located) started to appear. First, bands from the State of Espirito Santo, which is still south. Then bands from the western part of the country, Brasilia (the country's capital), and Goiania. And then bands from the northeast, from cities like Salvador, Aracaju, Fortaleza, etc. I think that nowadays there are bands everywhere, and we cannot talk about one sXe scene 'cause there are a lot of different ones.

Now about the other half of South America: in the early 90s, the only place that had a sXe scene besides São Paulo was Buenos Aires in Argentina. They had this big tradition of bands playing NYHC and kids emulating a NYHC lifestyle, so to them it was a "natural" step to have some kids interested in youth crew straight edge. It started there even a little earlier than in São Paulo. When the São Paulo scene became less political for the first time, around 95, two bands went to play in Buenos Aires — Self Conviction and Personal Choice — and the differences were interesting: in Buenos Aires people were totally into slower bands like those from Victory, New Age, etc., while we were into faster bands, what the Argentineans thought was passé. Buenos Aires also had a strong Krishna influence, while we were still kind of "vegan anarchist fundamentalists." But, on the other hand, the Argentineans thought that we were much more US-dominated than them 'cause our bands sang in English, while theirs sang in Spanish. After that year both scenes started to be more closely connected, and every summer we had tons of Argentineans on our couches.

In Chile, the sXe scene started later — in about 2000, and it was always more connected with Argentina than Brazil.

In Colombia, they already had tons of NYHC bands in 2000, which is kind of understandable 'cause a lot of people used to live in New York as aliens, some had even been in the infamous DMS hardcore crew. In 2001 or 2002, some bands from Bogota came to play in Brazil, and we started to be more connected. At the same time, they became more political. Nowadays there is an anarchist hardcore scene that is more modern crustie; but still related to sXe — and to CrimethInc. in a way.

Uruguay is a small country, pretty European, located between Brazil and Argentina. They had a political emo sXe scene in the beginning of the 2000s, strongly influenced by situationism and with kind of "French" visual aesthetics in a Refused-like way (although they didn't sound like Refused).

I have heard about some sXe kids in Paraguay, in the border area near Brazil, but I have never heard any band from there. I've heard about some hardcore crowds in Ecuador and Peru, but I'm not sure whether there is an active scene there, or whether these are only audiences for foreign bands touring.

That's a great overview, thanks! Let me ask you about Mexico too: Do you have any connections to the scene there?

Mexico seems like a very distant place to Brazilians, both geographically and culturally. I'm corresponding with some kids in Guadalajara and in Mexico City. And I have "friends" from Mexico on Point of No Return's MySpace. And I know that they have a scene there, but that's it.

Your essay was written from the perspective of a "young, white, middle class woman." Point of No Return was an all-male band. Why did you choose that perspective?

In a sense it was a rhetorical trick. The first draft of the essay was written by one of the band's members as a first person account. So the line in question probably spoke of a "young, white, middle class man." By turning it all into third person and adding a narrator, we thought that the piece would be more easily identifiable as a Point of No Return piece rather than the text of just one of us. So we, the band, narrated the woman's reflection.

The fact that we changed the gender reflected the scene here in São Paulo. When we toured Europe in 2000, we realized how many more women were active in our scene. We wanted the text to express this. The other parts — "young, white, middle class" — never got changed, simply because we probably saw no need to change them. To be honest, we simply thought less about these issues, even though there were a lot of people in the scene who were neither white nor middle class, including some members of Point of No Return.

Were class and race just less of an issue in the scene overall? Also compared to gender?

Yes, I would say that's true. Women were reclaiming their space and power in the scene, and we were sensitive to that. Gender issues were an important political topic, pushed by bands like Dominatrix, One Day Kills, and Infect. The same wasn't true for class and race issues. Class divides and racism are deeply embedded in Brazilian society, and they are reproduced in the scene. However, these issues just weren't addressed that much at the time, and our text reflected this lack of discussion.

How was class reproduced in the hardcore/punk community?

Even though social classes were mixed together when we played, there were also divisions. On the one hand, there were blue collar kids who spoke poor English and were less tuned into the latest developments in US hardcore; on the other hand, there were middle class kids with better education, more money, and the ability to emulate the European and North American scenes. Nowadays, though, the internet and capitalist globalization have blurred those lines, and the parameters of class identification may have changed.

What about divides along racial lines?

Racism in Brazil is peculiar. It's different to, say, the US. A Brazilian intellectual, Oracy Nogueira, has explained these differences in the 1950s by comparing a "prejudice of mark" in Brazil to a "prejudice of origin" in the US. This makes racial identities more fluid. For example, in Brazil you can be considered white even though your mother is black. It's your appearance that matters most, not your origin or your ancestors. And your appearance is not reduced to skin tone either. It's very much tied into class. This also means that people can change their "race" in the course of their lives. For example, with "brown" skin you might be considered black in Brazil as long as you are poor, and white once you have some money. People don't talk about this as racism in Brazil since Brazilians see themselves as non-racist people — even though most of them are racist.

Brazilian hardcore and punk have always followed an ideal of aesthetic whiteness — even if this was never clearly defined. This reinforces racist patterns that give whiteness particular value. It is something that needs to be addressed much more.

At the end of your essay you express a hope for "Latin American, Asian and African trends" within straight edge. Does this hope still exist? I mean, you have already said that you're not so involved with the straight edge scene anymore and don't say much about this publicly. But maybe you still have a general feeling when it comes to where the movement is drifting politically — or is it just drifting into many different directions?

I think that the essay and our statements about "third world hardcore" helped people and bands here to be aware of their own specific identity as sXe. But, again, I'm not so involved with hardcore nowadays, so I don't really know what's going on in other scenes.

I remember there was a point when I had a lot of pen pals from Southeast Asia, Indonesia, South Africa, and from all over Latin America. But these were still only places that were already "globalized" in a way. Thinking again about this topic, it's kind of arrogant to wish that every single corner of the map needs to be so integrated into the international world system that there can be a sXe or punk scene as a local imperialist counter-cultural manifestation.

I don't know if such a wish is necessarily arrogant. I mean, especially in the context of your essay I thought it was clear that this was not about globalizing a certain model, but about specific local manifestations of shared ideals. And globally shared ideals are still a good thing, I guess. Like, isn't that what the traditional meaning of internationalism builds on? In other words, maybe it's not so important that each place has its own "straight edge" scene, but a political scene that is also aware of the political dimensions of narcotics etc. How about that?

That's really the point. That's the point that most of the political movements miss, a point that used to be on the agenda of some traditional anarchist movements in the beginning of the 20th century.

Also here in Europe. In Sweden, for example, the "sobriety movement" was huge within the working class movement in the 1920s and 30s. Then it kinda disappeared. Like within the anarchist movement in Spain and apparently in Latin America, even though I know only little about that.

In São Paulo there was a big anarchist movement in the early 20th century. It was formed by Spanish and Italian immigrants who made up the majority of the population in the city back then. There was also a strong emphasis on sobriety.

And then what happened?

It seems to me that the early anarchists' emphasis on sobriety was part of a whole set of attitudes that aimed to create the so-called "men and women of the new society." They also propagated physical exercise, free love, etc. But it was more discourse than practice. It wasn't anything that was based on an identity, like sXe is nowadays. It was something that was much looser, if you know what I mean. Well, the anarchist movement in Brazil declined in the 1920s after the success of the Bolshevik Revolution. Some anarchists even turned to founding the first Brazilian communist party. And the whole thing with sobriety and staying healthy was mainly seen as naïve by the communists.

Do you think such movements — wide social movements with an emphasis on sobriety — might come back?

I don't believe history happens again. Now we have this thing called sXe which is based on sobriety. But as a fruit of the times, it isn't a movement. It is much more of a subculture, or maybe a counterculture, and a matter of identity; it has little to do with projections of a future society, as it was the case in the early 20th century. The Landless Workers Movement has an emphasis on being relatively sober in their communities, but this isn't anything that is part of their identity and has nothing to do with a projection of a future society either. It is mainly about keeping the militants from drinking so that they stay out of trouble.

I think that if there was something like a "straight edge social movement," a political movement with a strong critique of the legal and illegal drug industry and of legal and illegal drug consumption, it would be something totally different from what we had in the past.

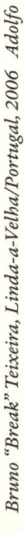

New Winds
Interview with Bruno "Break" Teixeira

New Winds became the best-known among a wave of radical Portuguese straight edge bands that turned the country into a center of political straight edge hardcore in the late 1990s. The album *A Spirit Filled Revolution* (2004), released with Poland's Refuse Records (see the interview with Robert Matusiak), was accompanied by a 170-page book covering an array of issues ranging from animal liberation to prisoner support to workers' struggles. New Winds disbanded in 2006.

Bruno "Break" Teixeira was the band's singer. He has since been a drummer for These Hands Are Fists (2006-2009), and currently sings in the all-acoustic act Arm the Spirit (2008 to present). He lives near Lisbon, Portugal.

Discography:
- *All Things Are Possible For Those Who Believe*, 1997, Dead King Records
- *Refusing To Live By Your Lies*, 2000, DIY distribution
- *A Spirit Filled Revolution*, 2004, Refuse Records
- *This Fire, These Words* 1996-2006, Refuse Records (includes first two albums plus other previously released material and three previously unreleased songs)

Let us start with a rather general question. While Sweden became known as a center for political straight edge in the 1990s, it seems as if Portugal has seen the strongest political straight edge scene in Europe of the last ten years. However, internationally this is not too well known. Would you mind providing us with a little background? Like, a very brief history of straight edge in Portugal — maybe especially in relation to political struggles?

I'm actually not sure whether Portugal had the strongest political straight edge scene in Europe of the last ten years. To some extent this is true, but not totally. We did have quite a big number of interesting bands with social/political/spiritual messages. But I would not want to divide between bands that were sXe and bands that weren't. I think it's more important to point out who made the hardcore scene a strong and political one. I can name bands like X-Acto, Liberation, Time X, Zootic, Sannyasin, New Winds, Worth The Fight, These Hands Are Fists, Shutter, and to some degree Day Of The Dead. Some of these bands accomplished a great deal in a scene that's increasingly concerned with aesthetics rather than with being an alternative threat.

I appreciate you not wanting to divide the scene into sXe and non-sXe bands. However, it seems to me that sXe was a big part of a lot of these bands' identity. In what way was it connected to their politics?

It's hard to talk about the other bands' motivations. To me, sXe was always connected to politics, since the beginning. Due to the bands I listened to in the mid-1990s — like Blindfold, Nations on Fire, ManLiftingBanner, Separation, or By The Grace Of God — I always saw sXe as a weapon of political resistance. The basic pillars were: no to alcohol, no to tobacco, no to drugs, no to dependency, no to a system of exploitation which sees you as a commodity and who acts as an oppressor. This was my sXe, the one I was living. It just made sense to me, and this was what I had always been looking for in my youth: something that made sense in my life and in my attempts to be active; something that provided me with a consciousness and an awareness of the reality around me; something that helped me go beyond just "having fun" and drowning in parties in order to fit into a group I did not identify myself with most of the time.

Most of the people in the punk scene were actually not sXe, but the scene still provided me with great opportunities for activities that I was looking for: doing shows, doing demos, informing others about what was going on in the world, feeding the homeless, building possibilities to focus on what I considered important. Unfortunately, I was not very open at the time to hanging out and working with people who were not sXe. I saw them as a part of the system I was fighting. I admit that I had an arrogant attitude, thinking I was better than others because I was sXe.

Later on, as I grew older, I found out and realized that I was just like everyone else in the scene, including the ones I criticized; I was also consuming things and caught up in the system. I started to realize that we all had many things in common and I stopped focusing on our differences. We all had the same goal: to bring meaning to our lives and to the lives of those around us. We just had different ways of trying.

I wish I had been more intelligent and aware earlier and had not acted in an arrogant way, but that was part of the learning curve. It took some time and quite some reflection to realize that I had to improve. In this process, it also became clear to me that my understanding of sXe was a lot different from that of most sXer's around me. I was really eager to work with people who wanted to make positive social contributions and who were looking for political alternatives — whether they were sXe or not didn't matter much anymore.

So, at that time, New Winds started to collaborate with a lot of people who were not sXe but who appreciated shows that included video or spoken word performances. These were the types of shows and actions we wanted to be engaged in. They made sense to me at the time, and they still make total sense to me today. sXe, on the other hand, does not make sense if it's just a personal choice and if we don't see beyond the limitations of it. sXe must stand as an attitude, as a way of life, and as an inspiration for others to make this world a better place. We must dive deep into the concept: it must be intelligent, bold, active, political, compassionate, and dedicated. This is how I see it.

You were starting to give us a short overview of the punk/hardcore history in Portugal. I kinda cut you off. Would you mind continuing?

The punk/hardcore scene started in the late 1980s with punk and skate trash bands in Lisbon and its outskirts. I can only remember the time from the early 1990s on. One of the most inspiring bands for a lot of old hardcorians in Portugal was X-Acto, who are still connected to the scene. I think X-Acto were pioneers in Portugal with respect to the punk/sXe philosophy. We even used the phrase: If it's not punk, then it's not sXe, and if it's not sXe, then it is not punk!

Can you explain this?

Punk and sXe have the exact same purpose: to defy a system that controls you and to provide a social alternative based on true values, a true sense of freedom, and the absence of oppression. The difference was the abstinence that sXe preached, which contradicted the habits of most early punks. sXe introduced the notion that sobriety, a clear conscience, and a rejection of drugs and intoxication (the system's poisons) can make it easier to develop a true (r)evolutionary consciousness and to have a deep impact on society.

In a world completely dependant on intoxication, sXe is a weapon of political resistance, it's the "UnDiscipline," the exact opposite of what millions of people do who consume products and have so-called "fun" at the expense of millions of suffering human beings and animals. This has very concrete dimensions, for example when indigenous populations are forced to run away from their homelands to plant drug or tobacco crops. The social costs of alcohol and tobacco are horrendous: alcohol as a drug is responsible for millions of deaths by car accidents and countless beatings in our homes; tobacco causes not only diseases in human beings but is also the excuse to intentionally infect innumerable animals with these diseases for "research purposes." And often enough the corrupt, greedy, and deadly industries behind these substances have connections to right-wing parties and so on.

This is the reality that sXe turns against, and that punk should turn against too. Both ideologies have a lot in common and I truly know that a lot of people who are not sXe do a great deal of excellent things. I just wish we could all move to the next level and stop supporting companies and substances that are not only dangerous and deadly but that also support a system of constant oppression. Those in power know that you are more dangerous when you are sober than when you are drunk, and they do a very effective job in keeping you separated from the real thing, in keeping you from fighting their rules and from fighting for those in need. They relentlessly force more and more products you don't need onto you and your home.

I chose not to participate in this because I know what it stands for. I'm not into their games. It's a personal choice but it's also a political choice. My hope is that people who drink or smoke at least think about all this. As I said earlier, after realizing that at some point in my life I was very prejudiced against people who did not make the choices I made, I think it is really important not to pass judgment. At the same time, I've always considered it important to speak my mind.

The fight is not about sXe, it is about overthrowing a system of oppression. What is most important is that we unite, now more than ever, and no matter what our differences are. I'm not going to make drinking or smoking a scapegoat for everything that's wrong with our world while hiding in my sXe comfort zone. I am committed to fighting the real enemy.

Take us back to the history of Portuguese punk/hardcore. You were talking about the mid-1990s and especially X-Acto…

All in all there was a good spirit at the time. I think that most of the people who remain in the scene today would agree. Many long-lasting contacts were established as a result of the type of punk/hardcore/sXe we lived.

X-Acto, with its originality both in music and lyrics, always remained very influential. Of particular significance was their CD *Harmony As One*. It dealt with global social issues and reflected a positive and strong way to look at what you could do for the earth, for animals, and for humans. It also showed how short-term projects and little things could have a big impact. It even had an eighteen-minute spoken word sequence at the end of the CD explaining why being vegan was the best choice for humans, animals, and the planet. It rocked! You could not be indifferent to that, it touched your heart. And it made complete sense — and still does, and always will!

Back then you could feel hope and you could feel that you were part of a big group of people willing to change reality by going to demos, distributing pamphlets, educating people in the streets, doing benefit shows to help the homeless, supporting dog or cat shelters.

Since X-Acto made people aware that a band is a powerful vehicle to share a message, a lot of other bands were formed. Punk, hardcore, crust, ska, and melodic hardcore bands appeared everywhere, and we experienced a hardcore boom. At the end of the 1990s, a lot of people were at shows, always! On average 300 to 500. This was unique in Portuguese hardcore history.

As time moved on, more bands joined, some bands broke up, some people went, other people stayed, new people came. From the year 2000 on, when X-Acto broke up and some of the band's members started Sannyasin, and when Time X and New Winds appeared, there was a lot of social/political/spiritual engagement and strong messages of human, animal, earth, and self-liberation.

Unfortunately a lot of that, if not all, is lost today. Most bands speak about hardcore and that's it. People are stuck to collecting T-shirts and records and hardly pick up a book or zine. No band speaks about anything except hardcore issues. No band takes a public stand with regard to social struggles, or, better yet, tries to engage people in action.

Of course some bands do good things musically and they make concerts an entertaining place to be. But I see no social issues. Anyone who expects to return home from a Portuguese hardcore show today with some social/political/alternative issue can forget it.

This is the current scenario. There are no "politicalities," no social issues, no one who speaks about anything except hardcore. There are no zines or books, videos or debates, spoken word performances or actions, nothing. This is definitely not what I spent years struggling for with New Winds and other people.

How about straight edge? Is it still alive?

It depends on what type of sXe we are talking about. If it's the type of sXe where bands speak about friendship and the guy who broke the edge, or about the problems and disappointments they have had within the scene, then it is certainly alive. Almost every straight edge band today talks about nothing but these subjects; subjects that in my opinion shouldn't be the most important. It's just never been my vision of sXe to stick to lyrical clichés that will never take you anywhere in terms of seeing the world differently and changing it. It's like pop music or any other "empty" style.

Whether politically inspiring sXe is still alive is a different question. However, I will say this: to me, political sXe will be alive as long as there are bands that address social, political, spiritual struggles and call themselves sXe. And this is still the case. My hope is that, as time moves on and as the world becomes an even sicker place than it is today, more and more bands will return to these struggles and organize resistance against those in power.

One more thing, though, just to clarify: I don't want to say that it's necessarily bad to talk about your friends, or about disappointments or broken relationships, or about the past or what happened within the scene. What I'm trying to say is that if we want to be a truly different and revolutionary movement, it's not these types of lyrics and issues that will get us there. They will not make us any different from the scenes we fight so much and want to distinguish ourselves from.

Across the Atlantic, a strong political straight edge scene has developed in Brazil, a former Portuguese colony. Do you think that the shared cultural heritage has anything to do with this? Or is it a mere coincidence? In any case, I assume you have good relations with the scene in Brazil, given the common language...

Of course the common language helps a lot with communication and with building strong bonds between the hardcore scenes. I also think you are right to some degree with regard to the cultural heritage. I can't really explain why, but when I went to Brazil for the first time I didn't feel that it was something new, it felt like a place I had already been to. It's strange but I think that Brazil has always been in my subconsciousness. At the same time, Brazil has a special way of making you feel like you have never felt before. People are very friendly and warm and society is completely different from what you're used to in Europe. It's something way out of everything you have known or lived. I think this is the main reason why most Brazilian bands — and I'm not just talking about hardcore — have such strong social and political lyrics. People are not spoiled like we are in Europe or in the US. A lot of people just try to survive. And many of them turn to music to spread revolutionary messages. The energy at a show in Brazil is completely different from what you're used to in this part of the world. People are not used to things being delivered or given for free, they have to fight for better living conditions every single day. I think what really touched me was to see first-hand something that I had only imagined but never experienced. I think this made me feel very connected to the country and its people. That's why I wanted to play there so much, I knew it would be the "right" audience for a band like New Winds. Shows there are simply amazing, everybody has a great time. People don't care so much about how well you play, they are just there to listen, to enjoy, and to make you feel at home.

How did you perceive straight edge in the Brazilian context?

sXe is Brazil is much more political than in Europe. People are involved in local as well as international issues, there is a lot of awareness and debate. Many shows include political information. I twice saw representatives of the Landless Workers Movement speak at sXe shows, sons of landless slaves who have been oppressed for generations. They spoke about their struggles. They are poor but they have a rare strength to fight for their rights to a home and to land to survive on. It was tremendously moving, I can't really put it into words.

It feels like the harsh social conditions in Brazil force people to be aware and focused and to stay informed, and this is reflected in the sXe scene. I always come home inspired when I go there — by the shows and by the people, especially by the dedication with which people follow their ideals. I feel blessed for these experiences and cannot thank the friends I have made there enough. I have been to Brazil six times and have learned so much as a human being.

Of course there are also people who don't care and who don't keep informed, and the sXe scene faces some of the same problems that sXe scenes are facing elsewhere: there is a tendency to be less and less focused on the "real enemy" and more and more on some conflict within the scene. However, in Brazil — as well as in other Latin American countries constituting the so-called backyard of the United States — there is a growing revolutionary movement on many levels. sXe is one of them.

What about your Iberian neighbor? I can't help wondering why a strong political straight edge scene would develop in Portugal, but apparently not in Spain. Do you have any explanation for this?

Don't really know, beats me. I guess smaller countries sometimes have an advantage as everyone knows everyone and people hang out together more often, so it's maybe easier to organize shows and other activities. In that sense, Portugal has great conditions for a concise, compact, and active scene. However, this alone can't really explain why Spain would not have a big and consolidated political sXe scene, especially when there exists an occupied territory within the country, such as the Basque Country. I think this and the fact that Spain was only recently freed from a dictatorship should be reason enough to have a strong political sXe and punk/hardcore scene.

I only played there once, in the Basque Country — a small show, sixty-seventy people, but it had some stalls with information and zines, and the bands we played with, Crickbat for example, were bands who spoke about other things than just music and hardcore.

I think people avoid playing there, at least small bands, due to the relatively weak political scene in general, although I know there are many anarchists and punks who do a lot of great stuff. I think that it all gets pretty much diluted because of the size of the country. But this is just my opinion, based on what I've experienced. Others might have different perspectives.

I went to see a show of the Gorilla Biscuits reunion tour in Spain. The venue was crowded, a big place with a lot of people, I think about 500. In other cities it was the same. But this is a classical and very well known band from the 80s. If "normal" hardcore or punk bands had played, I highly doubt that the venues would have been that full.

In the end, I think that the popularity of a philosophy, a lifestyle, an ideology, or even a band depend on the people involved and the places you grow up in and the amount of things that happen in your hometown. Sometimes it's just really hard to say why this happens in one place and not in another.

Geographically, Portugal is rather isolated. Your former band, New Winds, drew a lot of international attention. What were your experiences with reaching straight edge scenes — and, not to forget, activist communities — around the globe?

This is something I find extremely gratifying. It means the world to me. It is something that will be with me way beyond this life. When we started rehearsing in little garages, we never imagined that we would turn out to be one of the most talked-about bands in the worldwide punk hardcore and sXe scene. I never thought I would engage in such a powerful journey that would change my life forever.

What hardcore, punk, sXe, and New Winds has taught me is truly amazing, an achievement as a human being. The places I was able to visit, the people I was able to meet, what I was able to experience and learn, and what I was able to become as a person makes me feel truly blessed. I miss some of those days when everything was in such harmony, where we could sing songs of freedom and share dirty clubs with people screaming our songs as if their lives depended on it. I can hardly imagine another way than this. I can't see myself on any other path than the one I followed.

I believe that it was all supposed to be like this, so that I could become who I am today, thirty-three years old, feeling lot less angst regarding a whole bunch of things. Lyrics like those of "Young Until I Die," "In Praise Of Others," "Trust," "True Till Death," "Start Today," "Hope" by X-Acto, "For Those Who Crucify Us" by Sannyasin, and "Within 20 Years" by New Winds never made more sense to me than today. I was born without asking and I will die without wanting, but I'm really sure I made the best of what lay in between! These were amazing eleven years, they were all worthwhile. I'd live them again without blinking.

One of the things I'm most proud of is that New Winds was consistent with its message. That's what opened doors to us in terms of labels and got us relatively known. We promised we would speak up about social, political, and spiritual issues and put subjects like lost friendships or lost edges aside. And we did that. There was always something in the air when New Winds played. People always expected to hear about real life problems, and not about petty hardcore scene fights and trivialities. We always refused to "shoot against our own feet," as we say in Portugal.

Whenever we had the chance and the means to do so, we organized shows providing different cultural and political information. We used videos, spoken word, posters, books, texts, emails. We always had something on stage to share. It was all about words of action, about sharing thoughts, experiences, images, feelings. The ability to pick up a microphone and speak your mind about the world and to make people aware of things they weren't aware of before was always a reason to keep going.

We lived up to what we preached until our very last show on March 17, 2007, in the town where New Winds was born and where I have lived my whole life: Sacavém. The show was free, and we showed a video called *The 4th World War*, about globalization and its victims. The show was sponsored by some local organizations. We gave all of the money we got, 250 Euros, to a dog shelter. Until the end we kept doing what we thought was right.

We were never perfect and sometimes we screwed up big time. We said and did things that were wrong, but we always spoke out and acted. We never hid or shut up. We played more than 250 shows in eleven years, and participated in more than twenty benefit gigs for Food Not Bombs, dog and cat shelters, soup kitchens, prisoner support groups, Palestinian resistance, and animal liberation struggles. How could I ever forget such a band and the influence it had on me? If your life can change in one second, just imagine what eleven years can do, and you might be able to understand what I feel when New Winds is mentioned.

You said that the show was sponsored by some local organizations. Just out of curiosity: which local organizations sponsor hardcore shows in Portugal?

There are different groups, and they mainly let us use their space, especially in smaller towns. For instance, in many places around Lisbon, the Communist Party lets us use their head office for shows and social activities. It's not like we get support from local authorities or anything. They couldn't care less about us. Either they don't even know that we exist, or they send guys to shows who are disguised as hardcore fans but are actually from the police. The Portuguese government doesn't give a damn thing about education, health, or jobs, so why would they care about supporting groups who fight them? This would never happen. Very occasionally we get support (mainly in the form of equipment) by local authorities to organize benefit shows or youth festivals. But basically we rely on the people who arrange the shows to organize some kind of support from non-governmental groups.

Your latest musical project, Arm the Spirit, is all acoustic. This is an interesting — albeit not unique — development for a former hardcore band frontman. What made you decide to play acoustic? How is it working out for you? Do you think that you reach a wider — or at least different — audience? Have your messages changed at all?

I think the main reason was to do something different to reach other people. Hardcore is fast, furious, and it doesn't get that much into people's ears. You must be a fan of this type of music to like it. This acoustic project adds value to the message because it acts as a bridge between music and message. In what concerns the message itself, Arm the Spirit follows New Winds. Human, animal, earth, and self-liberation are at the core of our lyrics. We want to reach out to other people, spread hope and solidarity, compassion and love, awareness and attitude.

The band is going well for the moment. The idea to form Arm the Spirit was born by New Winds' second Bruno, who played guitar and who writes amazing lyrics. He started with some songs, and me and another friend, Nuno, worked on them, only changing a bit here and there, and we ended up with some good tunes. Later on in the studio, we added piano and violin as the songs needed some innovation and better quality. We are very satisfied with the four songs we recorded which will be released as a benefit CD for the Sea Shepherd Conservation Society. It will be called *September The Black* (not because of September the 11th).

As I said, our message did not change at all, it just grew stronger and wiser, I think. Screaming accusations or clichéd calls for change can be a little naïve. I think age and experience led to this, even if unconsciously. You just start looking at things from different angles. I have read more books now and I have experienced more in life. Time has passed, I've become different, and the world has become different too. Nonetheless, many issues are as pressing as ever and we will continue to address them: Palestine, Tibet, indigenous resistance, egoism, animals, the earth, Africa, war, racism, homophobia, sexism, the media, authoritarianism, lies and corruption, MOVE, political prisoners, humanity. The political focus doesn't change. It's just that we are making different, maybe "more accepted" music. We'd like to reach other audiences, people who usually listen to bands with empty lyrics or with coded messages that no one understands. We want to be simple, but direct and intelligent, positive, political, and powerful. I think this is the main intention.

While other members of New Winds have apparently moved out of Portugal recently, you still live near Lisbon. What are the most pressing issues that you have to deal with in Portugal as a political activist?

It is true that some members went looking for other places to live. It is not easy in Portugal, and expensive when you compare living costs to the salaries you are able to earn. I decide to stay nonetheless — for different reasons.

As far as being a political activist is concerned, I'm not sure if I still consider myself that. I did when I was in New Winds. During those years, I was active in many different struggles. Today, I'm only keeping updated — about SHAC, Mumia Abu Jamal, Jeff Luers, MOVE, Leonard Peltier, the Zapatistas and other indigenous resistance struggles, Palestine, etc. I'm addicted to reading now. I've never read as much in my life. I read every day, whenever I have time. I do answer emails and update the blog I maintain in Portuguese on www.armthespirit.wordpress.com, but I'm not writing letters to prisoners anymore, no longer organize spoken word performances or video nights, etc. I'm kind of taking a break from a ten-year period when me and some friends basically did this full-time. The beliefs and convictions are still there, they are right inside of me, but I'm just taking a break.

Because you exhausted yourself?

Well, actually, let me rephrase this: it's not so much that I'm taking a "break." I guess I just do things in different ways now. What has changed is that I no longer distribute pamphlets, brochures, and information material on a regular basis. This ended with New Winds breaking up, I can't exactly say why. But I remain politically active in my everyday life; I boycott companies who profit from the planet's destruction and from the suffering of human and non-human animals. I also volunteer at a soup kitchen for the homeless once a week and donate regularly to Sea Shepherd and Survival. I also spread political information through my blog.

Also, being in Arm the Spirit kind of demands a different way of activism. We do not have the same audience we used to have with New Winds. People who come to Arm the Spirit shows do not have the same political vein as hardcore kids, and you have to be a different kind of activist, you have to speak calmer, in a more constructive way, and you have to be more careful with words. It is challenging at times, but it's a challenge that I find important and that I enjoy.

Let us get back to the most pressing issues for political activists in Portugal…

I find that, not only here but around the world, the fences become tighter and tighter. We are more and more living in fascist states where punishment is brutal — physically, economically, and psychologically. Fear is sold more than solutions. Freedom is more and more restricted. Big Brother is on a never-seen level. We are totally controlled and punished because of some vague threat called "terrorism" — something that was started by the same governments who now say they want to protect us from it. All is "terrorism" now. Dissent is "terrorism." What a joke! Because governments can use the media as an enormous propaganda machine, people suck up their lies as if they are air to breathe. It's outrageous, frightening, and unbelievable, but it's happening. People are facing enormous difficulties in doing effective things to change the reality we live in.

At the same time, especially in Latin America, we find significant — and effective — uprisings and social struggles. One of the latest documentaries I watched, John Pilger's *War On Democracy*, illustrates this in an amazing manner. The earth and two thirds of its population are being robbed, humiliated, exploited, and killed by the same people who say that they are delivering democracy. "Democracy" is just a word that is either being used naïvely, or with the purpose of disguising tyranny. The US is delivering "democracy" in Iraq and in Afghanistan at the cost of more than a million lives. How can this be democratic? I don't want their war — but I sure don't want their peace either.

The fact is that people, including me and you, must continue to struggle if we want people who are much worse off than ourselves to have a better life and a more sustainable future. This concerns all generations. At the same time, we must never forget our past; we must learn from it. And we must remind the people who oppress us of the past as well. This is a constant struggle. As Milan Kundera so brilliantly put it: "The struggle of people against power is the struggle of memory against forgetting."

What do you think the future holds for political straight edge in Portugal?

I think there are three options, but this is just my personal view.

One: The scene stays as it is, lacking social and political struggles, focusing on T-shirt and record sales, "fun," "unity," and lyrics that talk about who has lost the edge, blah blah. The consequence would be the death of a scene with an enormous potential.

Two: The bands that exist today change, in the sense that sXe would be about action again, especially about acting differently. People would read and learn, and make information part of their shows and events.

Three: New bands come and turn the tide. They would go beyond today's mix of social/political apathy, mad consumerism, and disrespect for life. They would rekindle the struggles that make sXe what it really is, a (r)evolutionary alternative. As someone once said, "There is a war — here is a weapon." This is how I see sXe hardcore.

Scenes

- **Israel**
  Interview with Jonathan Pollack

- **Sweden**
  Interview with Tanja
  Interview with Gabriel Cárdenas

- **Poland**
  Interview with Robert Matusiak

- **USA**
  Interview with Kurt Schroeder

Israel

Interview with Jonathan Pollack

In Israel, the connections between straight edge hardcore and political activism have been strong since a radical hardcore underground with anarchist leanings emerged in the 1990s. Jonathan Pollack has been part of the scene almost from its beginnings. In 2003, he co-founded Anarchists Against the Wall, an Israeli direct action group that supports Palestinian resistance to the Israeli occupation. Jonathan lives in Jaffa.

It seems that anarchist politics and straight edge are nowhere linked as closely as in Israel. Would you agree? And if so, what do you think the reasons are?

The hardcore scene in Israel is tiny, and in the mid and late 90s there was indeed a very strong link to anarchist activism and politics, mainly due to bands like Nekhei Naatza and Dir Yassin. The atmosphere at shows was political in a very deep and in-your-face way, not something you could escape or consider as nothing more than cultural white noise.

Straight edge was part of that scene, even a prominent part at points in time, but never detached or separate. The fact that both of the aforementioned bands had Straight Edge members in them — while neither was a Straight Edge band as such — is a good example for that.

In a country that isn't much more than a huge military camp, it was clear how and why punk and politics mix, and for those of us with Xs on their hands, growing up in that scene, Straight Edge was politics years before I saw it on a Catalyst t-shirt.

A lot of what and who I am today is greatly indebted to that scene and its amazing people and spirit. While remnants of that attitude still endure today, I feel the scene — in general, and as far as Straight Edge goes — is much less overtly political today than it was then.

Would you say that the straight edge scene in Israel remains tied into radical politics though — or is there a straight edge scene today that distances itself from radical activism?

No, there just isn't really a separate Straight Edge scene in Israel. It used to be very rare to come across Straight Edgers who weren't, at least superficially, political. However, with today's general decrease in the emphasis that the Israeli hardcore scene puts on politics, you can now also encounter non-political Straight Edgers.

D9, Tel Aviv, 2007   Oren Ziv (Activestills.org)

Thinking about it though, for many of the "old timers" losing interest in Straight Edge seemed to be a precursor for losing interest in politics as well.

You yourself, however, remain a tireless activist and organizer. How do you see straight edge tied into this?

While I do see Straight Edge, in its essence, as a political choice, it doesn't interest me as a political movement or as a scene separate from the hardcore scene.

For me, Straight Edge is, and always was, a gut instinct. I remember being drawn to it as a teenager, long before I had the tools to dress my choice in the fancy robes of radical discourse and complex politics.

I was initially attracted to Straight Edge by the need to depart and distance myself — mentally, emotionally and politically — from the culture of my contemporaries; a culture obsessed with money and commoditization of leisure and personal interaction rather than with freedom; a culture in which the most upsetting thing you could do was to reject manufactured leisure.

Today, through the filter of years of activism, and with the ability to put Straight Edge in political terms, I am still not interested in doing so. It remains in the realm of clutched fists, red rimmed eyes and a raging gnash at the world around me, an instinct. Put again in the simple terms of a teenager, Straight Edge is the ultimate Fuck You.

So, in a wider political context, living straight edge has no real significance for you?

In a realpolitik context, the links between drug abuse or alcoholism and poverty, or between cigarettes and transnational corporations, are just another — and not even a very central — aspect of a fucked up world; another item in the endless list of boycott-worthy items if you'd like.

Straight edge's political importance lies in its explosive cultural charge. This is the real challenge that it presents, and why it connects so well with punk and hardcore. Unlike with more concrete political issues, there is no point in convincing people of Straight Edge's merits — being mostly instinctive, it is a fire that either burns within you, or it doesn't.

As a political idea, the Straight Edge of ebullient refusal to the decadence of our times is not that of an ascetic anchorite in the badlands of western civilization or of religious purity. The need to extract oneself from society, so prevalent in Straight Edge, is fuelled by the desire to see and live a different reality; a desire that can't subsist in the clubs, cafés and drug culture of mainstream society. Both my Straight Edge and my activism are strongly rooted in this passion, and neither is dependent on whether we will reach this different reality or not.

Can you explain more about the connection between this desire or passion, straight edge, and activism?

Activism sends one through the hollows and dells of failure and despair, and with all the positivism in the world, I doubt anyone seriously invested in a meaningful struggle can truly avoid these feelings at times. In my personal passage through the lands of political involvement, and especially through its lows, I've seen people shot dead for nothing more than demonstrating or breaking a curfew. Unfortunately, more than once, this happened meters away, right in front of me, and I couldn't do anything about it.

These are experiences that sink deep into one's soul. They occupy my nights and my sleep just as much as they occupy my days and waking thoughts. But still, despite its toll, I feel very fortunate to be part of such an intense struggle and to be satiated with its radiant passions, as well as its true sorrows.

For me, it is this choice, of real passions over the ready-made passions produced by the market, of true liberty over numbness and indifference, where Straight Edge and activism connect.

Help me understand how you relate straight edge to this passion: is it because you feel life more intensely when you are sober? Or because straight edge is a synonym for refusal and anti-consumerism? If the latter, I guess it would make drinking home-brew acceptable — but then that's hardly straight edge anymore...

I'd say it's closer to the latter. As I've explained before, while I don't ignore the ties between, say, alcoholism, poverty, and transnational corporations, I doubt they could justify the centrality Straight Edgers assign to alcohol consumption in our identity.

Whether a beer was produced by exploited laborers or a DIY microbrewery, is a question that should interest drinkers, not Straight Edgers. The real issue I recognize concerns not the on-the-ground economic circumstances of these products — these can indeed be circumvented — but rather the place that these substances hold within our culture, and what it means to reject them.

I tend to think that Straight Edge is a rejection of cultural consumerism in a way that goes beyond the mere ritual of monetary transaction. In my experience, alcohol, drugs and cigarettes have an important significance in the mainstream culture of hedonist indifference, in the acquisition of "cool," in the promotion of ready-made sterile rebellion-for-the-masses.

There is often a somewhat condescending tendency within radical circles, where we assume that once we've understood the context of things, we are in a way immune to them, as if we are in some way purer than the Average Joe. I think you can't expropriate drinking, smoking and drug use from the long dark night of trade, and it doesn't really matter if it's home-brewed or not. You just can't beat the system from within. For some reason, this is a commonly held view among anarchists with respect to, say, electoral politics, but not so much when it comes to cultural issues — where I think it's even more applicable.

How are your relations to both anarchist and straight edge scenes outside of Israel? And how do you perceive the politics of straight edge in other countries?

As I said before, Straight Edge doesn't really interest me as a movement. Over the years I've met some very interesting people and it is with them I keep in touch, not with their scenes.

However, even though the mainstream of Straight Edge, with its puritanism and macho attitude, isn't very interesting, the radical margins are full of beautiful, passionate and original people and ideas. Generally, as a rule, the farther you get from cleancut looks and fancy clothes the more interesting Straight Edge will probably get.

Isn't this what straight edge crust punkers are all about?

Yeah, I guess it probably is...

Anyway, despite the way I feel about jock culture in Straight Edge, veganism and animal rights' prominence in Straight Edge is not something to be ignored or taken lightly. While I don't really connect with a lot of things around bands like Earth Crisis, I treasure their contribution to transforming animal rights and radical environmentalism into a central issue for Straight Edgers.

Tell us more about your own political activities and about Anarchists Against the Wall...

Well, I'll try doing that without going into the depths of the complex and long history of Zionist colonialism in the Middle East. This history started at the very end of the 19th century, when a Jewish national movement began winning the hearts and minds of European Jews, with the aim of colonizing Palestine, which at the time was under Ottoman rule. Today — after establishing the "Jewish and democratic" State of Israel in 1948; after wars that have caused hundreds of thousands of Palestinian refugees, and after long periods of military rule — Palestinians remain either second class citizens in Israel, or subjects without rights in the Occupied Territories of Gaza and the West Bank.

The first outbreak of widespread popular resistance in the Palestinian Occupied Territories was sparked in December 1987 and became known as the Intifada — "uprising" in Arabic. It subsided with the signing of a so-called peace accord in Oslo in 1993. When the hopes and promises of the peace process were not met, a second Intifada erupted in October 2000.

Today, we are witnessing the perfection of a very sophisticated regime of racial separation (*Hafrada* in Hebrew, *Apartheid* in Afrikaans) in the Occupied Territories — a regime that's extremely brutal on the one hand, and, in many aspects, almost completely invisible on the other. Israel's acts are driven mostly by the desire to retain and strengthen its control over the land and the civilian population. Even the military withdrawal from the Gaza Strip was motivated by this: Israel practically retains control over the Strip and keeps it besieged, but is now provided with more international legitimacy.

One of the landmarks of the Israeli project of separation is the construction of the West Bank barrier ("The Wall"), which Israel started building in 2002, and which will practically annex about 10 percent of the West Bank to Israel when complete. The wall, together with the Jewish-only road system, Jewish-only settlements, prohibited zones, checkpoints and roadblocks, will secure the division of the West Bank into islands of territorial discontinuity, and ensure Israeli control over the scarce water resources.

The construction of the wall, with its grave implications on Palestinians, was also a catalyst for a new wave of popular struggle that started soon after construction had began, peaked in 2004, and continues to date.

The struggle against the wall, throughout the West Bank, mostly consists of almost daily demonstrations, riots and direct actions. People gather and march towards their lands where Israeli bulldozers are working, with the aim of disrupting and sabotaging construction. Demonstrators are usually met by military repression that varies from teargas and concussion grenades to rubber-coated steel bullets (very different from rubber bullets in most other places, often lethal) to, at times, the use of live ammunition.

In the past six years nineteen people, ten of them minors, all of them Palestinians, were killed in these demonstrations, in which firearms were only ever used by the army, never by protesters. Thousands of us, Palestinians, Israelis and internationals have been injured, many seriously. Hundreds have been thrown in jails, prosecuted and imprisoned. The Israeli army, like any army faced with a civilian uprising, knows no other way to deal with civilian dissent but to try and stifle it with extreme violence.

Anarchists Against the Wall is really just a side note in all this — Israelis joining an essentially Palestinian movement. I guess you could say that small bands of vagabond and treacherous Israeli anarchists roamed through the Occupied Territories from the early days of the second Intifada, drawn to the popular insurrectionary resistance to the occupation. These people later grew to become Anarchists Against the Wall, which is a more organized attempt of Israelis to join the resistance of Palestinians, as well as a means to enable others to do so.

As anarchists, many of us were obviously attracted to participate in an insurrectionary situation taking place right at our doorstep, but the rationale of joining Palestinians who put up resistance goes beyond that. The fact that we oppose the occupation, Zionism in general, and even the existence of nation-states per se, does not relieve us of our responsibility for what is done by our governments on the ground. Israelis, anarchists too, are the beneficiaries of Israeli apartheid, and it is being carried out in our name. Israeli apartheid and Israeli occupation will not end by itself — it will end when it becomes ungovernable and unmanageable. Being part of the effort to reach this situation is our moral duty. We can't cast aside the national identity with its privileges and moral obligations that has been imposed on us. Especially here, we are Israelis whether we like it or not.

Aware of our colonial position as Israelis, and the dangers such unequal political relationships carry, an important principle of our participation in the struggle is to do our best not to replicate the positions of occupied-occupier inside the movement. Though as Israelis the struggle is ours to fight, side by side with Palestinians, it is, in this colonial situation, definitely not ours to lead, and all major decisions are made by Palestinians.

Anarchists Against the Wall's importance is simply in being there, as Israelis; its importance is the shattering of borders — be they borders of national loyalty, or the ones between protest and resistance. In Israel such acts were not at all an obvious thing prior to Anarchists Against The Wall, even for anarchists.

Does straight edge sometimes become an issue in your collaboration with Palestinians? Like, in my experience, you often get respect in Muslim communities — which most of the Palestinian communities are, the significant Christian Palestinian population notwithstanding — if you don't drink as a non-Muslim.

> Sometimes, this can open doors and establish strong personal ties. At the same time, it seems difficult — for obvious reasons, I believe — to find many people in the Territories who'd rally behind the cause of vegan straight edge. So do you think that being straight edge helps or complicates transcending national, cultural, and religious borders?

It's kind of funny you mention that. It is well known that Muslims abstain from alcohol, but it is less known that devout Muslims also don't smoke or take drugs, because the Quran forbids one from harming her body. I guess that's where the stupidity of those hardliners who fluctuate towards fundamentalist Islam and try to give Straight Edge a religious touch draws from. In my opinion this trend is very counterproductive. I feel Straight Edge should be a passionate assault on our own mainstream culture rather than a way to connect our counterculture with fundamentalism.

I think it's rather problematic to equate Straight Edge with just abstinence, but having said that, abstaining from alcohol can definitely help in Palestine, no doubt, but I don't think Straight Edge is very relevant here. The non-Straight Edgers among us don't drink in Palestine either, out of a guest's respect for people's culture.

After years of Israelis using cultural-exchange and "dialogue" as ways to strengthen and profit from the occupation, Palestinians are very suspicious of normalization; i.e. the attempt to form normal relationships between Palestinians and Israelis under the occupation, as if the terms are equal. While disrespect for Palestinian culture would have definitely been detrimental for the attempt to build trust, I think such trust can only be built from the understanding that we do not seek normalization, but rather that we wish to take part, in the most literal way, in the fight against the occupation. Through the years, this trust was and still is being built through mutual respect and the sincerity of our wishes to take part in the struggle rather than to talk about guilt.

You are right — no, the Palestinian masses won't rally behind our libertarian causes, but this is not why we go. I understand anarchism not as an abstract idea confined to a hundred years of written thought, but, above all, as a fight against injustice in the here and now. I think that this is exactly what we are doing.

This does not mean, of course, that we don't have our own limits and principles. For instance, while most Palestinians, obviously, aren't exactly vegans, animal rights is very influential in the Israeli anarchist scene, maybe more than anywhere else in the world. I can remember a few times when this became an issue, for instance when we locked ourselves in a huge metal cage to block bulldozers from clearing the path for the wall, and one of the farmers brought a goat with him; or when donkeys are used to transport hundreds of kilos of olives during olive harvest. It is important for us to join Palestinians in their resistance, many times also at the price of ideological purity, but everyone draws her own line individually.

Alright, knowing you, I'm sure we'll get great answers to the final questions, no matter how general they are: what future do you see for anarchism, for straight edge, and for the Middle East?

I think the answer for all three is struggle.

For anarchism simply because struggle is its essence, and will, I hope, always be its future. I don't see anarchism as an escapist-utopian idea, but rather as one of the present; a never-complete pursuit of freedom and equality, with boundaries that are always expanding. It is not a movement based on the notion of "the good of man," rather the opposite: I see it based on the notion that there will always be oppression to fight, including after "the revolution."

As for Straight Edge — its intrinsic logic only has any meaning in the context of refusing society, in the context of discontent; as a tribal cry of war for the misfits and outcasts, the angry daughters of western pop culture.

And the Middle East? That's just too sad a story. We've already talked about realpolitik long enough in this interview, but there is simply no option for this region other than struggle — it is too succumbed by imperialism and internal corruption to offer any other solution, if there is to be a future for this place at all. From the occupation of Iraq to that of Palestine, from oppressive "authentic" regimes (as opposed to the puppet regimes of Iraq or Afghanistan) to religious fundamentalism, the light of hope is a very scarce recourse in the dark tunnel of the Middle East.

As far as the Zionist-Palestinian conflict is concerned specifically, I am not an optimist here either. Every effort at peace negotiations so far has been cynically used by Israel to mask the perpetuation of its apartheid regime as attempts to end it.

In the long term, the two state solution could never offer true reconciliation as it offers no solution to the millions of Palestinian refugees and is based on a racist notion of Israel remaining an ethnocracy where Jews will inherently have more rights than others.

The only point of dim light is that while racist and rejectionist tendencies on the Israeli side are rapidly growing, voices calling for the replacement of the national liberation struggle with one for equal rights become, slowly but steadily, louder on the Palestinian side. However, these voices are still a long way from representing the mainstream of Palestinian politics. Even if the agenda of civil rights will prevail over the nationalist one, long years of struggle are ahead of us.

Sweden

Interview with Tanja

Tanja is a northern Swedish political activist who was involved in the Swedish vegan straight edge scene of the 1990s (see also the interview with Dennis Lyxzén). Today, Tanja lives in a rural cooperative near Umeå, Sweden.

The infamous Swedish straight edge scene of the 1990s was very much concentrated in the town of Umeå in northern Sweden. I understand that you have been living in or near Umeå for some time now. But you didn't grow up there?

No, I grew up in Östersund — or close to Östersund, in the country. I moved to Umeå in 2000, after high school. But I had been there a lot before. There weren't so many towns near where I grew up, so Umeå was one of the closest.

But it was still pretty far, right?

About 400 kilometers.

And you mainly went to shows there?

Yes. As I said, there weren't so many options. I guess I started regularly traveling to Umeå in about 1997.

Why did you move there when you were out of school?

Well, I had been there a lot, and I already knew people in town. Besides, there was still a pretty strong vegan straight edge scene in Umeå at the time which gave me something to connect to — this seems important when you set out to create your own life.

Was Umeå the only town with a strong vegan straight edge scene?

Umeå was definitely the center. But there were smaller towns in the north too: Luleå, Piteå, Sundsvall. There was a scene in Östersund as well. But it was very different to Umeå. Umeå is a college town with a lot of student activists. That's very characteristic for the place. You don't have that in Östersund at all. We had a house called Tingshuset where we could hang out, put up shows, and organize festivals. However, the bigger and more exciting things always happened in Umeå.

In Östersund — and this might be true for the other smaller towns as well — there was always some kind of a "little brother complex." Like, we had our own bands, but most shows were still played by bands that came from other places. The scene always seemed to revolve more around people who organized shows rather than people who were playing in bands themselves.

Umeå, Sweden, 2000   Nora Räthzel

What was interesting, though, was that a vegan straight edge identity in Östersund was really important to me because you had to be very active to keep a scene going. Once I had moved to Umeå this changed. There wasn't anything to prove there. Everyone was vegan straight edge. This also meant that I got a different perspective on the scene. Like, certain aspects of it really started to bother me; things I hadn't even thought about much before.

For example?

Mainly all the macho aspects — and how far they reached. This was one of the reasons why I chose a rather separatist feminist milieu.

Were these aspects particularly strong in the Umeå scene, or was it just that they started to bother you more once you had moved there?

The latter. I think you find these aspects in almost all hardcore scenes — or everywhere in a patriarchal society, for that matter. As I said, it was just that my overall perspective on the scene changed after I had moved to Umeå. I think that I had this image of moving there and getting really involved. I even did a course in sound engineering. But I became disillusioned soon, because as a girl I felt welcome only under certain circumstances.

How did this become obvious? Were there any decisive experiences you had?

It's hard to say. I thought about this before meeting for the interview. Like, why is it still self-evident to me to live drug-free, yet I decided to leave that scene?

I can't really remember any particular events that triggered the decision. But I remember one incident, for example, that I believe illustrates the problem well. This happened even before I moved to Umeå. I was talking to some guys in Östersund who never seemed to take me seriously. Like, they always made it pretty clear that they didn't wanna have me around when they met with the bands that came through town. But this one time they were really excited and said, "Wow, Tanja, we found this band that's really great for you! They are on Victory, and it's an all-girl hardcore band!" They were talking about Baby Gopal. You know, their album was rather poppy, they had these pretty female vocals, the cover was blue and pink — and I was just like, "This is not okay!"

There was a pretty influential all-girls band from Umeå, though, right? The Doughnuts.

Yes, of course! They unfortunately stopped playing before I moved there. But they really meant a lot to many girls. They were very important.

I mean, of course, there were girls in the scene, but it was difficult for them. Like, when they started to organize Punkfesten, a big annual punk festival in Umeå — and it was really big at the time, with people coming from all over Sweden and beyond — I remember having many conversations with girlfriends of mine when we were just like, "This is not really an atmosphere where everyone feels welcome."

Girls were always a minority. In Östersund, for example, it sometimes seemed that the only girls were me, my best friend, and then some guys' girlfriends. There was always a huge gender gap. I think it's the responsibility of both sides to change that, and that you gotta take power if you have none, but still, the way I experienced it, there were a lot of guys who had the means to make a positive change, but they didn't do it. They didn't do what they could have done to change things. To the contrary, they usually did not allow others, in particular girls, to share power with them. There were a lot of missed opportunities. I think this is what became really obvious to me once I had moved to Umeå. It was certainly no coincidence that there were so few girls in the scene.

When you speak of macho elements, does that also mean violence?

I never really witnessed any fights. But there was definitely a lot of violent posing and dancing. You know, the whole "brotherhood" thing. And it wasn't just talk. The whole notion of brotherhood became very concrete in terms of how the power in the scene was divided.

If these elements were so strong, what was attractive to you about the scene to begin with?

Well, first of all, I come from a left-wing home, so the rebellious attitude of punk struck a chord with me. Then I was interested in animal rights, which was big at the time. And finally I met this friend, Kickan, who got herself well established in the scene. I don't know how she did it 'cause it certainly wasn't easy, but she was basically the one who showed me that you could be straight edge without being Christian. She was a little older and I was very influenced by her.

So early on, straight edge and hardcore punk were kind of one and the same thing for you?

Yes, I would say so, even though this was not typical for the hardcore scene in Östersund. To be honest, it sometimes seemed that it was only Kickan and I who lived drug-free — even though there must have been others too.

Did that create problems? Being drug-free in a scene that predominantly wasn't?

No. We got respect for living drug-free. While I was questioned for living drug-free in basically all social contexts I ever found myself in, this was really never the case within the hardcore scene. Being straight edge was kind of an ideal to aspire to — even if many couldn't live up to it.

What bands did you listen to at the time?

I definitely had my phase — when I was like fifteen — when I would only listen to what came out on Victory. But I pretty soon stopped to only listen to self-identified straight edge bands. In general, I never really put much time into all the scene stuff. None of the girls I knew really did. The girls I knew weren't nerdy enough to collect all those special edition seven inches and zillions of zines. There was a girl somewhere in central Sweden who tried to organize a straight edge network for girls toward the end of the 1990s. Not much came of it, but those were the kinds of things that I was always much more attracted to than all the nerdy stuff.

What happened after 2000? It seemed that the mighty Swedish straight edge scene suddenly disappeared very fast.

I really don't know, to be honest. What I do know, however, is that there seems to be hardly any place where living drug-free is still as much of a norm as it is within left-wing, radical circles in Umeå. This is definitely true for the circles I move in, which mainly consist of feminist women. But I think it applies pretty generally — to the point where I can see it being a problem for radical people who do not want to live drug-free. I would not be surprised if some folks even ended up moving from Umeå because of this. Umeå is really special that way. As far as I can tell, you can't even compare with what's going on in Stockholm, for example.

So living drug-free is not just accepted in the circles you're moving in, but it is seen as something positive?

Absolutely, there is no doubt. It is socially not really acceptable to use alcohol or drugs openly. Being considerate and taking care of each other is really important. Drug consumption just doesn't seem to fit in.

That's interesting because I have a friend who grew up in Umeå but has been living in Stockholm for a while now, and from all I know she never had anything to do with the hardcore scene but lives totally drug-free and sees that as a big part of her life.

I think that's very typical. I mean, out of the people I have to do with in Umeå, I really have to think of someone who does not live drug-free. There aren't many. At the same time, most of my friends are not linked to hardcore at all.

But them living drug-free is still related to the straight edge scene of the 1990s?

In a certain way definitely. I mean, to this day there are people who move to Umeå because of its reputation for a drug-free radical culture. I guess this culture was created here in the 1990s and it is now culturally reproduced even if the original label might largely be gone. That's why you get to meet kids who are like eighteen years old and who are proud of being drug-free. They certainly weren't around in the hardcore scene in the 1990s, and they wouldn't call themselves "straight edge" either. But living drug-free is still something they got taught when they grew up.

Why did many of the folks who were part of the scene in the 1990s also drop the straight edge label?

I think many — especially many women — went through a development similar to mine. They just got turned off by the macho character of it all. Besides, there were always some who were into living drug-free but never embraced the whole hardcore thing. Whether they had particularly negative images of straight edge I can't tell, but they certainly had a pretty strong critique of hardcore culture in general. In any case, living drug-free in Umeå is certainly not bound to any particular taste in music...

Just to make sure: when you say drug-free, this also means that people don't drink or smoke?

Yes, that's part of it.

How about vegetarianism and veganism?

That's also part of it. Definitely. I don't even know many vegetarians. Almost everyone I know is vegan. Animal rights are still really big. There are quite a few folks who live outside of town in old farm houses that have partly been turned into animal shelters.

What about your personal approach to straight edge? Before you came to identify as straight edge, was there a time when you didn't live drug-free?

I never drank. There was a period when I attempted to chew tobacco, which is quite popular in Sweden — but that didn't last very long.

So living straight edge kinda came as a natural thing?

Yes. Even family-wise. I think I was fortunate that way. There were basically no drugs in my family, and it was easy for me to live drug-free. I guess I also never liked the feeling of losing control. In any case, I never had to force myself to be straight edge. There was never anything I had to remove from my life. It was easy and did feel kinda natural. In this sense I'm also really grateful that the straight edge wave was so big when I was a teenager. Otherwise it would have been much harder to live drug-free.

Because straight edge provided some kind of support or legitimacy for living drug-free?

Exactly. Even kids who didn't live drug-free knew that there was this thing called straight edge and that it was something cool. As I said before, I never hung out with many straight edge kids. It wasn't even particularly important for me to be in contact with other straight edge kids. It was important, however, that the straight edge movement, and the fact that people knew about it, justified what I was doing. This was maybe the biggest meaning straight edge ever had for me. It just made things easier. Like, I never had to explain why I didn't drink. I could say that I was straight edge and that was enough.

How about the few straight edge friends you had? Did straight edge come naturally for them too?

Hard to say. I guess it was a mix. What seemed evident, though, was that those who had to force themselves to be straight edge didn't stay straight edge for very long…

This seems to be the case very often. Just like the fact that some of the most militant straight edgers don't stay straight edge for very long either. And when they do change, they often go off the deep end and become drug dealers or whatever…

Yes, I've seen that happen too. Same with the ones who get the "Straight Edge for Life" tattoos. Very few of them still live drug-free.

What about straight edge and politics in the 1990s? Was there a direct link? Like, when you heard that someone was straight edge, did you immediately think that this person was left-wing?

Absolutely. Like, I have never met people who called themselves drug-free or straight edge without calling themselves left-wing. I think this has a lot to do with the strong social democratic — and partly socialist — history that Sweden has. I guess straight edge was just linked to that tradition.

At the same time, the political dimensions of straight edge weren't necessarily explored very deeply. To many, straight edge was just part of the identity kit, if you will. Look at economic analysis or class analysis, for example. I mean, I certainly didn't have such an analysis at the time. Of course, there might have been discussions that simply passed me by. But my impression was that while everyone embraced very general notions of solidarity and justice, deeper analyses were really lacking — for example in terms of gender, and maybe especially in terms of class. I had an understanding of feminism, but I think it was really class-blind. Which, again, might all be very typical for Umeå and the scene that developed there: Umeå is really very much a university town; most of the activists have middle class or academic background.

Is this also the reason why, like in many other countries in the 1990s, animal rights were really a dominant issue within the straight edge scene?

Probably. I mean, it's definitely true that animal rights were very dominant as a political issue. And, I guess, class does play into that. Like, I would say that there are enough activists in Umeå now who reject their class privilege and do not become academics or whatever. But their backgrounds remain clearly non-working class. I also think, though, that things have changed a bit and that people have developed a deeper economic analysis of society and of their own class position.

Also in connection to living straight edge or drug-free?

Yes I think so. I believe, for example, that living drug-free is seen by many — in particular by many women — as a form of solidarity with underprivileged social groups because these groups often seem to be affected the most when it comes to alcohol and drug addiction.

At the same time, I still see the original motivations for living drug free within radical circles in Sweden as a mainly personal or individual thing. Like, even for us women with a feminist analysis, living drug free was seen as part of our individual liberation — taking control of our bodies, being independent, developing strength.

What really struck me, for example, when I first read "The Antifa Straight Edge," which I think will also be in this volume, was that the text made a strong link between straight edge and collective politics. The idea that living drug free might allow you to do more effective work for other people really spoke to me. I mean, of course, my friends and I had always seen the connections between different forms of oppression, but in my understanding straight edge still had predominantly individual dimensions — something that primarily had to do with how you related to yourself, to your body, your health etc.

It always seemed that the Swedish vegan straight edge scene was particularly strong in the north of the country...

Definitely. The scene was really concentrated in northern Sweden. There was a bit of a scene in central Sweden, but it didn't amount to much. At least that's what it seemed like from our northern perspective.

The "northern thing" was really important in all this. Like, there was definitely a sense of "northern pride" involved. We preferred to travel to some small town in northern Norway or northern Finland to see a show rather than to Stockholm.

Everything in Sweden is concentrated in the center and in the south. The north often seems overlooked and neglected. So the whole vegan straight edge movement really meant a lot for the north and for northerners' self-esteem.

It seems like this even went beyond radical circles. I remember getting a ride from Umeå to Stockholm once by someone who certainly wasn't a hardcore or straight edge person. But he knew all about the vegan straight edge scene and was particularly proud that Dennis, "a boy from Umeå," had become some kind of a celebrity in Sweden.

Yes, I think that's pretty typical. There were of course a lot of people who did not agree with some of the militant animal rights actions of the 1990s — which happened in connection with the straight edge scene. Some still see veganism associated with militancy, but I think that's a minority. Overall, I think there has always been a sense that it's much better for kids to be straight edge and vegan than... I don't know, a lot of other things they could be. I mean, there are always folks who don't like youth movements, no matter what kind, but generally there has been a pretty strong sense of acceptance in the north. And people definitely know what straight edge means. It's a common and familiar term, not only in hardcore or activist circles.

The scene was never really that isolated in Umeå. It was recognized by everyone and everyone understood what it implied. Especially the vegan thing caught on really quickly. I remember news clips on TV about how 30 percent of all the students of this or that Umeå high school had turned to eating vegan food. It was something that everyone took notice of.

Do you have any explanation for why all this happened in the north of Sweden rather than in other parts of the country?

I'm sure that there are folks who have very smart theories about this, but I don't. However, I can think of a few factors that might have played into this: first, I already talked about how the strong social democratic tradition in Sweden might have provided a basis for straight edge — this tradition has always been particularly strong in the north; secondly, people in the north live in a pretty harsh natural environment they identify strongly with — so for some kids, a vegan straight edge lifestyle might have just been an extension of this; thirdly, there was a real economic boom in the north in the 1980s and 1990s — this might have made people more aware of consumer issues and related exploitation; and finally, Umeå just plays a pretty dominant role in the region — developments there usually have a pretty strong influence on the north as a whole.

I once talked to a guy who wrote a university paper about the Umeå vegan straight edge scene. He claimed that the explanation for why such a strong vegan straight edge scene developed in northern Sweden was very simple: Dennis Lyxzén. I guess he was suggesting that the phenomenon was just an example for what individuals can achieve if they are really dedicated — especially in rather small communities. Umeå, for example, has a population of just about 75.000...

I think this is a little difficult. On the one hand, dedicated individuals can certainly achieve a lot — but on the other hand, especially from a feminist perspective, I'm a bit hesitant to credit one guy with creating a whole movement. You can't have a movement if you don't have many individuals who take care of all sorts of things; things that might often go unnoticed, but that are no less important.

I mean, it is certainly true that Dennis was very influential. But one person alone can never make a scene, if you know what I mean.

Opposite: Stockholm Vegan Straight Edge Crew, May 1 Demonstration, 2009 "Don't drink away the class struggle: drug-free organizing!" mang (mang.se)

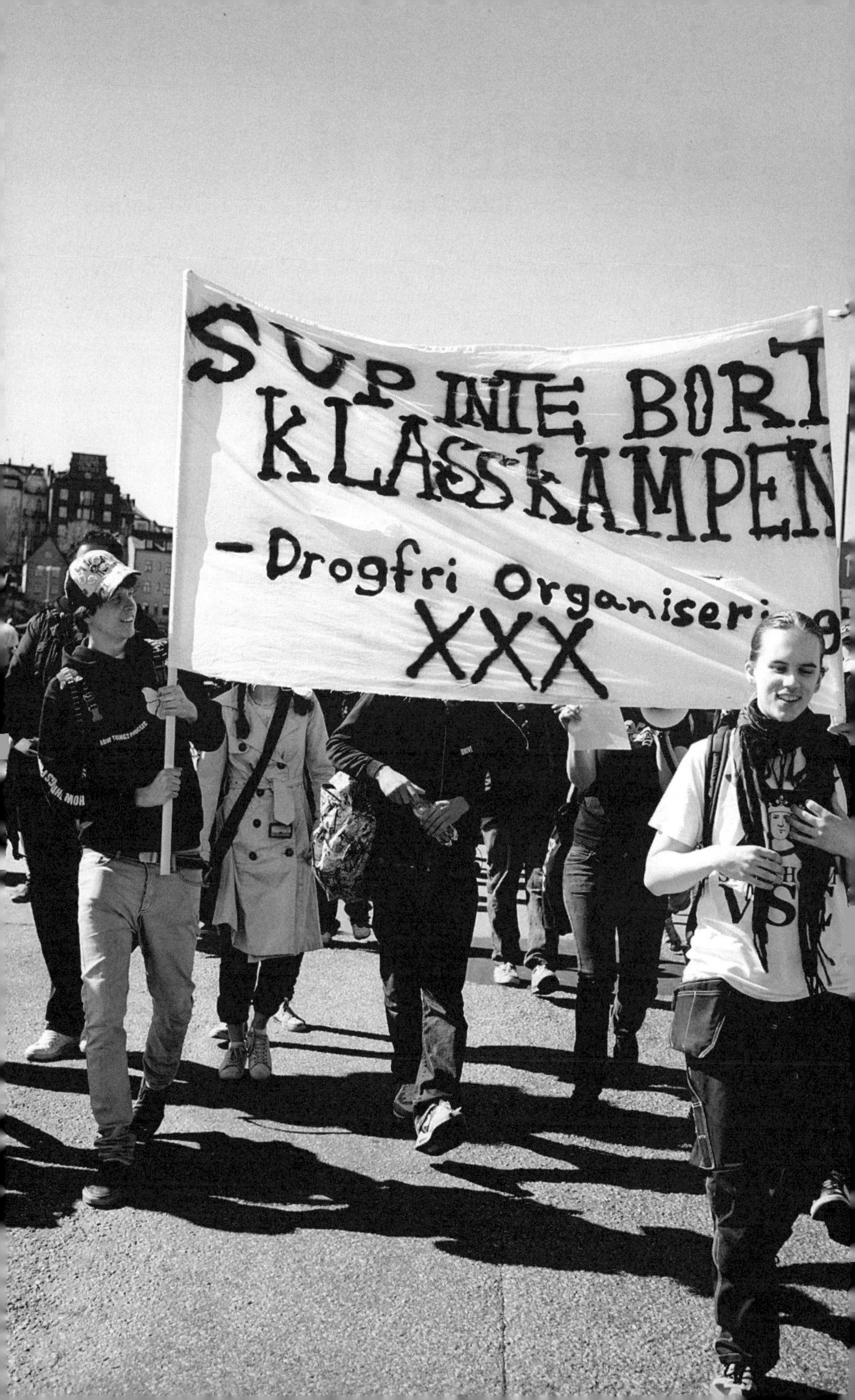
SUP INTE BORT
KLASSKAMPEN
–Drogfri
XXX

Sweden II
Interview with Gabriel Cárdenas

Gabriel Cárdenas is the initiator of the Stockholm Vegan Straight Edge Crew, representing a new generation of Swedish straight edge activists.

When did the Stockholm Vegan Straight Edge Crew form?

We got together a couple of years ago. But it's mainly a name for individuals who share similar ideas. We're not that active as a group.

It still seems to be an indication that the straight edge movement is alive in Sweden...

Yes, definitely. I guess it's not as big as it was in the 1990s, when I was too young to be a part of the scene. But there were still straight edge bands when I started going to hardcore shows in 2004, and I think it's gotten stronger again in recent years.

So when we talk of the Swedish straight edge movement today, does this automatically mean vegan straight edge, or are not all of the straight edge kids vegan?

In Stockholm most kids are vegan, or at least vegetarian. But that might be different in smaller towns.

In the 1990s, the Swedish straight edge scene was pretty much centered in the north of the country. Is this still the case?

No, I think it has diversified. There is probably a stronger legacy of the 1990s scene in the north. For example, it seems pretty accepted within the left not to drink there — or there might even be a majority of left-wing folks who don't drink. It's not the same in Stockholm. When the Stockholm Vegan Straight Edge Crew announced its plans to bring its own banner to this year's syndicalist May 1 demonstration, there was quite some resistance from other leftist activists. This might not happen in a place like Umeå.

However, as far as self-identified straight edgers go today, it's not that much centered in the north anymore, it's pretty spread out. There are bands and crews active in various places: from Lund, which is in the very south, to Gothenburg, Jonköping, Linköping, Stockholm — and of course you still got straight edge bands in Umeå too, like Forever Young.

Do most people in the straight edge scene see themselves on the left politically?

At least for Stockholm I'd say that's definitely true. Despite the resistance I mentioned, we did have our own little bloc at this year's syndicalist May 1 demonstration. So in Stockholm the connections between straight edge and leftist politics are really strong. Me personally, I've grown up with leftist politics. My father, Gabriel Cárdenas Schulte, was a high-ranking activist in Peru's Túpac Amaru Revolutionary Movement — he's serving a life sentence for his involvement in revolutionary politics. Not everyone has that kind of a personal connection, but all the straight edge activists I'm in touch with here in Stockholm identify as leftists. I think that's pretty much true for the rest of the country too, but I can't say for sure 'cause I don't know the other scenes that well.

Poland

Interview with Robert Matusiak

Poland developed into a center of Eastern European straight edge in the 1990s, not least due to the efforts of Robert Matusiak, who has been running Refuse Records in Warsaw since 1993. The label counts as a stronghold of political European straight edge hardcore and has released bands like Seein Red, Nations on Fire, New Winds, and several important compilations. Robert is also a concert and festival organizer and strongly involved in antifascist action and other radical campaigns and projects. Here he talks about the history of his label and the Eastern European straight edge scene.

Refuse Records has served as a cornerstone of political straight edge hardcore for a long time. Can you tell us a bit about the history of the label?

Refuse started in 1993 with the intention to support the scene and its ethics. I wanted to get people excited about the things that were exciting to me. I got into hardcore/punk culture in the late 1980s. I saw my first show as a young kid in 1989. I was influenced by both the international and the local Polish scene.

The late 1980s and early 1990s were a very good time for DIY hardcore punk in Poland. There was a massive number of bands and zines, and there were a lot of active people. It was a real counterculture. This also had to do with the political changes in the country: under the old so-called communist system in Poland, it was hard for a real DIY scene to grow because it was illegal to release records on DIY terms. Bands and promoters always had difficulties. And there were economic challenges: buying instruments, amps, etc. Relatively speaking, everything was much more expensive than it is now. So with the political changes at the end of the 1980s, there was a literal explosion of DIY shows, zines, and bands: The Corpse, H.C.P., U.O.M., Trybuna Brudu, Chaos, S.K.T.C., and Political Vermin are just some examples. A serious underground network was on the rise.

After four years of attending shows, I finally decided to become involved more actively and to return something to a scene that had made me aware of many important issues and that had changed my life in many important ways — after all, it was due to this scene that I became first a vegetarian, then a vegan, straight edge, etc.

Regres, Osiwecim/Poland, 2008   courtesy of Refuse Records

Even if the 1990s are now often portrayed as a bad time for hardcore/punk — especially in light of a 1980s revival — I think that there was a great feeling of community in the early 90s and that many great and positive things were happening on an international level. Like, when I decided to become straight edge, there was a huge wave of European straight edge hardcore with bands like ManLiftingBanner and Feeding The Fire from Holland, Nations on Fire, Blindfold, Shortsight, and Spirit Of Youth from Belgium, Spawn from Germany, Refused from Sweden, Open Season from Italy, X-Acto from Portugal, or Cymeon X from Poland. Many of these bands were politically aware and linked straight edge to anticapitalism, antifascism, anarchism, and left-wing politics. This was particularly appealing to me as I was inspired as much by sXe hardcore bands like Minor Threat or Youth of Today as I was by UK anarcho-punk bands from the Crass era. I was interested in the political side of punk, but I always felt that a lot of potential got lost due to alcohol/drugs and violence.

Many new bands came up in the DIY hardcore scene in Poland in the 1990s: Apatia, Inkwizycja, the above-mentioned Cymeon X, Hooded Man, or Kto Ukradl Ciastka. At the same time, there was also a great political hardcore/punk scene with bands like Homomilitia, Amen, or Post Regiment. Hardcore/punk was pretty much connected with social and political activism on all levels. I think what happened at the time can be compared to the 1960s anti-establishment revolts in Western Europe — a period that had no equivalent in the East. People involved in hardcore/punk founded a great number of progressive projects, groups, and collectives: from antiracist and antifascist initiatives to environmental or animal rights organizations to anarchist activities and squatting houses. Attending anti-fur protests, supporting pro-environmental campaigns, partaking in antifascist demonstrations, or joining actions against compulsory military service were as much part of being a hardcore/punk kid as going to shows. There was not much debate about whether these activities were useless or not — being involved in them was just a part of the thing we called hardcore punk.

It was very inspiring for me to fight collectively and to meet all the people I've met, no matter what exact movement they belonged to. I still draw from the spirit and the friendly and supportive environment of that time. It is what keeps me going today and what makes me want to give back at least some of what I got from this community.

I was always interested in many different aspects of hardcore punk culture and strongly avoided getting caught up in the creation of various sub-scenes. In the early 90s, there wasn't much of a division. It was still normal for regular punks, hardcore, and sXe kids to hang out together, to have a good time at the shows together, or to fight Nazis on the streets and to kick them out of our shows.

In 1993, I started working with some friends on a zine. At the same time I started a small distribution of music, zines, literature, and other things. This was the beginning of Refuse. In 1994, I started booking hardcore/punk shows in Warsaw, together with my friend Stasiek from Qqryq Productions and the local sXe crew. Qqryq was one the first labels and distributions in Poland and made the best Polish fanzine. The folks there were also responsible for booking many great shows in the late 1980s and early 1990s. I was working in their mail-order group and everyone was very supportive. They were great teachers in punk rock! Stasiek unfortunately died in July 1994 which was a big loss for all of his friends and for the local scene. I kept on booking shows on my own and booking shows is still one of the most important activities of Refuse Records.

Between 1993 and 1996 there were more people involved in Refuse than there are now, for example Jarek and Hoody, both members of Kto Ukradl Ciastka, a band that appeared on the first Refuse Records release. Many friends were helping out.

On a summer evening in 1995, I was hanging out with friends, and some of us had the ingenious idea to start a small tape label and release some of the local bands in which our friends played. It was nothing too ambitious in the beginning. I would have never imagined that I'd still be doing it so many years later; neither that it would provide me with the opportunity to work with so many great international bands.

Our first tape release was in 1996 and all the bands were from Poland: Kto Ukradl Ciastka, Cymeon X, and Zlodzieje Rowerow. Zlodzieje Rowerow became one of the most important Polish hardcore/punk bands and the best-selling band ever on Refuse. It helped establish the label on a local level and motivated us to do more releases. In 1998, our first CD was released and it was a turning point for us as everything became more serious and Refuse Records turned from a small tape label into more of a record label.

Today, after fifteen years of Refuse, we have over fifty releases with bands from all around the world: Belgium, Holland, Germany, Sweden, and Portugal in Western Europe; Poland, the Czech Republic, Macedonia, Serbia, and Belarus in Eastern Europe; plus the USA and Brazil. We have also released some worldwide compilations. We have booked many shows, tours, and festivals like Straight Edge Fest, Walpurgis Night (Noc Walpurgii in Polish), and Open HC Fest. The distribution is still active. We do mail-order and we table at shows. I have worked with countless bands and individuals.

How did straight edge play into all this?

My personal involvement in straight edge started in early 1992, but I already knew about the movement since around 1988 and had tried to live this way a few times before. I drank only occasionally and never smoked, so it wasn't that difficult to become sXe. Minor Threat and other early DC bands, as well as Youth of Today, Gorilla Biscuits, or Insted were all influential of course, but so was Lärm from Holland and the first sXe band in Poland, U.O.M. There were also fanzines in Poland like *Usta* or *Mysha*, which were a great source of information about straight edge, bands, and political issues.

At about the time that I became straight edge, Cymeon X appeared on the scene, and soon there was a really strong straight edge culture in Poland with many kids getting connected and forming networks. This was a very inspiring time and people really felt like they were part of something positive and radical. There were a lot of bands, tours, zines, everyone was vegetarian and many were active in antifascism and other political struggles (the Nazi scene was very strong in Poland in the late 1980s/early 1990s). There was no division between sXe hardcore and the rest of the hardcore/punk scene, and many straight edge kids were politically aware. Bands like ManLiftingBanner or Nations on Fire were as important for many of us as all the classic 80s US straight edge hardcore. All this changed with the rise of the new school and the popularity of Victory Records and all that.

How so?

It came naturally because there was a wave of new hardcore in the US with commercially more successful bands who could afford coming to Poland to play shows. Many DIY-oriented hardcore and straight edge bands couldn't do that. At the same time, some former DIY bands also become more visible in the media, were played on MTV, etc. They turned more mainstream. Many new kids got interested in hardcore through these channels, and DIY, ethics, or politics were not that much of an issue for them.

Then there were also some people who were involved in the DIY scene who lost interest in hardcore altogether — not least because of the new developments. The meaning of the term "hardcore" changed — it began referring to a different kind of music, to different goals and interests.

From what I gather, you always saw punk/hardcore, and also straight edge, directly connected to politics?

Right on. When I started Refuse and all the activity around it, it was clear to me that it will promote straight edge (and hardcore punk generally) in connection with radical politics. Most of the shows — at least during the first years, until I started losing lots of money — were benefits for a local animal rights collective called FWZ, for the antifascist struggle, and for other activities. Even today, when most of my money goes into the record label and the distribution, I still sometimes donate money from the shows to support a good cause, whether it's an anarcho-syndicalist collective, the local Food Not Bombs chapter, or African migrants in need after their main hang-out was attacked by Nazis.

As I grew up in the Cold War era when Poland was still ruled by the so-called communist regime and its non-democratic authoritarian government, with the Solidarnosc protests and martial law in the early 1980s, politics were impossible to escape. So they became part of me no matter what. When I heard bands like Crass, Dead Kennedys, or M.D.C., and especially Polish bands like Dezerter, they opened my eyes with respect to many issues and made me more aware of how the world around me worked; they inspired me to read more about social movements, political issues, and to start questioning things on my own. In the late 1980s, there were many protests here; living in Warsaw you were always confronted with many types of protests on the streets. In 1989, when the old system collapsed, it was great to see bands and publications form an underground that was commenting on reality in a way that you would never find in the mainstream media.

As I said before, at that time going to hardcore/punk shows was inevitably connected to being engaged in antifascist or anarchist politics. I was involved in struggles concerning many issues, also women's liberation, homophobia, and environmental issues. I just felt that anything we could do to make the world around us a little bit better was a worthwhile effort.

The political work I did was always very present at the shows we organized. We had different political groups and organizations tabling, we had speakers on stage, we had films and videos, spoken word, workshops, etc. In this spirit, Jenni from Emancypunx and I started the Walpurgis Night Festival in 1996 with a focus on sexism, girl/women liberation, and homophobia. It became one of the biggest DIY-oriented festivals in Poland and retains its blend of music and information to this day.

Most bands that are released on Refuse Records are politically aware, or at least care about important issues. Many of our releases include booklets — or, like in the case of the New Winds album *A Spirit Filled Revolution* and the Birds of A Feather album *The Past The Present*, properly bound books — with writings, articles, thoughts, opinions, comments, explanations, useful contacts, etc.

Today, as the label and the distribution have become bigger and as I'm often organizing shows or touring with bands, I can't be involved in too many things anymore because of time. However, I'm still attending actions, demonstrations, or meetings whenever I can, and I'm still in touch with many people involved in all sorts of activism.

You have already pointed out how you are connected to political straight edge activists around the world through your label. One region that people interested in politics and straight edge often don't know much about is Eastern Europe. Can you tell us a little about what's happening there?

For the most part, punk and hardcore scenes are still very much oriented towards Western Europe and North America. In fact, I'd say today even more so than about ten years ago. I think at that time people were more curious about discovering scenes in new places and making punk and hardcore an international phenomenon. Today, when everyone can find out about what's happening in the US and some Western European countries by clicking on some online link, people just turn their attention there. The increasing number of documentary material on the early US hardcore scene also cements the image that hardcore is predominantly a US phenomenon — even compared to Western Europe, let alone South America or Japan. This despite the fact that thousands of bands from South America, Asia, or Eastern/Central Europe are on MySpace today, and that many places in the world have hardcore scenes that are almost as old as the scene in the US. Of course there have been countless incredible bands and activities in the US, but I'd consider it a big loss if all the other scenes disappeared behind this history.

In the case of Eastern Europe — or let's say, the "ex-communist bloc" — the region was indeed isolated for a long time, as we lived behind the Iron Curtain and found it hard to exchange ideas, music, contacts, etc. Today, the highest obstacle for us is to realize our potential and to develop a strong community — a community that would also make us more aware of other countries and scenes.

The scenes that exist in Eastern Europe today do not look very different to their counterparts in other places. And they are very similar from country to country within the region. If you go to a show in Warsaw, Budapest, or Prague, the vibe is certainly very similar. Overall, the hardcore/punk scene is well established in the region. In the big cities, there are punk or hardcore shows almost every day and the infrastructure of the scene is well developed, from DIY shows to squats. However, there are still some places where hardcore punk is fresh and unique.

Straight edge isn't popular here at all right now. Much less so than it used to be for the last twenty years. It seems like no one wants to be "ideological" anymore, and that includes being straight edge. On the one hand, you can see it as today's kids just being against "rules" of any kind, a sort of postmodernist end of ideology. On the other hand, you can see it as kids shying away from anything serious; from anything that demands deeper involvement. The result is that radical cultures are turned into commodities.

From my perspective, it's impossible to stay away from all "ideologies" — if you try to, you usually just end up following mainstream ideology, often deceptively hidden behind "free consumerism for all." As a result, there is not much counterculture left in hardcore. In fact, certain parts of the scene have turned into microcosms of mainstream society where obsessing over your outfit, a fixation on fashionable brand names, or collecting shoes has become more important than content, ethics, and a sense of community. Having said that, examples of genuine hardcore, punk, and straight edge are still visible and solid in Eastern Europe too.

Poland used to have the region's strongest sXe scene. I guess not too many know that one of the very first sXe bands in Europe was founded in 1985 right here: a band called U.O.M. In the 1990s, we had many sXe bands like Cymeon X, Respect, Awake, Sunrise, or Inflexible. In recent years, there were Second Age, Regres, Only Way Out, Insurrection, X's Always Win, and others. Today, there are hardly more than one or two bands left, like the young sXe kids from Cervantes. However, there remains a fair number of bands with straight edge members. There is also still a number of sXe zines, like *Second Vision, Chaos Grrlz, Passion To Destroy, Screaming At A Wall, Awaiting The End, Kiss My Edge, The Heat, Back In The Day*, or *In Full Swing*. Most of them are about music, political, and personal stuff. Many straight edgers are also involved in booking shows, there are some labels run by sXe individuals — Refuse, Emancypunx, In Our Hands, Spook, City To City, Living Disaster — and some straight edgers are still involved in different kinds of non-music related activism, from

Poster for Noc Walpurgii (Walpurgis Night) Festival, Warsaw, Poland

animal rights to anarchism to antifascism to feminism. So I think it's still pretty good compared with other countries.

The Czech Republic is a place where many bands go to play as it is on the way to the south of Europe. There are also many festivals, including the annual three-day Fluff Fest where every summer around 3000 hardcore kids gather. Most of the people behind the festival are related to straight edge, so there are always some sXe bands on the bill as well as stalls with animal rights or Antifa groups. No Reason was probably the most important band there in the 90s. In recent years, there was an influential political anarchist vegan sXe band called Spes Erepta, but they broke up a short while ago. One of the reasons was that some of the band's members wanted to focus more on political activism than on doing music. Other bands that have been active in the last two years were Lakme (emotive vegan sXe hardcore) and Nidal (vegan sXe metalcore). Also worth mentioning is Balaclava, a band that has some sXe members — people who also played in Spes Erepta — and that has been active for ten years, promoting veganism and radical politics. It's great to see that there are still many kids from the sXe scene there who are involved in activism. I have the impression that sXe is more meaningful in the Czech Republic than in Poland and that it still has substance.

Hungary has been known for having some youth crew bands like Hold True or, more recently, Motivation.

In Croatia, Vaseline Children were active in recent years, but they split up in 2008. They played raging hardcore with critical and political lyrics — they always sounded really pissed off. All of the members were involved in doing zines and booking DIY shows.

In Serbia there are The Truth Of XXX and Lets Grow — they are not 100 percent sXe anymore but they did a lot for the DIY hardcore/punk and sXe scene in the ex-Yugoslavian region.

In Macedonia there was F.P.O. who also split up recently. They were very successful and did many releases both in Europe and in the US. They toured Europe three times and tried twice to visit the US. Unfortunately, both times their visas were denied; this is an example that demonstrates the difficulties that some bands from Eastern Europe are still facing. Former members of F.P.O. have started new bands like Smartbomb and Barney's Propaganda. They're super active in the local DIY hardcore/punk and anarchist scenes, doing shows, radio programs, zines, and everything you could possibly think of in order to keep the scenes alive.

In countries like Slovenia, Slovakia, and Romania, sXe is rather small, and there are almost no sXe bands, even though some individuals are active locally.

Belarus is the last non-democratic country in Europe and the scene that developed there in the mid- to late 1990s has always had a strong focus on political issues and DIY culture. As it's not that easy to visit the country — especially for US citizens who pay a lot for a visa — there aren't many bands able to play shows there. Whenever a band does manage to play some gigs, the reception is overwhelming. Kids are extremely friendly and positive — maybe a phenomenon of such isolated places.

It is as hard for bands from Belarus to leave and play outside the country as it is for bands to come in. The first sXe band there was Jiheart. This was a great political female-fronted hardcore band that sang in Belarusian. There were other bands in their wake — not all of them sXe — like I Know, Devil Shoots Devil, and Pull Out An Eye. The only 100 percent sXe band there right now is Apple Shout. Given the political situation in Belarus, I think the hardcore/punk bands there are amazing. You can learn a lot about living in non-democratic states from listening to them. I have heard stories about everyone attending a show getting arrested, or about zine editors being picked up for interrogation by the local KGB. One of the ex-members of Jiheart got arrested at an anti-government protest and spent a week in prison where he got seriously beaten. Maybe these are all reasons why shows there are among the best you can imagine.

The Ukraine always had a very small, mostly traditional punk scene. The hardcore scene has grown there over the last two years or so, and some new distros promoting veganism and straight edge have appeared. There are also some sXe bands now, like

Keep On Fighting, Declaration, and Deviant, as well as the sXe-related Clearsight.

Lithuania, Latvia, and Estonia have only a couple of individual kids involved in sXe and no bands or zines.

Russia has developed quite a big hardcore scene with a good amount of sXe bands. In fact, it kinda feels like a renaissance of sXe in Russia. In the 1990s, bands like B'67, Posadil Derrevo, Skygrain, or Trikresta were active, and now there is a really huge new wave of Russian sXe with bands like Flawless Victory, Verdict, Engage At Will, Haram, Margaret Thrasher, High Hopes, Frenzied Kids, and others. There are also some sXe-related bands like Fight For Fun or Save Remains, as well as labels — for example Hard Times Rec — and some zines.

This is not reduced to Moscow and St. Petersburg. I'm in contact with people from places like Perm, which is literally at the end of Europe, right by the Ural mountains. Recently, a sXe-oriented hardcore/punk distribution, GivexBlood Records, opened in Krasnoyarsk in Siberia. It's like three days by train from Moscow — much closer to Mongolia than to any European country. There are bands, shows, and activists in towns like Novosibirsk (Feel The Pain) or Irkutsk (Margaret Thrasher). It's amazing to be in contact with people from these places, sending them records and zines and organizing shows for them. If someone from Petropavlovsk-Kamchatsky — at the very eastern end of Russia — will order anything from Refuse I will consider my mission accomplished and quit!

Seriously, though, I'd say that Russia has one of the strongest straight edge scenes in Europe at the moment, and it seems quite political. People are involved in different activities from Food Not Bombs to animal rights to militant antifascism. They give the right meaning to the term straight edge. This seems particularly important because, unfortunately, Russia also has the strongest Nazi-sXe movement in the world.

I meant to ask you about right-wing adaptations of straight edge in Eastern Europe. There is the phenomenon of what you referred to as Russian Nazi-sXe, and there are similar developments in other countries. Also in Germany, some right-wing youth groups — particularly among the so-called "National Autonomists" — have recently tried to claim straight edge for their political cause. How do you see these developments?

I think the roots of the problem lie in hardcore becoming apolitical and avoiding to take a stand concerning certain issues. When this happens, it is just a matter of time until some conservative or right-wing attitudes will become attached to it.

The first big conservative wave in hardcore was certainly connected to the hardline movement. In Poland, it started to become visible in around 1995. Ultra-moralistic and self-righteous views on homosexuality, abortion, feminism, civil liberties, etc. become commonplace in straight edge. For a period of about two years, I'd say that most sXe bands and sXe kids were hardline and pro-life. There were many conflicts and discussions which ended with a serious division within the scene. I was involved in it as someone who was very critical of hardline and everything I saw associated with it: pro-life, homophobia, intolerance, and just blind hatred. It was all very intense and I even got death threats from local hardline chapters. Luckily it all pretty much calmed down in the late 1990s, even though straight edgers who are pro-life or prejudiced towards someone else's sexuality are still around.

What emerged as a bigger problem in the late 90s was that bands like One Life Crew and some NYHC skinhead bands became popular. It was inevitable that this strengthened conservative and right-wing views within the scene. There was a comeback of all the tough guy stuff and people thought it was funny to provoke "PC" types. To me it was just a bunch of people trying to draw attention.

In recent years, terms like "conservative punk" or "conservative hardcore" have started to appear on message boards. This is interesting as neither hardliners nor One Life Crew fans claimed such terms for themselves in the 1990s. So now we have these elements within the scene that are obviously proud of their patriotism, their conservatism, their reference to traditional Polish Christian culture, etc. Some of these folks seem linked to extreme right-wing and neofascist groups — which disqualifies them even more.

Luckily, there has been a lot of resistance against active attempts by right-wing extremists to co-opt the hardcore straight edge scene. Many kids were ready to support antifascist activities even when they themselves weren't necessarily all that political. I remember that in 2004/2005 neo-Nazis appeared at some shows, but a successful "Good Night White Pride" campaign was organized and they were soon gone. To be honest, for a long time I didn't think that it was a really strong movement and considered it more of a message board phenomenon. However, now there are at least five Nazi hardcore bands in Warsaw who organize shows regularly. It seems to be a very different scene. I have never seen any such kids at the shows I go to.

Generally speaking, the Polish Nazi scene seems on the rise again. In fact, I would say that it's almost as strong as it was in the mid-90s. I hear more and more stories today about people who are attacked outside punk shows; or just anywhere on the street, for that matter. Racist attacks are also on the rise. A lot of this is organized by groups like the Celtic Front — basically a right-wing streetfighting unit. In Bialystok, a region in eastern Poland, Nazi gangs and Antifas battle regularly. Migrants from Africa and Georgia are also involved due to the many hostilities they have to endure. I think that right-wing extremism is on the rise worldwide, also fuelled by the economic crisis.

In Germany, right-wing extremists are increasingly involved in hardcore and straight edge. A similar trend is developing in the Czech Republic. There too, straight edge has become part of some reactionary notion of "purity." It might happen in Poland as well. However, nothing compares to the situation in Russia, where the Nazi-sXe movement has stolen all of the symbols and principles of straight edge and mixed them with nationalism, racism, and fascism. There is also a Nazi-hardline movement.

It is disgusting to see how right-wing extremists reclaim symbols of the left, of antifascists, or of straight edge culture. However, this is typical for right-wingers. We know that they are not very creative individuals and always steal from others, whether it was Roman architecture in the 1930s, the swastika symbol, or punk rock — no matter that they play it worse than the worst real punk band could ever play it. The artwork on their releases confirms this: nothing reveals better how untalented and non-creative they are. And not only that, they are ignorant too. Friends in Russia tell me that people in the Nazi-sXe scene have no knowledge about the history of straight edge. They do not know who Ian MacKaye is, and they have never heard of Minor Threat. Besides, they don't seem to take their straight edge beliefs very seriously either. For some of them, not smoking is enough to qualify as straight edge, even when they are still drinking; others smoke, but don't drink, etc.

Any ideas on why these movements are strongest in Russia and Germany?

I think the history of both countries might play a major role here. I think it's obvious in the case of Germany because of the country's past and the legacy of a particularly disastrous ideology that has never been fully defeated and was ready to explode again when the Berlin Wall came down. In Russia there was never a strong democratic or liberal tradition, and the country did not share the debates and achievements of other European countries.

Both countries have strong traditions of superiority towards other countries and this tradition is easily passed on to younger generations. In Germany this is at least discussed and the history is not hidden. We can't say the same in the case of Russia. In Russia, a lot remains to be disclosed and clarified. For example the relations of the Soviet Union to other countries from the so-called communist bloc; countries that were controlled and occupied by a regime based in Russia. The different level of awareness also means that there is stronger resistance to the extreme right in Germany than in Russia. It also seems that the Russian government is exploiting right-wing sentiments to justify their violence in Chechnya and in some ex-Soviet Union republics.

Of course there have always been extreme right-wing, fascist tendencies in other European countries too. Some people collaborated with the Nazis or the Stalinists, while others — for example in Poland — formed independent nationalist movements as a reaction to the threats posed by powerful neighbors like Germany and Russia. When state socialism collapsed and many Eastern European countries gained their political independence again, concepts of national identity seemed particularly important and ghosts from the past were able to return. However, despite these tendencies, in most of these countries the democratic process has developed much better than in Russia, and people remain overall more vigilant towards totalitarian extremism because they have experienced it at the hands of German Nazism and Soviet state socialism — for most people in Eastern Europe totalitarianism is connected to foreign occupation, domination, and war.

So you think that the co-optation of punk/hardcore and straight edge culture in these countries is mainly related to a generally stronger right-wing scene?

Yes. What is really peculiar is the mentioned use of the radical left's symbols in right-wing youth culture. We have hardly seen this in other places yet. And it's not only symbols, also tactics, slogans, and issues. The way in which hardcore punk and straight edge are used is part of that.

How do we best tackle this danger?

To begin with, we have to be very vigilant concerning the infiltration by right-wing and neofascist groups. We also have to be very outspoken about the issues and values we hold dear. We have to remind people of the roots of punk, hardcore, and straight edge culture, and of these movements' antifascist history. We also have to keep the memory of our fights alive. In the late 1980s and early 1990s, there were Nazis at almost every single hardcore punk show in Poland, and there were many fights; there really was a lot of violence. It takes a lot of strength and effort to kick Nazis out of the shows and to keep them off the streets. But it needs to be done, and we did it, and we will do it again. So, basically, the simple answer to your question is: we have to keep the fascists away from our shows! This is the basic thing. If we don't follow this simple principle, our hardcore scene will be destroyed.

Another aspect I consider extremely important for the defense of our scene is to keep hardcore crowds educated, no matter what kind of hardcore they're listening to. At our shows, this can mean everything from having antiracist and antifascist literature there to putting up posters and flyers about upcoming demonstrations to inviting political speakers. We also have to create direct contact to minority groups

F.P.O. (Macedonia), somewhere in Spain, 2006   courtesy of Refuse Records

and migrants — to everyone who is affected by neofascist violence. We can help each other and we can learn from each other. We are strongest when we are united.

Finally, we have to remind people that apolitical attitudes breed ignorance and apathy and hence provide an opening for conservative and right-wing infiltration. It is much easier to keep hateful, intolerant, and violent idiots from entering our scene than to kick them out once they've got a foot in the door.

You said that Poland was the country where the strongest sXe scene in Eastern Europe developed. Any theories on why this was the case?

As Poland was the country with the strongest hardcore punk scene in Eastern Europe, I think it was natural that there was a high interest in straight edge as well. It might also be a reaction to the many alcohol-related problems in Polish society as well as to the extensive use of alcohol and drugs in the punk movement. Refusing to drink has always been and still is a big deal here. It's probably similar in Russia.

Another question about the Polish scene: I once talked to Jenni from Emancypunx Records about the reactions I got from a

number of Polish anarchists when I talked to them about radical political straight edge. They basically said that no such thing existed in Poland. This struck me as odd because I had met a fair number of Polish straight edge kids who were definitely politically conscious and active. You also said that there exists a strong traditional link between hardcore/straight edge and anarchism in Poland. Jenni explained this apparent contradiction by saying that there was a strong divide between a self-declared "serious" political scene in Poland and — an allegedly "unserious" — political hardcore and straight edge scene. Would you agree with this?

I can agree insofar as there are certainly prejudices between certain circles. I guess on the one hand it is true that the hardcore and straight edge scene today often appears apolitical. On the other hand it is also true that there exists a certain "ultra-activism" tied to arrogance and disrespect for everyone who is not on the same level of education, activism, or commitment. Being politically active can be very hard for people; not only because of governments, cops, or corporate capitalism, but also because of other activists! However, I don't think that this is peculiar to Poland. I'm pretty sure that one can find such patterns everywhere.

Polish anarchism in general is a touchy subject that we could discuss for another few hours. I prefer not to generalize about the radical scene here as there are many caring individuals who dedicate their time working for a good cause. Many do wonderful things. However, I am very skeptical when it comes to certain individuals, and I try to keep a clear distance from them. As I said, I don't wanna go into details, but some of the experiences I've had with these people can't even compare to the worst experiences I had in the punk/hardcore scene. This was a major reason why I distanced myself more and more from the "activist types" in the late 1990s, and concentrated on my involvement in punk and hardcore. I was convinced that we could have at least as big a political impact on people's lives as federations or discussion groups haggling over petty details.

Concerning the reaction you got from the anarchists you talked to, I'm not surprised. To be honest, they might think that no one is truly political but themselves — this goes for many individuals or groups, not just straight edge kids. There is a certain competition about who is the most righteous, the most radical, the most committed. Then there are also fights over the issues that one deems most important. These issues change also within the anarchist scene. Ten years ago many anarchists here were influenced by libertarian free market policies and neglected the anticapitalist struggle — today it seems like all they care about are workers' rights. There has also been a change with respect to the antifascist struggle. This is slowly gaining acceptance in anarchist circles now after it has been ridiculed for a long time. I can't help thinking that many anarchists just never met any Nazis — and hence never understood the struggle's necessity — since they rather attend universities than punk shows.

Sometimes productive relationships can be established between anarchists and hardcore/punk kids, but it is true that such relationships often crumble because the anarchists don't take the hardcore kids' political beliefs seriously and only see them as the result of some "subcultural" involvement. They try to act as "leaders" of the movement, based on what they've read in books or simply on their middle class background. There are even some who have come out of the punk/hardcore movement, but now turn their back on it since they have "evolved." As if reading Bakunin and Kropotkin makes you a better anarchist than listening to Crass. Interestingly enough, these folks still maintain ties to the punk/hardcore kids, because it is still there were they can find an acceptance of their political beliefs that they do not find in mainstream society.

As far as I am concerned, many anarchist theories that we find in books, pamphlets, or magazines are *lived* by the punks who organize squats and alternative cultural places, who serve food to the homeless, who do benefit shows, who live their lives guided by cruelty-free ethics. The same is true for many straight edgers. I guess some people who are not familiar with the scene just never see beyond the drinking, fighting, and vandalizing — which, unfortunately, I can understand to a certain extent.

Let's talk about these aspects within the scene. You've pointed out that there has always been a strong connection between hardcore/straight edge and politics — in Poland as much as in other places. At the same time, when you and I first talked about this book, you welcomed the idea because you thought that there was too little political consciousness in the hardcore scene today. Do you think that this has simply changed over the years, or have there always been "two strains" in the scene, so to speak?

I'd say that in the mid-90s, the hardcore scene started to become more separated from its punk origins. It was no longer "hardcore punk" but plainly "hardcore." Many of the original ethics were lost, and fashion, record sales, and merchandise became increasingly important. It was only a logical consequence that certain parts of the hardcore scene turned their attention more and more to better known bands, often released by major labels. This is still the case today. Many people in the hardcore scene just want to identify with a musical scene and they can't be bothered with reflecting on their favorite band's record label. They want "professional" entertainment and don't care about high prices at the door, security gates, or corporate sponsorship. To them, DIY just spells "amateurism." Many bands pick up on this, consciously avoid "controversial" issues, and water down the political contents of the entire scene.

Partly this might be a reaction to the holier-than-thou attitudes of many political activists. Partly it might be a reaction to all the discussions and conflicts that politics caused in the scene in the 1990s. In any case, a whole culture of communication has disappeared. I believe that the internet and its message boards contribute to this. On these forums, communication between people is often reduced to posting a few lines of nonsense which render any meaningful exchange impossible. Personal animosities become more important than respectful political debate. As a result, the educational infrastructure — the info tables, the speakers, etc. — are disappearing from the shows, while clothing companies are replacing DIY zines and distros. A few years ago most sXe kids were still vegetarian or vegan — now we are witnessing an "anti-PC" backlash where ethics are considered an irritating nuisance. The logos of multinational corporations, including those of Nike or McDonald's, no longer raise immediate concerns. They are all around the scene. In this sense, the scene has become an integral part of consumerist mainstream culture. Quite a few straight edge kids make Coke their beverage of choice. It's like hardcore has turned into a Shangri-La for corporate advertising — and no one's even getting paid!

You said that many kids might have lost their interest in politics because of holier-than-thou activists and many heated discussions. Do you see any other reasons — like in a wider social context?

It's hard to say. Overall, politics don't seem to be less urgent than in the 1980s and 90s. We have the so-called "War on Terror," US-imperialism, corporate globalization, climate change. I guess many privileged people — and this increasingly includes certain classes in Poland and other Eastern European countries — just have fairly easy lives and are able to escape into some kind of virtual reality where they think these things don't affect them. As a result, you also have bands, including hardcore bands, that prefer to talk about personal issues, relationship problems, etc. I don't want to say that the personal is not important, and neither do I want to write a rule book on how to be hardcore, but when did the political cease to be personal? Being "apolitical" is a myth, every single choice we make in our lives has a political dimension, and our personal situations are all affected by politics of the past, present, and future, there's no escape. Besides, if we live in privileged countries and come from privileged classes, we must be aware of our privileges and of what they are based on.

I must not generalize of course. There remain many individuals and bands in the scene who are interested in politics, and there are always new kids appearing too. Some of the more recent political straight edge bands have even been successful with a wider audience, like Verse in the US. There is certainly still a demand for such bands. The big interest in the 2005 Trial reunion shows also confirmed this. We also got tremendously positive feedback on the New Winds album that we published with a 170-page book about political issues. There are always people who write to us or talk to us after shows, who say that they got interested in certain political questions because of some band they have heard. This still feels fantastic. It has also been interesting to see how bands like Gather, Wait In Vain, 7 Generations, or Anchor have mixed vegan straight edge ethics with radical politics. Bands like Limp Wrist, R.A.M.B.O., or I Object are also all extremely interesting bands that are straight edge, political, and strongly DIY. All this shows that, no matter how watered down many parts of the scene have become, there is still a demand for bands with serious agendas, thoughtful messages, and caring principles.

What does the future of Refuse Records hold? You've been active for a long time already, but it doesn't seem like you're losing steam...

Thanks, I'm trying to keep on track. There are always new bands, zines, or actions that impress me and motivate me to continue — just as there are older bands and past experiences that never cease to inspire. There is always some great band that I'd like to release or book shows for. I can't live without hardcore and punk, without my friends in the scene, the community, the shows, the touring and traveling, etc.

I will keep on releasing bands that play loud music, show a good spirit, and have important things to say. One of our next releases is the mentioned LP by the Dutch band Birds of A Feather with members who have been straight edge for fifteen to twenty-five years. The LP will be released with a book about the history of European straight edge. I'm super excited about this!

2008 was the fifteenth anniversary of Refuse and we had eight new releases that year, three festivals, and some shows and tours, two of which were European-wide. Unfortunately, I'm not able to keep up this schedule because of work. It's not always easy to have time for everything: two jobs, the label and distro, booking shows and tours, personal life... But I already have ideas for upcoming releases. And I finally want to visit Brazil after years of planning! All these goals and adventures are well worth the sacrifices.

Anything else you'd like to add?

I'd like to say that whoever claims that straight edge is in no way connected with radical politics just wants to write their own history. You can imagine that such claims really upset me — especially in the Polish context. Often it's just a matter of definition. Some people say that being straight edge can't make you a serious political activist, because you "only" deal with music or "(sub)culture." First of all, that's not true. Secondly, artists can have a much bigger impact on people than thousands of flyers handed out during demonstrations. It's interesting too how certain "formalities" might give you political credibility even if they are not related to content at all: for example, some folks might be seen as "political activists" because they live in a squat, even if all they ever do there is sleep. On the other hand, a straight edge show is not considered "political" even if you are distributing radical books and magazines and have political speakers on stage.

In any case, let us just take the example of Poland: throughout the years I have known straight edge kids who were involved in anarchist and left-wing politics, in the squatting movement, in Food Not Bombs, in human rights issues, in feminism, in gay/lesbian/queer struggles, in environmental campaigns, in veganism and animal rights, in radical antifascism, in black blocs, in antiracist activities, in the fight against anti-Semitism, etc. They have done everything from tedious legal work to direct action. It'd be ludicrous to deny this history, even if a lot of sXe kids might have limited themselves to music and drug-free living. So what? It doesn't make the great work that others have done less valuable.

USA

Interview with Kurt Schroeder

Kurt Schroeder has been involved in the US straight edge scene for roughly two decades. In the early 90s, he co-founded Catalyst Records, a label that has fused the 1990s vegan straight edge scene with a broad radical agenda, including the fight against sexism, racism, and homophobia. Catalyst describes itself as "a label that still believes that hardcore is as much about communication, hopes and ideals as it is about music." It has released bands like Birthright, Gather, and Point of No Return, and has turned into an international hub for politically oriented straight edge hardcore.

It always seemed to me that the 1990s vegan straight edge movement was a politically curious phenomenon. On the one hand there was definitely a genuine intention to fight cruelty and suffering and make the world a better place — on the other hand there was self-righteousness, puritan ethics, and political conservatism. The line between these two sides often seemed very thin; so thin that many progressive-minded drug-free kids distanced themselves from the straight edge movement as a whole. It seems that Catalyst Records was an attempt to keep progressive politics in the movement. Would you agree with this perception? Tell us a little about the label's history and its political aspirations.

At the very least I can say that Catalyst Records was formed as a way to promote ideas and bands with a strong message within the straight edge scene. As time went on this definitely progressed as my own understanding and political awareness progressed. From the beginning I believed that straight edge was a revolutionary concept, and saw it in that framework, as opposed to those who did — and many who still do — see it in a more fundamentalist/ conservative light.

This was compounded by the introduction to the ethic of veganism into the straight edge scene, and my own involvement in living vegan and my introduction to other fundamental concepts such as feminist principles.

As far as aspirations go, they are basically the same as they were at the start: to present other options, to promote critical thinking, and to help out bands that support similar ideas.

How did this play out for you? Did you feel that you got your message across, or was this a frustrating venture at times?

It can definitely be frustrating, especially when there is a totally anti-progressive current in the hardcore scene, depending on what is popular at the time. However, I feel like as long as I continue to stay true to the goals of the label and do things on my own terms, the label is successful. The point has never been to be big, to make money, or to be most popular, but to continue to provide an alternative voice in the context of the hardcore scene.

How would you say that the scene has generally reacted to Catalyst and its bands? Did you ever feel isolated or was there always a sense of respect even from folks who did not share your political commitments?

The reaction the label and the bands we work with receive is often really dependent on the flavour of the current hardcore scene. This scene goes through phases and cycles, and the whole point of the label is to remain steady and to not follow trends. With that said, there are most definitely times when Catalyst Records seems a little out of place in the overall hardcore scene, especially when the scene is at its least progressive. Fortunately there seems to have been a big resurgence in more progressive/vegan/intelligent hardcore in the past five years or so, and a growth of people interested in critical thinking and in the underground/DIY hardcore scene in general.

On the other side of things, for a time there was a noticeable backlash against political and vegan bands, and I think this attitude remains to a great extent in the more "mainstream" portion of the hardcore and straight edge scenes today.

Let's go back to the scene of the 1990s: one thing that always bothered me was that some of the most popular vegan straight edge bands did not draw stronger lines between themselves and the sometimes frighteningly conservative tendencies within hardline — especially militant anti-abortion attitudes or blatant homophobia. Like, I had a feeling that even though some of these bands never actively endorsed such views, they didn't take strong enough stances against them either. Does this resonate with you in some way?

I think a lot of the attitude you are referring to is just a product of the huge influence that hardline and hardline bands had on the vegan straight edge movement in the beginning. Most of the vegan bands in the hardcore scene either had members who were hardline (or paid lip-service to the ideology), or were influenced by earlier hardline bands. At the time it was just an inherent part of what was going on, the movement was very new, and there were very few bands or zines that were presenting an alternative view.

I think this has changed to some extent as the movement has continued to mature and grow, to incorporate new ideas, and to rely less upon the more puritanical influences.

When one checks the Catalyst forum today — arguably a focal point for political straight edge debates, at least in the US, but internationally too — animal rights issues remain very prominent, and there are discussions about racism and sexism. Other issues relevant to radical politics like, say, workers' struggles, are almost completely absent. Do you see this as a problem? I mean, you're familiar with the critique of (vegan) straight edge being a "middle class" movement, etc...

As far as the common subjects of the forum goes, I don't really put too much thought into it, primarily because it is a message board, and I don't really have any kind of high expectations — even though I think it does operate on a different level than most other forums.

I do think that those subjects — animal rights, for example — are more prevalent. I would just guess that they are the issues that many of the participants are the most well-versed in and that most of the users have in common.

Of course vegan straight edge is mostly a middle class movement, there is no getting around that. Hardcore itself is a primarily middle class phenomenon. I think we just have to understand that many progressive movements are essentially middle class, accept it and keep trying to move forward. I think there are a lot of cultural factors that maintain the ability for people of relative privilege to get involved in such ideologies, and I'm not sure how to effectively expand the base to individuals of different socio-economic backgrounds.

Do you think that geography also plays a role here? I mean, it seems to be a common perception that political straight edge bands in Europe or Latin America are often more tied into "socialist," "leftist" or "class" politics, because such aspects are generally more present within countercultural movements, while radical politics in North America are often critiqued for their "lifestyle" character.

I'm sure this is a factor. The political spectrum of the U.S. is definitely more to the right than most of the other countries where hardcore has taken root. In addition there is a strong fundamentalist undercurrent in American culture. I have no doubt that the lack of real information about these subjects in the U.S. has a great effect, and I'm sure that there is a huge difference in both the level of basic education here versus European nations, and also the amount of basic information that Americans receive about the importance of historic socialist/populist movements — these are almost totally absent from any school here.

There has been a long tradition of social conservatism here for over fifty years now, even though it remains detrimental to the majority of the population. I see it as a form of institutionalized social control, and a perpetuation of false consciousness.

> Speaking of geography and the international straight edge movement: it is also a commonplace that, compared to North America, straight edge in Europe or Latin America has always been more political, as in: socially aware and tied into wider social movements. Would you share this perception? After all, Catalyst has a rather impressive catalogue of political straight edge bands, many of which hail from the US. But maybe all the political straight edge bands from the US end up on Catalyst and are the exceptions that prove the rule?

I definitely think that Europe and South America have a much more politically-influenced straight edge and hardcore scene, this is really without question. I really think that the abundance of U.S. bands Catalyst released is mostly due to the ease of finding these bands close to home at one point in the label's history. As the label and the scene expanded, and as I was introduced to more international bands, I think that changed to a great extent. Of the last ten to fifteen releases on Catalyst, around half have been for (or include) non-U.S. bands.

I will say that it can just be much easier to communicate with bands from the same country and who are native speakers of the same language. It is easier to really know what the band is about, to catch their live shows, etc. It's really not that huge of a barrier at this point, but that, and the amount of vegan straight edge bands that once existed in the U.S. scene, kept the label roster fairly U.S. heavy at the beginning.

> Finally, the Catalyst website states that the label is "dedicated to more than just releasing records. Catalyst is also about ideas and the meaning behind the music, such as straight edge, veganism, feminism, the DIY concept, as well as fighting intolerance and injustice." How are all these aspects connected for you personally?

Personally I believe that there are no separations between all of the struggles listed there, they are all basically intrinsically tied to the same principles: that everyone and every being has the inherent right to live its natural life, free from oppression or unnecessary suffering. I believe that the DIY ethic is a vehicle for this because capitalism is a flawed system at its most basic level, one which cannot function without inequality. Of course I do not operate under the illusion that any of this is perfect, or that I do not contribute in some way to inequality or injustice — this is inevitable for any individual living in this culture — but I, through the label, remain dedicated to presenting alternatives, and promoting the questioning of our current culture and different ways of thinking.

Manifestos

- **The Antifa Straight Edge**
  XsaraqaelX

  Interview with XsaraqaelX

- **Wasted Indeed: Anarchy and Alcohol**
  CrimethInc.

  Interview with CrimethInc. agent Carrie No Nation

- **Towards a Less Fucked Up World: Sobriety and Anarchist Struggle**
  Nick Riotfag

  Afterword: Towards a Less Fucked Up World: Five Years and Counting
  Nick Riotfag

The Antifa Straight Edge

XsaraqaelX

"The Antifa Straight Edge" was first published as a pamphlet by Alpine Anarchist Productions (AAP 003, 2001), a radical DIY-publishing outfit. It formulates one of the most explicit critiques of conservative tendencies within the 1990s vegan straight edge movement and is a rare example of drawing concrete parallels between straight edge and antifascist action. As most AAP pamphlets, the text was published under a pseudonym — a current interview with the author follows the text.

I'm just about to turn twenty-seven and I've been straight edge for over a decade. I've been feeling alienated from the scene for quite a few years now, mainly due to well-known developments commonly referred to as Hardline and/or Christian Straight Edge (I'm aware of the differences between and within the two, but to get a message across I will admittedly focus on the similarities here which mainly consist of promoting conservative — to say the least — ethics and politics). At first, my reaction pretty much was to retreat. It was kinda like, well, a new generation of kids is taking over, what can I do? But recently, the idiotic and highly irritating militancy of many straight edgers seems to have got totally out of control, and I feel that it might be worth to clarify at least a few things about sXe.

Having said that, this is not about a revival of the "original" or "true" meaning of sXe, not about some "old" versus some "new" school, an "alternative" interpretation of straight edge's ideas, or an attempt to reclaim the scene for people like myself. Terms (and movements signified by them) are never fixed and clearly defined, they're always dynamic, open to different interpretations, and hence changes. I can't (and don't want to) forbid other people to call themselves straight edge, to X up, wear sXe shirts, or listen to Youth of Today, as much as I might disagree with their attitudes, beliefs, and actions. There's no universal criterion for defining what sXe really means, and I'm the last person who'd wanna do such a thing.

So, what is this all about then? Basically, just about a clarification that being straight edge doesn't necessarily mean you are a violent semi-fascist gay-bashing macho dick, maybe even with an obscure obsession with an oppressive, patriarchal religion. In fact, being straight edge can mean quite the opposite: it can be all about trying to be involved in antifascist politics. So, the Antifa Straight Edge will try to explain how to be straight edge in this sense.

What motivates me to do this if not — as dismissed above — "reclaiming" or "purifying" the term?

1. To remind antifascist straight edgers out there that there are still other like-minded spirits within (or at least at the fringes) of the scene.

2. To remind the militants that there is still disapproval of and resistance against their "war" within straight edge ranks themselves.

3. To allow non-sXedgers a wider understanding of sXe, so they might not have to disrespect it immediately just because it experiences unfortunate and disturbingly strong trends of stupidity at this point in time.

Supporting antifascist politics to me means fighting for anti-authoritarian, self-determined, and economically just communities in which a diversity of people can coexist in solidarity, mutual respect, and peace.

Straight edge to me means an attempt to develop certain personal virtues that might prove beneficial in the fight for antifascist communities, namely responsibility, awareness, and independence.

It seems practically impossible to establish, maintain, or defend antifascist communities without the individuals constituting them taking on responsibility, since the whole point behind the idea of such communities appears to be that we don't need leaders or people who tell us what to do because we take on the responsibility to think, decide, and act for ourselves. Awareness seems like an inevitable quality in this respect. It's hard to act responsibly in a community if we don't know shit about what's going on. And awareness seems hard to be developed without at least a certain sense of independence, meaning: to be able to find and figure out for ourselves what's going on and not depend on some big brother's indoctrination.

Based on these thoughts abstaining from intoxicants (and that's all sXe originally meant) can make sense to certain individuals: A lot of intoxicants lower your levels of awareness and responsibility pretty much right after consumption. Others may contribute to a rather phlegmatic personality in the long run.

And some might cause serious addiction, often leaving individuals completely detached from any community. So, if one values being responsible, aware, and independent, it might be understandable to choose sobriety over the consumption of intoxicants.

Another aspect to consider is that the consumption of especially alcohol and cigarettes usually supports big corporations that stand against the idea of economic justice and participate in turning individuals into consumerist slaves (maybe the most widespread form of capitalist control today denying us true individual independence).

Combining these aspects we can see that abstaining from intoxicants has a symbolic significance that goes beyond simply abstaining from intoxicants. It's a statement for being unwilling to let others control your life: not just drugs, but corporations, politicians, cops, your parents, whatever gets in the way of your self-determined way of doing things. It's a statement of taking your life into your own hands. It's a statement for uncompromising DIY ethics, in the original spirit of DIY punk and DIY hardcore. And in this sense it might very well be seen as a revolutionary statement, being about consciousness, fighting the system, liberation, determining your own destiny.

On this basis, all the social movements and activities a lot of straight edgers have participated in over the years could grow strong because they were strongly grounded: homeless support, minority support, vegetarianism/veganism, environmentalism, to name but the most obvious few. It is in this sense that I can see straight edge being a part of an antifascist movement, and I know that this is what sXe has always been about to many individuals involved in the scene.

But this also means that sXe is nothing but a lifestyle. It is not an ideology. There are no natural moral laws against drinking wine or lighting a pipe. I happily leave such arguments to totalitarian and oppressive political and/or religious schools of thought. If I didn't wanna drink for such reasons I'd become a Seventh Day Adventist or something. I don't abstain from drinking 'cause god or the universe or whatever tells me not to; not because it's inherently evil or sinful; not because we're not meant to drink, or because alcohol is no "natural" food source. I don't drink (or smoke dope, etc.), because I personally don't want to. It seems to interfere with my abilities to promote antifascism.

Seen this way, being sXe is purely pragmatic. I'm sXe, because I think it helps me being an antifascist and allows me to make an antifascist statement, and because of no other reason. If I felt being sXe wouldn't support antifascist action, I wouldn't give a shit about it.

This has, I think, some important implications, especially in the light of ongoing developments within the sXe scene:

1. It's a personal decision. I do think that being sXe generally provides a good basis for an antifascist lifestyle, but neither does it automatically make you an antifascist (as, unfortunately, we have to witness today), nor is it the only way to be an antifascist (which seems so obvious I almost feel silly to point it out, but sometimes it seems one has to make the most trivial things explicit). In simple terms: There are lots of great and decent individuals/antifascists who are absolutely not sXe — and who am I to question these people's personal lifestyle choices?

2. Straight edge was born out of a mainly white middle class American movement, namely hardcore; therefore it is the result of a specific time and place and social setting, and therefore its negative reaction to intoxicants is a result of specific socio-historical circumstances. In other words: we are not too fond of intoxicants because our society uses them in shitty ways, and in particular because they started to destroy our punk and hardcore scenes. That, however, does not mean that intoxicants can't function differently under different cultural circumstances. I'd find it embarrassingly pretentious to disrespect, for example, the use of peyote in many Native American nations, or of ganja in the Rastafarian community. There are different worlds with different rules.

3. Nobody is ever "wrong" or "bad" because of not being sXe. We might not like it, or we might want to confront people who do shitty things under the influence of intoxicants, but the actual consumption itself doesn't mean shit, and we have no right whatsoever to judge people who like to drink or smoke or shoot up.

Unfortunately, many kids today don't see sXe this way. They don't understand it as pragmatic, modest, and open-minded. They understand it as an ideology, a law, a true way of life, a universal moral code. You are sXe, you are good — you are not, you are bad. People are divided into different moral categories depending on whether they drink beer or fruit juice, whether they smoke a joint or chew licorice, whether they eat their muesli with dairy or soy. This is a fascist mentality. Pure and simple. An ideology with its claim to exclusive truth and righteousness is by definition an antifascist's enemy. Whether it's Catholicism, capitalism, or straight edge. Straight up: If I get in a situation where some fucked up sXe kids in Salt Lake City (or anywhere else for that matter) start a fight with some dope-smoking kids for no other reason than them smoking dope, I wouldn't hesitate a second to join the ranks of the latter, who are, in this case, nothing but innocent victims of a bunch of fascist hooligans.

But it's not only the scary self-righteousness, intolerance, and militancy that sXe as an ideology breeds. It's also that its ideas become repulsively narrow-minded: instead of understanding the complexities of global food production and distribution, nutrition, ecological balance, and social division, they become idiotic vegan fanatics; instead of considering the patriarchal character of our societies, they become anti-abortion; instead of embracing diversity as an intrinsic social value, they become homophobic; instead of seeing the interrelations between environmental destruction and economic injustice, they become Eurocentric racists in deep-ecological colors; instead of being committed to antifascism, they hype bands like Vegan Reich; instead of holding up the tradition of innocent early sXe self-defense with shirts like "It's OK Not to Drink," they sport martial "True till the End"-bullshit; instead of generally being socially and politically aware, they reproduce American middle class family values; instead of being progressive, they revive Christianity in its most conservative and frightening forms; and instead of being unassuming, decent, and peaceful, they become arrogant, bigoted, and violent. It's a sad affair.

Anyhow, this text probably won't change any of that. I'm too aware of the little impact my humble self can have. Nonetheless, I want people to know that there's still a different X out here. One that does not represent ideological (and, by now, physical) terror and sectarianism, but pragmatic antifascist politics:

> *The Antifa Straight Edge believes in a sXe lifestyle of abstaining from intoxicants as an actual and symbolic mode of promoting a life of responsibility, awareness, and independence through regaining self-control and shunning dependency on the political, social, and economic powers of a capitalist society. It furthermore supports like-minded social action based on this self-control, mainly in the fields of women and minority rights, social justice, animal rights, and environmentalism.*
>
> *The Antifa Straight Edge does not, however, believe in a sXe lifestyle as a necessity for antifascism. It does not judge people by their personal habits, but relates to them according to their general social conduct. It also does not evaluate people's habits without taking cultural and social circumstances into consideration. In fact, the Antifa Straight Edge respects and even encourages a diversity of lifestyles as an essential aspect of creative antifascist communities.*
>
> *Furthermore, the Antifa Straight Edge fully and uncompromisingly supports a woman's right to choose, a person's right to engage in the sexual relations of their choice, and*

the priority of social issues over animal rights or environmental protection.

Finally, the Antifa Straight Edge does not believe in forcing anybody into, or reprimanding anybody for a certain lifestyle, let alone by violent means. The Antifa Straight Edge commits itself to modesty, open-mindedness, and respect, and contemplates the use of militant resistance only where antifascist values, such as self-determination or social and economic justice, are under immediate and obvious threat.

Generally, the Antifa Straight Edge acts by example alone. Militant action is a last resort, and its use must follow strict notions of sensitivity, responsibility, and measure.

Fight the Power!

Interview with XsaraqaelX

What was the motivation behind writing "The Antifa Straight Edge"?

Basically a frustration with the straight edge scene of the 1990s. Although I can't say that the early scene was better because I only got into straight edge in about 1991. I only know about the 1980s from hearsay.

Straight edge really meant a lot to me when I first got involved because where I grew up there was no straight edge scene and drinking was the standard. I was always the only kid who didn't drink apart from the church crowds — which made me weird in the eyes of everyone. Discovering that there were other kids like me out there, kids interested in underground culture but not in alcohol and drugs, and that there was even a whole movement of these kids was one of the most exhilarating experiences in my life. And I'm not exaggerating.

However, when I immersed myself into straight edge culture, I already had very solid political beliefs. And very soon these beliefs clashed with a lot of what I encountered in the straight edge scene: ignorance, religion, bigotry. I couldn't believe that there were straight edge kids who were against abortion or homosexuality! It was really incomprehensible to me.

Around 1995, I began to feel really embarrassed for identifying as straight edge and distanced myself from the scene completely. I never changed my habits though in terms of not drinking etc. Then a few years later — not least because I had met a number of people with similar personal histories — I decided to make a "last stand" as a straight edge kid and wrote this piece. I guess the rest is explained in the text.

Did this bear any fruits? Did your essay have any impact?

Yes and no. I got some very encouraging and supportive feedback from various places: people from New Zealand to Israel to Poland got in touch to say that the text summed up their frustrations and beliefs and that they would reprint it in their local zines, in English or in translation. As you know, these things don't always happen and I didn't follow up on where the piece ended up, but it must have got out there at least to some degree. I just recently ran into someone from the States who was like, "Oh, you're the guy who wrote the 'Antifa Straight Edge'!?" I have no idea where he had gotten the text from.

On the other hand, the essay certainly didn't have a huge impact. It just never had the forum for it either. Maybe if it had been published in *HeartattaCk* or something... I guess I didn't work hard enough to spread it widely. I wrote the piece, but then didn't really put a lot of effort into distributing it.

The essay was eventually published by a collective I was involved with, called Alpine Anarchist Productions (AAP). They brought it out as a pamphlet, but didn't focus much on distribution either. They mostly published political texts and short fiction. "The Antifa Straight Edge" was the only straight edge text they put out, and it was never advertised much. Like, while a number of AAP pamphlets were distributed through outlets like AK Press, "The Antifa Straight Edge" was never even considered for such distribution. I guess there was some sense of not wanting to be labeled as a "straight edge project" — despite the radical contents of the piece and the fact that AAP was largely drug-free. The negative connotations of straight edge certainly played an important role there.

I guess the text meant something for certain individuals. I remember one friend writing that he hoped it would lead to a "coming out" of political radicals within the scene. This was one of the nicest acknowledgments I got, but the coming out hardly occurred. As I said, the overall impact on the scene was not strong.

Why the focus on antifascism?

This largely had to do with my European background. Although most of my experiences with straight edge culture stem from the US, I spent the main part of my teenage years in Europe and was politically very much influenced by the continent's antifascist youth movements, especially the Antifa groups in Germany. I guess I wanted to apply this principle to straight edge.

In the text you suggest that at least parts of the 1990s straight edge movement displayed fascist tendencies? These are strong words.

I guess so. At the time, the poles of fascism and antifascism very much defined my perception of society and politics. Either you claimed that you had the truth and the right to implement it — this is what I saw as fascism; or you were committed to open, diverse, and self-determined communities — this is what I saw as antifascism. Within this picture, a lot of the attitudes I encountered in the 1990s straight edge scene registered on the fascist side.

But I understand that these are strong words, and I admit that they might not have much analytical value. I can even see a certain contradiction in using such language in a text that argues for tolerance and that criticizes self-righteousness. In other words, "The Antifa Straight Edge" might be considered a pretty militant text for turning against militancy. I guess I was very angry and disappointed. As I said, straight edge had really meant a lot to me.

One of the most controversial passages in the text is where you demand "the priority of social issues over animal rights or environmental protection." Do you still stand behind these words?

The statement certainly has to be understood against the background of the militant animal rights movement that had become extremely influential within the 1990s scene. It just seemed to me that many people focused so exclusively on this one political issue that their overall political analysis became really screwed. This was very graphically exemplified to me when I saw small migrant-run butcheries smashed while the banks and chain stores next door remained untouched. This just seemed wrong.

It was mainly a gut feeling I had. I never cared much for debates of whether "human life" was "worth more" than "animal life." Such questions never interested me and I don't think there can ever be an answer. I mainly experience such debates as divisive. For me, it was more that enormous apparatuses of oppression seemed overlooked because of the exclusive focus on animal rights. At the time I wrote "The Antifa Straight Edge" this seemed particularly obvious to me because I had just spent a number of years in so-called Third World countries, living in poor fishing and farming communities. To take African villagers to task for the means by which they try to scrape together a living and feed their children just seemed absurd to me — even if it often contradicted my own animal rights sensibilities. I just saw different priorities.

To paraphrase Bertolt Brecht, your diet only becomes an ethical issue once you have enough to eat. By no means, however, do I want to suggest that animal rights are not important. I have been a vegetarian and an on-and-off vegan for almost twenty years. Although I do not believe in veganism as a requirement for anarchist societies, I have deep respect for vegan ethics. I also doubt that I would use the words you quoted today. However, at the time I wrote the piece they seemed important.

Can you tell us more about Alpine Anarchist Productions? Are you still involved in the project?

AAP was a very loose collective of traveling kids. We were all politically active but not connected to any particular scenes because we were moving so much. The only way to stay involved in a more continuous project seemed to run a small-scale DIY publishing outfit that we could coordinate via email. Given the less than ideal circumstances we were fairly successful, I suppose, and published thirty pamphlets. The last one, the "Anarchist Football (Soccer) Manual," was by far the most successful. Today, nearly all the folks who have been involved have turned to other things and the project is pretty much on ice. Most of the work we've put out is archived on our website.

How do you see the straight edge scene today? Have things improved?

There have certainly been big changes in the almost ten years since I wrote "The Antifa Straight Edge." The dogmatism of earlier eras seems to have softened and the scene has become more diverse. At the same time, it almost feels like there has been a sort of regress to the 1980s rather than a progressive leap — I find the predominant problems in the scene today to be machismo and de-politicization.

Having said that, this is really the impression of someone who is looking from the outside in. I have long stopped actively participating in the scene. As I said, there is certainly diversity and I keep on meeting awesome and politically very aware straight edge kids — you know, the kind of kids who have always been there, even if they weren't the loudest and most visible. To confirm their presence had been a major reason for writing "The Antifa Straight Edge."

Wasted Indeed: Anarchy and Alcohol
The CrimethInc. Ex-Workers' Collective

"Wasted Indeed: Anarchy and Alcohol" has been the most widely read critique of intoxication culture articulated within the contemporary anarchist movement. The CrimethInc. Ex-Workers' Collective is, according to its website, "a decentralized anarchist collective composed of many cells which act independently in pursuit of a freer and more joyous world." It is best known for books like *Days of War, Nights of Love* (2000) and *Recipes for Disaster: An Anarchist Cookbook* (2004). The journal *Rolling Thunder* has been published biannually since 2005. Aside from such publishing projects, "CrimethInc. agents" have been involved in organizing numerous festivals and acts of resistance.

"Wasted Indeed" was issued as a pamphlet in 2003. The same year it also appeared in the final issue of *Inside Front*, a radical hardcore zine; an abbreviated version was published in the Spring 2003 issue of the anarchist *Fifth Estate* magazine. This reprint lacks the original appendix. The collective explains: "'Wasted Indeed' originally appeared with a hypertrophied appendix, 'The Anarcho-Primitivist Case for Straight Edge' — a sort of sendup of primitivist historical revisionism, though based on kernels of truth. It is not included here, for fear it could be taken too seriously outside its original context."

Peering through the fog behind his eyes, he saw an alcohologram: a world of anguish, in which intoxication was the only escape. Hating himself even more than he hated the corporate killers who had created it, he stumbled to his feet and headed back to the liquor store.

Ensconced in their penthouses, they counted the dollars pouring in from millions like him, and chuckled to themselves at the ease with which all opposition was crushed. But they, too, often had to drink themselves to sleep at night — if ever those vanquished masses stop coming back for more, the tycoons sometimes fretted to themselves, there's gonna be hell to pay.

Ecstasy v Intoxication: For a World of Enchantment, or *anarchaholism*?

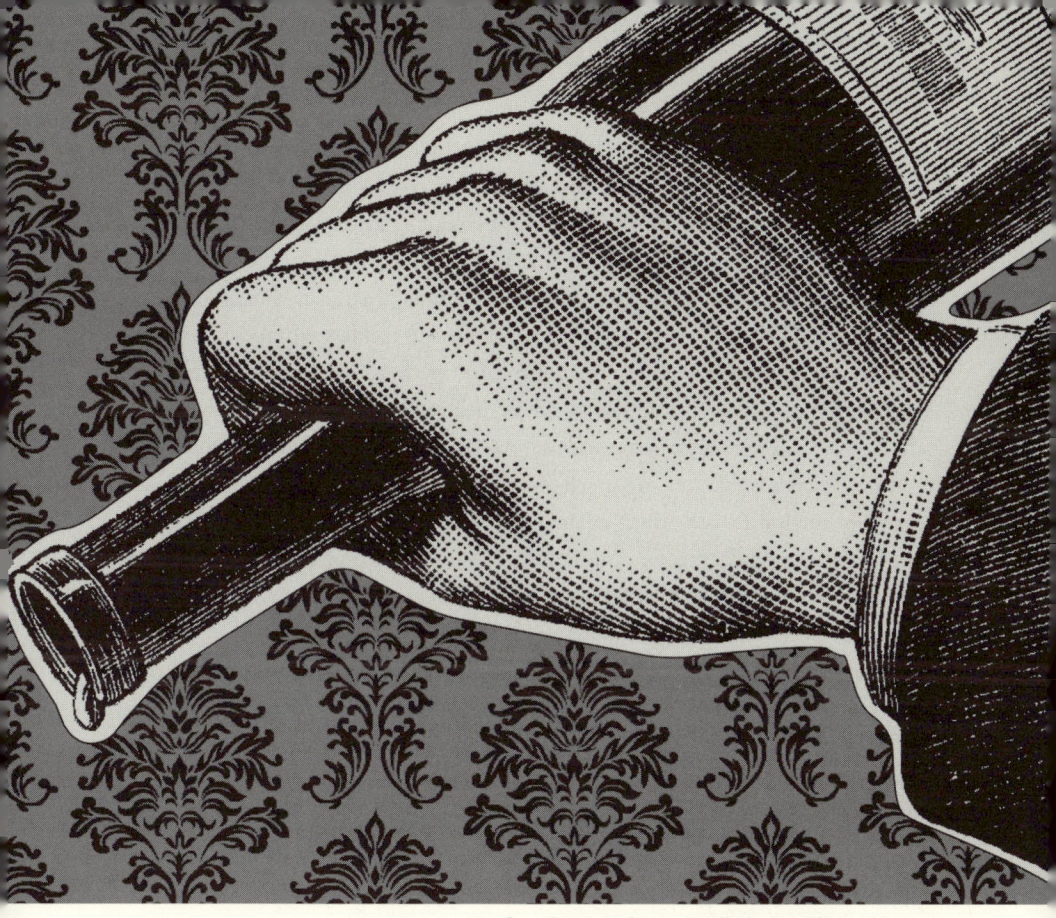

Art from the original Wasted Indeed! pamphlet

Sloshed, smashed, trashed, loaded, wrecked, wasted, blasted, plastered, tanked, fucked up, bombed. Everyone's heard of the arctic people with one hundred words for snow; we have one hundred words for drunk. We perpetuate our own culture of defeat.

Hold it right there — I can see the sneer on your face: *Are these anarchists so uptight that they would even denounce the only fun aspect of anarchism — the beer after the riots, the liquor in the pub where all that* pie-in-the-sky *theory is bandied about? What do they do for fun, anyway — cast aspersions on the little fun we do have? Don't we get to relax and have a good time in any part of our lives?*

Do not misunderstand us: we are not arguing against indulgence, but *for* it. Ambrose Bierce defined an ascetic as "a weak person who succumbs to the temptation of denying himself pleasure," and we concur. As Chuck Baudelaire wrote, *you must always be high — everything depends on this.* So we are not against drunkenness, but rather against drink! For those who embrace drink as a route to drunkenness thus cheat themselves of a total life of enchantment.

Drink, like caffeine or sugar in the body, only plays a role in life that life itself can provide for otherwise. The woman who never drinks coffee does not require it in the morning when she awakens: her body produces energy and focus on its own, as thousands of generations of evolution have prepared it to do. If she drinks coffee regularly, soon her body lets the coffee take over that role, and she becomes dependent upon it. Thus does alcohol artificially provide for temporary moments of relaxation and release while impoverishing life of all that is genuinely restful and liberating.

If some sober people in this society do not seem as reckless and free as their boozer counterparts, that is a mere accident of culture, mere circumstantial evidence. Those puritans exist all the same in the world drained of all magic and genius by the alcoholism of their fellows (*and the capitalism, hierarchy, misery it helps maintain*) — the only difference is that they are so self-abnegating as to refuse even the false magic, the genie of the bottle. But other "sober" folk, whose orientation to living might better be described as enchanted or ecstatic, are plentiful, if you look hard enough. For these individuals — for us — life is a constant celebration, one which needs no augmentation and from which we need no respite.

Alcohol, like Prozac and all the other mind-control medications that are making big bucks for Big Brother these days, substitutes symptomatic treatment for cure. It takes away the pain of a dull, drab existence for a few hours at best, then returns it twofold. It not only replaces positive actions which would address the root causes of our despondency — it *prevents* them, as more energy becomes focused on achieving and recovering from the drunken state. Like the tourism of the worker, drink is a pressure valve that releases tension while maintaining the system that creates it.

In this push-button culture, we've become used to conceiving of ourselves as simple machines to be operated: add the appropriate chemical to the equation to get the desired result. In our search for health, happiness, meaning in life, we run from one panacea to the next — Viagra, vitamin C, vodka — instead of approaching our lives holistically and addressing our problems at their social and economic roots. This product-oriented mindset is the foundation of our alienated consumer society: without consuming products, we can't live! We try to buy relaxation, community, self-confidence — now even ecstasy comes in a pill!

We want ecstasy as a way of life, not a liver-poisoning alcoholiday from it. "Life sucks — get drunk" is the essence of the argument that enters our ears from our masters' tongues and then passes out of our own slurring mouths, perpetuating whatever incidental and unnecessary truths it may refer to — but we're not falling for it any longer! Against inebriation — and *for* drunkenness! Burn down the liquor stores, and replace them with playgrounds! *For a Lucid Bacchanalian, Ecstatic Sobriety*!

Spurious Rebellion

Practically every child in mainstream Western society grows up with alcohol as the forbidden fruit their parents or peers indulge in but deny to them. This prohibition only makes drinking that much more fascinating to young people, and when they get the opportunity, most immediately assert their independence by doing exactly as they've been told not to: ironically, they rebel by following the example set for them. This hypocritical pattern is standard for child-rearing in this society, and works to replicate a number of destructive behaviors that otherwise would be aggressively refused by new generations. The fact that the bogus morality of many drinking parents is mirrored in the sanctimonious practice of religious groups helps to create a false dichotomy between puritanical self-denial and life-loving, free-wheeling drinkers — with "friends" like Baptist ministers, we teetotalers wonder, who needs enemies?

These partisans of Rebellious Drunkenness and advocates of Responsible Abstinence are loyal adversaries. The former need the latter to make their dismal rituals look like fun; the latter need the former to make their rigid austerity seem like common sense. An "ecstatic sobriety" which combats the dreariness of one and the bleariness of the other — false pleasure and false discretion alike — is analogous to the anarchism that confronts both the false freedom offered by capitalism and the false community offered by communism.

Alcohol & Sex in the Rape Culture

Let's lay it on the table: almost all of us are coming from a place where our sexuality is or was occupied territory. We've been raped, abused, assaulted, shamed, silenced, confused, constructed, programmed. We're badasses, and we're taking it all back, reclaiming ourselves; but for most of us, that's a slow, complex, not yet concluded process.

This doesn't mean we can't have good, safe, supportive sex right now, in the middle of that healing — but it does make having that sex a little more complicated. To be certain we're not perpetuating or helping to perpetuate negative patterns in a lover's life, we have to be able to communicate clearly and honestly before things get hot and heavy — and while they are, and after. Few forces interfere with this communication like alcohol does. In this culture of denial, we are encouraged to use it as a social lubricant to help us slip past our inhibitions; all too often, this simply means ignoring our own fears and scars, and not asking about others'. If it is dangerous, as well as beautiful, for us to share sex with each other sober, how much more dangerous must it be to do so drunk, reckless, and incoherent?

¶ Speaking of sex, it's worth noting the supporting role alcohol has played in patriarchal gender dynamics. For example — in how many nuclear families has alcoholism helped to maintain an unequal distribution of power and pressure? (All the writers of this tract can call to mind more than one such case among their relatives alone.) The man's drunken self-destruction, engendered as it may be by the horrors of surviving under capitalism, imposes even more of a burden on the woman, who must still somehow hold the family together — often in the face of his violence. And on the subject of dynamics...

The Tyranny of Apathy

"Every fucking anarchist project I engage in is ruined or nearly ruined by alcohol. You set up a collective living situation and everyone is too drunk or stoned to do the basic chores, let alone maintain an attitude of respect. You want to create community, but after the show everyone just goes back to their rooms and drinks themselves to death. If it's not one substance to abuse it's a motherfucking other. I understand trying to obliterate your consciousness is a natural reaction to being born in alienating capitalist hell, but I want people to see what we anarchists are doing and say 'Yeah, this is better than capitalism!'... which is hard to say if you can't walk around without stepping on broken forty-ounce bottles. I've never considered myself straight-edge, but fuck it, I'm not taking it anymore!"

It's said that when the renowned anarchist Oscar Wilde first heard the old slogan *if it is humiliating to be ruled, how much more humiliating it is to choose one's rulers*, he responded: "If it's humiliating to choose one's masters, how much more humiliating to be one's own master!" He intended this as a critique of hierarchies within the self as well as the democratic state, of course — but, sadly, his quip could be applied literally to the way some of our attempts at creating anarchist environments pan out in practice. This is especially true when they're carried out by drunk people.

In certain circles, especially the ones in which the word "anarchy" itself is more in fashion than any of its various meanings, freedom is conceived of in negative terms: "don't tell me what to do!" In practice, this often means nothing more than an assertion of the individual's right to be lazy, selfish, unaccountable for his actions or lack thereof. In such contexts, when a group agrees upon a project it often ends up being a small, responsible minority that has to do all the work to make it happen. These conscientious few often look like the autocratic ones — when, invisibly, it is the apathy and hostility of their comrades that forces them to adopt this role. Being drunk and disorderly all the time is *coercive* — it compels others to clean up behavior when you are too fucked up for dialogue. These dynamics go two ways, of course — those who take *all* responsibility on their shoulders perpetuate a pattern in which everyone else takes none — but everyone is responsible for their own part in such patterns, and for transcending it.

Think of the power we could have if all the energy and effort in the world — or maybe even just *your* energy and effort? — that goes into drinking were put into resisting, building, creating. Try adding up all the money anarchists in your community have spent on corporate libations, and picture how much musical equipment or bail money or food (-notbombs ... or, fuck it, bombs!) it could have paid for — instead of funding their war against all of us. Better: imagine living in a world where cokehead presidents die of overdoses while radical musicians and rebels live the chaos into ripe old age!

Sobriety & Solidarity

Like any lifestyle choice, be it vagabondage or union membership, abstention from alcohol can sometimes be mistaken as an end rather than a means.

Above all, it is critical that our own choices *not* be a pretext for us to deem ourselves superior to those who make different decisions. The only strategy for sharing good ideas that succeeds unfailingly (and that goes for hotheaded, alienating tracts like this one as well!) is the power of example — if you put "ecstatic sobriety" into action in your life *and it works*, those who sincerely want similar things will join in. Passing judgment on others for decisions that affect only themselves is absolutely noxious to any anarchist — not to mention it makes them less likely to experiment with the options you offer.

And so — the question of solidarity and community with anarchists and others who do use alcohol and drugs. We propose that these are of utmost importance. Especially in the case of those who are struggling to free themselves of unwanted addictions, such solidarity is paramount: Alcoholics Anonymous, for example, is just one more instance of a quasi-religious organization filling a social need that should already be provided for by anarchist community self-organizing. As in every case, we anarchists must ask ourselves: do we take our positions simply to feel superior to the unwashed (er, washed) masses — or because we sincerely want to propagate accessible alternatives? Besides, most of us who are not substance-addicted can thank our privileges and good fortune for this; this gives us all the more responsibility to be good allies to those who have not had such privileges or luck — on whatever terms *they* set. Let tolerance, humility, accessibility, and sensitivity be the qualities we nurture in ourselves, not self-righteousness or pride. No separatist sobriety!

Revolution

So anyway — what are we going to do if we don't go to bars, hang out at parties, sit on the steps or in front of the television with our forty-ounce bottles? *Anything else!*

The social impact of our society's fixation on alcohol is at least as important as its mental, medical, economic, and emotional effects. Drinking standardizes our social lives, occupying some of the eight waking hours a day that aren't already colonized by work. It locates us spatially — living rooms, cocktail lounges, railroad tracks — and contextually — in ritualized, predictable behaviors — in ways more explicit systems of control never could. Often when one of us does manage to escape the role of worker/consumer, drinking is there, stubborn holdover from our colonized leisure time, to fill up the promising space that opens. Free from these routines, we could discover other ways to spend time and energy and seek pleasure, ways that could prove dangerous to the system of alienation itself.

Drink can *incidentally* be part of positive and challenging social interactions, of course — the problem is that its central role in current socializing and socialization misrepresents it as *the* prerequisite for such intercourse. This obscures the fact that we can create such interactions at will with nothing more than our own creativity, honesty, and daring. Indeed, without these, *nothing* of value is possible — have you ever been to a bad party? — and with them, no alcohol is necessary.

When one or two persons cease to drink, it just seems senseless, like they are ejecting themselves from the company (or at least customs) of their fellow human beings for nothing. But a *community* of such people can develop a radical culture of sober adventure and engagement, one that could eventually offer exciting opportunities for drink-free activity and merriment for all. Yesterday's geeks and loners could be the pioneers of tomorrow's new world: "lucid bacchanalism" is a new horizon, a new possibility for transgression and transformation that could provide fertile soil for revolts yet unimaginable. Like any revolutionary lifestyle option, this one offers an immediate taste of another world while helping create a context for actions that hasten its universal realization.

No war but the class war — no cocktail but the molotov cocktail ! Let us brew nothing but trouble!

Postscript: How to Read this Tract

With any luck, you've been able to discern — even, perhaps, through that haze of drunken stupor — that this is as much a caricature of polemics in the anarchist tradition as a serious piece. It's worth pointing out that these polemics have often brought attention to their theses by deliberately taking an extreme position, thereby opening up the ground in between for more "moderate" positions on the subject. Hopefully you can draw useful insights of your own from your interpretations of this text, rather than taking it as gospel or anathema.

And all this is not to say there are no fools who refuse intoxication — but can you imagine how much more insufferable they would be if they did not? The boring would still be boring, only louder about it; the self-righteous ones would continue to lambaste and harangue, while spitting and drooling on their victims! It is an almost universal characteristic of drinkers that they encourage everyone around them to drink, that — barring those hypocritical power-plays between lovers or parents and children, at least — they prefer their own choices to be reflected in the choices of all. This strikes us as indicating a monumental insecurity, not unrelated to the insecurity revealed by ideologues and recruiters of every stripe from Christian to Marxist to anarchist who feel they cannot rest until everyone in the world sees that world exactly as they do. As you read, try to fight off that insecurity — and try not to read this as an expression of our own, either, but rather, in the tradition of the best anarchist works, as a reminder for all who choose to concern themselves that *another world is possible*.

Predictable Disclaimer

As in the case of *every* CrimethInc. text, this one only represents the perspectives of whoever agrees with it at the time, *not* the "entire CrimethInc. ex-Workers' Collective" or any other abstract mass. Somebody who does important work under the CrimethInc. moniker is probably getting sloshed at the moment I'm typing this — and that's ok!

Interview with CrimethInc. agent Carrie No Nation

"Wasted Indeed" was first published some years ago and has been reprinted several times in various forms and forums. What have the reactions been like? The radical political scene is not exactly known for abstinence…

Actually, nowadays some anarchist communities in the United States do very little drinking. Anarchism used to be really associated with drinking in some places here, but many of those scenes have collapsed; that lifestyle can be hard to sustain. Many younger anarchists seem to have learned from this — not that they are totally sober, necessarily, but drinking and drug use are not central to their social lives.

The anarchist community in my home town, for example, is almost entirely sober. Drinking is not a part of any of our regular social activities, so we find ourselves exploring other ways to relax and create intimacy together. I think this is becoming more common in other parts of the country as well.

The most ironic reactions to "Wasted Indeed" have been snide dismissals from people who drink, to the effect that people in our circles must have a real problem with drinking or else we wouldn't take that stance. This strikes me as projection.

I understand that you have also conducted workshops on living alcohol/drug-free in radical contexts. What were your experiences there?

I've been invited to participate in a few panel discussions about sobriety and radical politics, yes — but I think most of those panels have been missed opportunities, because they were composed entirely of sober people. People who have chosen lifelong sobriety are not the best positioned to speak on the subject to a mixed audience; it would be better to hear from a variety of perspectives. The people most qualified to speak about drug use and sobriety are those who have just quit using or are trying to quit, not those who haven't ever used or who quit long ago. It's the same with talking about quitting one's job and changing one's lifestyle—people who are currently trying to do that have much more useful perspectives on it than full-time anarchists who dropped out ten years ago.

How strong are non-alcohol/non-drug sentiments within CrimethInc. circles? What happens at your convergences, for example? Are these alcohol/drug-free?

There's a fair bit of diversity around this issue in CrimethInc. circles, but habitual reliance on intoxicants is uncommon — it's just so boring and typical, so consumerist! Perhaps the best test case to examine is the CrimethInc. convergences, which are explicitly sober spaces. This policy has been developed for a variety of reasons. For one, it makes it easier to deal with security issues: it denies the authorities a pretext to raid the site, and makes sure no one's drinking leads to loose lips and subsequent entrapment by informants. It also seems to make non-consensual social or sexual interactions somewhat less likely. Finally, as the convergences are intended to be an experimental laboratory for non-standard interactions and relationships, the sobriety policy ensures that people don't simply do what they do the rest of the year in other spaces. In this regard, the CrimethInc. convergences are distinct from practically every other anarchist gathering around the US, most of which are marked by a fair bit of drinking and predictable behavior.

People with a wide range of relationships to intoxicants come to the convergences — straight edge kids, people who only drink occasionally, and people who are struggling with addiction. The one thing everyone has in common is that they all choose to be in a substance-free space for the duration of the convergence, and thus to experiment with other forms of pleasure, intoxication, and interaction. This has been surprisingly successful — many participants who otherwise choose to drink, even to drink a lot, are supportive of the convergence being a sober space and argue strongly for this approach. Some of the people who snuck off into the woods to drink at the 2006 convergence were among the most vocal proponents of the sobriety policy in 2007, arguing that they regretted all they missed and felt there was a lot to be gained from everyone experimenting with sobriety together at least once a year.

It is noticeable that there are hardly any explicit references to straight edge in your essay. I assume this was a conscious choice. What were your reasons for not using the label?

Straight edge is a useful reference point in a specific subcultural context, but CrimethInc. texts circulate far outside that context. Also, in the spaces in which people are most familiar with it, it is also the most freighted with associations, not all of which are good. Some of the culture associated with the straight edge scene has not been particularly anti-authoritarian, anti-capitalist, or liberating.

Still, I assume there has been some influence on CrimethInc. agents by the 1990s vegan straight edge scene...

I think the 1990s vegan straight edge scene has the most influence on the younger kids who were not around to experience it. For them, Earth Crisis is just a hardcore band they listened to in high school, with the good associations everyone has with high school rebellion. For older participants who were active in the 1990s, Earth Crisis and the vegan straight edge scene in general are much more problematic; they were characterized by a single-issue focus that often obstructed the discussion of broader-based liberation struggles, and at worst directed energy towards reactionary phenomena such as so-called "pro-life" politics and self-righteous middle class consumerism.

I think that one of the most memorable points made in "Wasted Indeed" is the reminder that while one or two persons who stop drinking might end up as outcasts, a community of non-drinkers could, and I quote, "develop a radical culture of sober adventure and engagement, one that could eventually offer exciting opportunities for drink-free activity and merriment for all." Have you seen this happen? Do you think that straight edge at its best was able to provide this — at least in certain places and at certain times? Is it something that you see realized within CrimethInc. circles today?

I wouldn't rule out that some straight edge scenes may have resembled this description, but I can't say it resonates with my experience from the days I traveled in those circles. I remember there being a handful of us positioned between the heavy-drinking anarcho-punk scene and the consumerist straight edge scene who wished to combine the best aspects of both, but I don't know that that ever came to fruition on a large scale. I'd say my current community is the best example I've experienced of a radical sober space. It's exciting to be connected to a lot of people for whom sobriety is a starting point for a passionate exploration of life.

Sticking with the straight edge theme: when you decided to publish *Evasion*, how important was the fact that the book's protagonist was straight edge?

I don't think that was mentioned a single time in the course of discussing whether to publish that book. On the other hand, it probably influenced the decision on an unconscious level — if the stories in *Evasion* had been about stealing liquor, drinking by the railroad tracks, and waking up with a hangover, it would have been a very different story, and less promising as a vehicle for spreading a counter-consumerist message.

The book's anonymous author — known to many as Mack Evasion — complained in various interviews and zine columns that the straight edge message of the book was widely overlooked. Did you have a similar impression?

Again, I think the message did come across on a subconscious level. One indication of this is the defensiveness the book created — if it had included a lot of generic stories about getting drunk, it would have fit much more neatly into the stereotypical punk traveling zine format, and people would have reacted less strongly to it. The implication that one need not drink to enjoy life — or, for that matter, to rebel — often provokes defensiveness, even if that defensiveness ends up being framed around entirely different issues.

In his *HeartattaCk* column, Mack took an increasingly outspoken straight edge stance. What is your take on the discussions that this caused?

Honestly, I fear I wasn't paying close attention, so perhaps I'm not qualified to speak on this. If I had to hypothesize about the controversy, I would guess that someone brought up the issue of privilege, arguing that it was self-centered and oppressive for white males in the US to endorse sobriety as a universally applicable stance. To some extent, I agree with that critique, though I don't think it's necessarily oppressive for a white male to suggest to a community predominantly composed of other white males that they should consider sobriety as an aspect of their radical practice.

I believe the question of context is an interesting one. Like, what audience did you have in mind when publishing "Wasted Indeed"? And would you say that there are any cultural contexts where the message is not really applicable, so to speak?

If memory serves, "Wasted Indeed" was originally written for the "Food and Drink" issue of *Fifth Estate*, North America's longest-running anarchist periodical. *Fifth Estate* has a sort of hippy reputation, so it was a deliberately provocative submission; the editors were actually quite hesitant about putting it in, shortened it, and included a disclaimer saying that they loved to get drunk themselves. It appeared after that in the reunion issue of *Inside Front*, an anarchist magazine that had developed in the straight edge hardcore scene, which was a context in which it was somewhat less controversial. I think it's written to speak to people who are already somewhat familiar with radical ideas, in order to draw the connections between liberation and sobriety for that particular readership.

I think the further away one gets from one's own cultural context, the less likely it is that one's opinions will be applicable to others. So I certainly can't say whether anything in "Wasted Indeed" would be relevant to women in Zapatista communities or underclass bankrobbers a century ago in France. At the same time, women in Zapatista communities are well known for pushing for sobriety in their communities as part of their struggle, and in France a century ago the anarchist bankrobbers who invented the getaway car (nowadays known as the Bonnot Gang) were sober and strictly vegetarian... so who knows, maybe it's an idea with wide relevance! The point is, that's up to others to decide, in their own contexts, not for us to decide from ours.

Towards a Less Fucked Up World:
Sobriety and Anarchist Struggle

"Towards a Less Fucked Up World: Sobriety and Anarchist Struggle" was first self-published as a pamphlet in 2003. The text proved to be pivotal for contemporary connections between radical politics and sobriety. The author, Nick Riotfag, revised the original version for this book and has added an afterword.

Nick Riotfag is an anarchist, queer, and straight edge activist/writer who lives in North Carolina.

Introduction

This zine is an ongoing project I've been writing in my head and on paper for several years now. Since I decided to become permanently sober several years ago, I've constantly struggled to find safe spaces; I hoped that when I started to become a part of radical, activist, and anarchist communities, that I would find folks who shared or at least respected my convictions. Instead, I found a painful paradox: radical scenes that were so welcoming and affirming in many ways, yet incredibly inflexible and unsupportive around my desire to be in sober spaces.

I have plenty of reasons for being substance-free that aren't "political," per se. Some are more personal or internal: I love my body and want to preserve my health; I'm personally terrified of addiction; I tend towards extremes, so I think that if I did drink or drug I'd overdo it; my family has had alcoholics and drug abusers who have ruined lives. Others are more pragmatic: as an activist I participate in actions that could put me at risk for arrest, and the legal risks of drug possession just aren't worthwhile; I have better things to spend money on; and so forth. However, my primary reasons for choosing this lifestyle are specifically connected to my political beliefs as a revolutionary, a feminist, and an anarchist. I don't think that most folks with whom I work on political projects realize or acknowledge that my choice to be sober isn't just a personal preference or an annoying puritan dogma. This zine is my attempt to articulate why I consider sobriety a crucial part of my anarchism and feminism.

I've tried to put it together in a way that combines theory and analysis with my personal experience. The first few sections explore the connections I see between intoxication and different kinds of oppression (sorry if it gets a little wordy at times); the next bit talks about how intoxication fits into radical communities; then I offer two stories from my life and my reflections on them before the conclusion.

TOWARDS A LESS FUCKED UP WORLD:

SOBRIETY AND ANARCHIST STRUGGLE

I realize that sober folks have traditionally not been known for presenting our views respectfully, with open ears and loving hearts. I'm definitely among those who stand guilty of bludgeoning people with my beliefs. Hopefully this zine will at least in part rectify that tendency by explaining my views without judging or blaming non-sober folks or seeming to set myself up as superior to others. If it fails in this, I apologize in advance, and welcome folks to call me out on it. That said, please know that much of my anger that manifests in a "judgmental" or "preachy" tone comes from constant denial of safe space, refusal to recognize the legitimacy of our feelings and opinions, alienation in most social environments, and general ignoring of our concerns and desires and needs. I write with love and rage, and I apologize for neither.

A Quick Note On Words

I like the term "straightedge," not because I'm especially invested in the bands and the scene, but rather because I like the way it places my decision not to drink or take drugs in the larger context of a positive radical social critique. Of course, I've found that most folks — probably many of y'all, too — have nothing but negative associations with sXe: macho white dudes beating up people, crappy music, super dogmatic and preachy assholes, or even anti-abortion extremists. Even though I completely reject all of those things, I still think there's hope for reclaiming the term as something positive. But because for most folks I've asked it's often more of a stumbling block than a help, I'm going to stick with "sober" or "substance-free" for the purposes of this zine.

Here are some definitions for some of the key concepts I'll be talking about:

- **Intoxication:** an artificially altered state of mind produced through drug and alcohol consumption
- **Intoxication Culture:** a set of institutions, behaviors, and mindsets centered around consumption of drugs and alcohol
- **Patriarchal Masculinity:** a way of behaving and understanding oneself as a man based on fucked up sexist values
- **Anesthesia:** artificially-induced numbness to sensations and feelings

Masculinity, Rape Culture, and Intoxication

Dear readers: please know that this section includes discussion of sexual violence and other things that may be difficult or triggering for some folks. Please use self-care to determine if and when it makes sense to read this. Thanks!

I saw a billboard once as I was riding my bike through downtown New Orleans. It was advertising some kind of fancy liquor, whiskey I think. The slogan was, "It's what men do." The message was almost reassuring to me; the only possible conclusion, I supposed, is that I must not be a man. The mass media encourages folks socialized as men to affirm our masculinity through intoxication, specifically through capitalist alcohol consumption. The whiskey billboard I saw, along with Budweiser ads that show "male bonding," various beer companies whose commercials use men objectifying women, and countless other advertisements, show alcohol as the common theme that links men as they engage in the most manly of activities. How surprising is it, then, that alcohol is almost always involved in some of the "manliest" pursuits of all — male violence against women, including domestic violence, sexual assault, and rape?

The relationship between intoxication, gender, and violence is complex. A significant proportion of gendered violence — specifically sexual and relationship violence against women — is committed by men while intoxicated. Of course, this doesn't mean that intoxication causes violence, but it would be equally foolish to ignore the correlation. In heterosexual interactions, men who have learned from media and pop culture to understand themselves as initiators and seducers use alcohol as a tool for overcoming resistance both from the desired sexual conquest and from their own conscience. At the same time, in this harshly puritanical, sex-negative culture, many rely on alcohol as their only means of overcoming the shame they feel about our sexual desires. Generally speaking, I think that the broad dependence in this society on alcohol in the process of finding partners and having sex obscures our sexuality, negatively impacts communication, reduces our ability to give and receive meaningful consent, lessens the probability of safe sex practices, and supports rape culture. When this dependence, and all of the dangers it entails, connects with patriarchal notions of sexuality, including male senses of entitlement, the hunter/hunted dynamic, and "no means yes" myths, the result can be disastrous.

As a man, part of my decision to live a sXe or sober lifestyle stems from my recognition that patriarchy and intoxication culture go hand in hand. Intoxication is used as an excuse to justify (and legally, a mitigating factor in the prosecution of) a wide range of unacceptable behaviors, including sexual harassment and rape. In my personal experience, many people I've known — most often men — have significantly altered their behavior while intoxicated in ways that directly reinforce oppression (i.e. becoming more openly homophobic and misogynist in speech, more sexually aggressive, etc), and expected the fact that they were intoxicated to somehow alleviate their responsibility for these behaviors. The idea that being intoxicated somehow makes one less able to make rational and compassionate decisions should be a reason to abstain from using alcohol and drugs.

In saying this, I want to make clear that I do not intend to blame victims; there is absolutely no excuse for sexual or relationship violence, regardless of the intoxication or not of the assaulter or the survivor. I refuse to allow one's intoxication to reduce one's culpability for fucked up behavior. If there's any possibility that drinking or taking drugs could increase, even the slightest bit, one's capacity to be violent or abusive, then I consider that more than enough reason to be substance-free. If you're making the decision to get intoxicated or fucked up, and you care about living your ideals in any meaningful way, you need a plan for how you can be held accountable, by yourself and others, for how you behave when you choose to do so, in sexual situations and beyond.

I want to emphasize that this is not something that exists only in the "mainstream," as if anarchist or radical communities were immune from its effects. Women in our communities are speaking out about sexual harassment and assault and rape at the hands of "radical" men. In virtually every case of which I'm aware, alcohol played a major part in these incidents. One of my dearest friends has been sexually harassed on multiple occasions and sexually assaulted by intoxicated anarchist men, who, while sober, expressed serious and firm anti-patriarchy convictions. Yes, anarchist men, feminist men, men who say they are fighting patriarchy with all their might, that means us: if we take seriously the charge to be responsible, anti-sexist allies to women, I strongly believe that we must look very critically at the ways we get intoxicated.[1]

This pattern of boundary-crossing while intoxicated doesn't always fall predictably along gender lines. Sometimes women take advantage of men sexually using intoxication; at times the intoxication of both or all parties makes it difficult to sort out accountability; sometimes participants don't neatly fit gender boxes and power dynamics play out with more complexity. Alcohol-based coercion and blurry consent also exist in same-sex relationships and interactions, in some especially difficult to escape ways due to the particular stranglehold of intoxication culture in queer communities.[2] Although the conditioning that men receive in our patriarchal rape culture contributes to higher rates of men crossing boundaries without consent, all of us — men, women, and others, transgender and non-transgender — have the capacity to violate others. But more importantly, we also all have the capacity to become allies

---

1. To clarify: I don't want my focus on calling out men who drink alcohol to examine their behavior to falsely imply that sober men are generally off the hook, not likely to sexually assault, and not in need of examination of our patterns of consent and sexuality. That's pretty elitist, in terms of how it puts sober men (especially me) on some sort of different, less guilty level, and also dangerous, in its implication that we somehow need to be less vigilant about owning up to our capacity to violate folks' boundaries. All of us, regardless of gender, sexuality, or substance use, have been raised in a rape culture, and in particular folks socialized as men have been subjected to especially harmful messages about masculinity and violent sexuality. Although alcohol, in combination with media's linking of masculinity and intoxication, can be used by men as a tool to facilitate the expression of this rape culture, choosing to drink or not drink does not make any of us less subject to the socialization we've received, nor less in need of a critical look at consent and sexuality.

2. For a more in-depth exploration of the intersections of intoxication and sexuality in queer communities, see "My Edge is Anything But Straight" in this volume.

in the struggle to undermine patriarchy and construct a society based on consent. I think that because of this, all people who are committed to fighting rape culture and patriarchy can benefit from critically examining our patterns of intoxication, and discussing ways to be held equally accountable for behavior while intoxicated as well as while sober.

Oppression and Anesthesia

Maintaining privilege and continuing to oppress a group of people is only possible when oppressors can see the people they oppress as less than fully human. A major tactic in the dehumanizing process is the oppressor's anesthesia, numbing oneself so as to be unable to empathize with the people they are relegating to a sub-human status. Mab Segrest wrote a moving essay about how a key strategy for maintaining white privilege is the anesthesia of white people towards the suffering of people of color, through distance (out of sight, out of mind), rationalization, intoxication, and other methods. Likewise, masculinity operates by forcing men to stay detached and impassive in the face of physical or emotional pain, setting up sensitivity and empathy as "female" (and therefore inferior) characteristics. Constructing masculinity as unfeeling — anesthetized — makes possible the incredible suffering inflicted by men upon women (and other men) through violence, rape, child abuse, denial of access to birth control and medical care, the patriarchal nuclear family, and so many other means. In this context, it makes perfect sense that intoxication would be linked with masculinity. Intoxication often reduces the ability of people to empathize with others, an integral part of being an oppressor.

A friend of mine pointed out that when she was in high school, most of the kids that she knew who had any idea of what was happening in the world were getting completely fucked up as often as they could to neutralize the pain of that awareness. I can understand how activists, who (theoretically) operate by refusing to ignore the suffering and oppression in the world, face an incredible temptation to try and numb themselves, even temporarily, to the pain they see and feel and struggle against every day. However, I also strongly believe that if everyone in our culture was both fully aware of the full extent of how fucked up our society is — and refused to simply ignore the pain of that awareness though various methods of intoxication and anesthesia, from booze to television — then people simply would not stand for it.

Even providing for the (minority, I think, of) people who are simply cruel and hateful, I truly believe that a population honestly facing the realities of poverty, oppression, and misery rife in this culture cannot do so with both clear heads and clear consciences. When heads are not clear, clear consciences become less and less important. When people refuse to be numb and truly live the pain of this culture, it motivates action. I believe that our task as activists or people who feel a call to change this culture is first and foremost to be open to that deep pain, to feel it and mourn it and hate it, so that it lights fires in our chests that burn for our participation in revolutionary struggle.

Youth Liberation and Sobriety

The most well-known icon of sXe, the Xs that some edgers draw on their hands, originated out of a gesture of solidarity with youth. To this day, kids at shows and other all-ages events that serve alcohol often have black Xs drawn on their hands by the people taking money at the door as a sign that they aren't allowed to drink. In the early 1980's, when Minor Threat began bringing the substance-free message to the punk scene, people who noticed kids marked with these Xs as symbols for prohibition of alcohol started drawing them on their hands, regardless of age, to show solidarity with youth and a commitment to sobriety. Because of the prevalence of intoxication culture, shows and other events often cost more for young kids, or don't allow them in at all. The drinking age serves as a legal tool for enforcing segregation and discrimination directed towards young folks, setting up an entire system around consumption of alcohol that simultaneously devalues youth and glorifies intoxication, constructing it as "mature" and advanced and all of the other positive traits associated with adulthood.

As a result, among young people, the mystique of intoxication culture leads to semi-secretive consumption of alcohol and other drugs, often to a destructive degree. For kids around the ages of eighteen to twenty-two or so, just before and after the drinking age, the ability to finally partake in the highly coveted "privilege" of intoxication culture leads to cults of hyper-intoxication, reinforcing the mystique even more. When the destructive consequences of getting fucked up manifest dramatically in young folks, as shown by the number of deaths from binge drinking, clueless and patronizing adults wag their fingers and bemoan "peer pressure" as the cause, when it's blatantly fucking obvious that the causes lie in their own actions.

The entirely adult-constructed mystique around intoxication, hypocritical and inconsistent policies promoting potentially fatal intoxicants while violently suppressing less harmful ones, and the oppression and devaluing of young people in general frequently lead to the desire to emulate the destructive fucked up patterns of adult intoxication with the vehemence of youth. Fuck "peer pressure" — I've felt consistent and unrelenting pressure from every sector of adult society to intoxicate myself through every possible means for as long as I can remember. Do adults honestly think that a "drug education program" in 5th grade and some condescending guest speakers in a high school health class would cancel the effects of an entire social system based on oppression requiring intoxication and anesthesia to survive?

My decision to abstain totally from intoxication culture has a lot to do with my desire for youth liberation. Maybe I don't want the privilege that comes with adulthood to destroy my body legally. Maybe I don't buy the argument that only adults — being naturally superior to kids, according to adult chauvinist logic — are responsible enough to handle getting fucked up. I think the impressive thing is being strong enough to survive without getting fucked up — if becoming an adult means accepting the need to numb myself into accepting the status quo, then fuck it, I'm following Peter Pan and never growing up.

Intoxication and Social Life

Seriously, one of the reasons why living in a community that drinks constantly bugs me is that it makes conversation so damn boring! I can hardly ever hang out in a large group without conversation turning for a substantial period of time to drinking, getting fucked up, what so and so did when they were fucked up, how fucked up so and so's going to get, blah blah blah. Who fucking cares? Are people really so boring most of the time that they don't merit conversation without corporate-induced altered consciousness? Can we really not think of anything more interesting to talk about than our self-destructiveness? What about our dreams, our passions, our crazy ideas and schemes, our hopes and fears? I hate going to parties where intoxication numbs individuality into mush, so that I can have the same mindless banter with 100 people but not a conversation of any substance with a single person. Am I anti-social for staying home with one good friend or a book when that's the alternative?

Beyond boring conversation, dependence on alcohol limits our social lives in other ways. In bar culture, public interaction is limited to contexts where we have to buy something in order to spend time with other people. It makes us less well equipped to enjoy one another's company in ordinary mindsets or without corporate intervention. We bond over buying, consuming, numbing, and things rather than creating, experiencing, feeling, and personalities. Instead of challenging it, we accept the proposition that we need consumer capitalism to be able to "loosen up," have a good time, and get past the hang-ups and self-restraint that constrain our lives.

Intoxication and Corporate Culture

I know a disturbing amount of folks in radical communities who spend their entire income on alcohol and tobacco. People who shoplift from the local food coop because they don't want to pay for food will head down the street to the chain convenience store and pour the tiny bit of money that they do have into some of the most wicked fucking corporations in operation today. There seems to be an incredible blind spot around tobacco and booze with regards to ethical consumption; kids who'll demonstrate against Wal-Mart or Exxon for their labor or environmental practices will then turn around and buy cigarettes and beer from stores that have devastatingly negative impacts on local communities and that were produced by companies that are central to everything that's awful about global capitalism. Kudos to kids who at least make an effort to buy local, grow/brew their own, and such, but the industry feeds off of them just as much, knowing that the more dependent they are on chemical stimulation the less they'll care where it comes from.

Growing tobacco is incredibly destructive to land; after three years of hosting a tobacco crop, soil is so depleted that nothing can be grown there for the next twenty. Tobacco (grown by indentured servants and slaves) was the single reason why the first English colony in America managed to survive, and with increasing numbers of white settlers requiring new swaths of land every three years to sustain the colonial economy, it's not a stretch to say that tobacco-motivated theft of native land was one of the major catalysts for the genocidal campaign against the indigenous people of this continent that continues to this day. This process continues around the world, as tobacco corporations constantly absorb new plots of land to feed the cravings of the millions of addicted around the world. To get this land, corporations steal it from public lands or indigenous tribes, "buy" it from peasants so impoverished by global capitalism that they have no choice but to sell it (so that they can be more easily forced into the new factories), or convert land that previously grew food crops that actually nourished rather than poisoned people.

In most nations in the global south, tobacco is flue-cured, a labor-intensive process that requires massive deforestation; one researcher estimated that tobacco cultivation and processing accounted for one of every eight trees cut down in underdeveloped countries. As more and more land becomes ecologically devastated from tobacco cultivation, the cycle accelerates, less and less land is available for food production, and more and more deadly chemicals and genetically engineered strains are required to grow anything. Tobacco companies offer subsidies and technical support to farmers in underdeveloped nations to switch from food to tobacco, and since IMF structural adjustment programs have decimated public support of agriculture, many farmers have no choice but to convert, accelerating hunger within their nation and increasing their dependence on the global capitalist market. Tobacco is at the heart of the horrifically pathological global system of capitalist agriculture that prioritizes the right of First World people to poison themselves over the right of Third World people to eat.

Intoxication In Oppressed Communities

Drugs and alcohol are used as colonial weapons against folks of African descent in the United States. Frederick Douglass pointed out in his slave narrative that on holidays, masters would encourage slaves to drink to excess specifically to skew their perceptions of what freedom was and to promote passivity the rest of the year. From absentee-owned liquor stores in black neighborhoods to the CIA's introduction of crack as a weapon against black communities, white people have profited from the economic drain, physical debilitation, and social conflict and violence exacerbated by alcohol and drugs in black communities. The black revolutionary tradition in the US has strong tendencies towards sobriety, from the Malcolm X to the Black Panthers to Dead Prez, drawing specific links between black oppression and intoxication culture.

When a slave was drunk, the slaveholder had no fear that he would plan an insurrection; no fear that he would escape to the North. It was the sober, thinking slave who was dangerous, and needed the vigilance of his master to keep him a slave. — Frederick Douglass

The native communities that survive in North America are almost all absolutely devastated by alcoholism. Alcohol abuse has severely disrupted what positive community structures have survived the European genocide. For the past several hundred years, alcohol was used by opportunistic whites as a way to con native people into signing "treaties" robbing them of their land, and as an intentional strategy of sowing discord into previously unified, harmonious, and sober communities. Currently, alcoholism is one of the leading causes of death among native people; around reservations that have prohibited alcohol, primarily white "drunk towns" have sprung up with dozens of bars and ABC stores just past the reservation borders to turn indigenous addiction into capitalist profit, often with fatal consequences.

Queer and trans communities struggle with astronomically high rates of alcoholism, due both to an attempt to escape the pressure of hiding their sexuality from family, friends, and society, and due to the emphasis on alcohol as a form of recreation throughout mainstream queer culture. Beer companies are among the largest sponsors of "Pride" celebrations and advertise extensively in queer publications; in most areas of the US, the primary social spaces for queer-friendly (or even queer-safe) interaction are bars whose primary function is selling intoxication. One of the first specifically gay and lesbian organizations in many towns is a chapter of Alcoholic Anonymous. Substance abuse rates among queers are also severe, as untold numbers of ravers and club queens burn out on cocaine, crystal meth, ecstasy, and other substances. The epidemics of AIDS and other STDs continue, in spite of the incredible efforts of educators and activists throughout the country, largely because of risky sex while intoxicated. For sober queers, virtually no physical or social space exists.

Intoxication and Radical Communities

The reluctance of "activist" or "anarchist" or "radical" communities to acknowledge how fucked up (pun intended) intoxication culture can be genuinely baffles me. Ever since I got involved in radical politics, these connections have seemed obvious to me, but the fact that so few people appeared to agree made me wonder whether perhaps I was the one who had it all wrong. Alcohol (ab)use, tobacco smoking, and varying degrees of drug use have been central institutions in the lives of the vast majority of the radical folks with whom I've worked. Only recently have I begun to make connections with other sober radicals apart from scattered acquaintances, and nearly all of us relate to the feelings of isolation within our communities, alienation from our peers, and frustration with the lack of support we feel for sober safe spaces.

Yet the fact that we're the few, the lonely, and the sober by no means indicates that we're the only ones who see or complain about the problems caused by intoxication culture's infiltration into radical communities. My individual conversations with many distinctly non-sober folks often reveal a genuine anxiety about the negative consequences of their personal and the scene's social dependence on drugs and alcohol. My personal experience and the experience of numerous women, people of color, and queer and trans people with whom I've discussed the issue confirms to me how hypocritical people can be who claim to be fighting oppression yet participate proudly in intoxication culture. More and more, this issue seems like the elephant in the corner that no one's willing to point out.

I think it's high time (ha ha) that our communities started meaningful dialogues around issues of sobriety and intoxication — and there are going to have to be non-sober allies who step up and take active roles alongside the substance-free folks for it to work. We need to be negotiating agreements for collective houses and spaces, social gatherings, shows and events, and other spaces in our lives that respect the needs of folks both sober and not, with a particular emphasis on respecting the requests of women and trans folks, whose needs are least frequently considered in developing community standards. This is not something that many of our communities are used to, but in my opinion it's absolutely essential. This process has the potential to be a revolutionary transformation, as we move away from a loosely associated group of people who work together to an actual community where we respect each others' needs and hold each other accountable.

Intoxication and "Autonomy" vs. Accountability

In the process of developing community agreements, some folks may feel that they're being denied their "autonomy," their right to live their own lives how they want, including the right to get fucked up if they so desire. Personally, I wholeheartedly support the right of any individual to fuck themselves up with chemicals as much as they want to, without sanction from the state, organized religion, or self-righteous zine writers. However, I only support that right so long as you contain the destructiveness of your choices to yourself; as someone wise once said, "Your right to swing your fist ends where my nose begins." And I'd argue that very few people who do choose to get fucked up honestly and completely look at how their choices to do so impact others, particularly oppressed folks.

From the financial support of really fucked up corporations, to the targeting of people of color and queer communities and the increased rates of addiction and devastation in these communities, to the relationship between intoxication and patriarchal masculinity, to the fucked up behavior towards women that so often arises with intoxication… it's NOT just a simple personal choice you make yourself, in a bubble, to smoke or drink or take drugs. There's an incredible amount of baggage that goes along with the decision to get fucked up that activist communities, in my experience, rarely acknowledge.

Some anarchists see anarchy as the ability to do whatever they want without having to be accountable to anyone else for their actions. I personally think that that kind of attitude is just the standard American "rugged individualism" bullshit repackaged as a faux-radical alternative, because it doesn't challenge the fundamental alienation from each other we suffer under capitalism and the state. If our society replaces genuine community with consumer culture, authority, and oppression, that kind of anarchism simply rejects any idea of community at all. For me, anarchism is about replacing the false community of the state and consumer culture with a community based on mutual aid rather than competition, gift economy rather than capitalism, and collective agreements based on full consent and voluntary association rather than rules or laws based on state coercion and violence. Instead of being accountable to authority, I want us to actually be accountable to each other. A pretty important part of that is being able to come together as radical communities and have conversations about how alcohol and drugs impact our work, our spaces, our relationships, and our unity, and to figure out what sorts of agreements and boundaries make sense for us.

As a perfect example of the kind of community-based response to alcohol and drugs I'm talking about, look at the Zapatista movement in southern Mexico. During the weeks I spent in Chiapas learning about their struggle, I learned something that most of the kids in the Subcommandante Marcos t-shirts don't mention: all autonomous Zapatista communities are 100 percent alcohol free. No alcoholic beverages are sold or consumed in any of the autonomous municipalities, and on the signs indicating that you are entering Zapatista territory in rebellion against the Mexican government, many specifically say that these are alcohol and drug free spaces. I learned also that the reason for this is because it was a central demand of the women involved in discussion about the new society they were building. Mexican women feel most acutely the effects of alcoholism, in terms of domestic and sexual abuse, and because being financially dependent on men in a patriarchal society means that when husbands spend the family's money on booze, the wife has to struggle to pay for food for her and her children. The director of a feminist collective in San Cristóbal with whom I spoke said that male alcohol abuse is one of the central problems facing women in Mexico today.

Consequently, the communities agreed to the demand of the women for drug and alcohol free communities, in spite of the fact that many of the men wanted to be able to drink. Some villages even split around this issue. Currently, the no-alcohol agreement is enforced by the community, and it is almost always respected; folks who refuse to respect the prohibition are ostracized or, if they refuse to change their behavior, face expulsion from the community (incidentally, it's almost unheard of for it to reach that point). A traveler I met who had passed through Guatemala and parts of southern Mexico on his way to Chiapas mentioned that in most of the rural villages he'd passed through, the majority of the men would be drunk by 10 AM, every day. The Zapatista communities, he observed, had a completely different vibe; people got far more done and treated each other with more respect.

I mention this example for a number of reasons. For one, I think that many anarchaholics who supposedly idolize the Zapatista struggle could stand to learn about how those communities deal with alcohol and drugs. Also, I suspect that a lot of North American anarcho folks might find such a prohibition "authoritarian" or worse. This gets at the heart of how I see the difference between hyper-individualist and community-based anarchism. There's nothing authoritarian, in my opinion, about an agreement reached collectively to abstain from individual behaviors that the community collectively decides are harmful to itself as a whole. The key to the Zapatista autonomous project is that it's totally based on voluntary association; no community or individual is forced to participate. Many villages have chosen not to be an official part of the network of autonomous municipalities if they don't consent to all of the agreements made by the Zapatista movement, and that's fine.

Furthermore, the Zapatista agreements on alcohol are an example of actually acknowledging and directly respecting the autonomy of women. How many anarchist groups or communities in the US who claim to be feminist have actually adopted the desires and needs of women into their practice — or even bothered to ask? All in all, the people involved in that struggle decided to place the good of their community, as determined through consensus, above the unlimited "freedom" of individuals to do as they please. I would challenge our anarchist communities in the north to think critically about our priorities and grapple with these difficult questions about individual and community, autonomy and accountability.

Story #1

My primary activist community when I first moved to the town where I now live operated out of a collective bookstore, an awesome space full of radicals working on positive projects. Just a month or two after I'd become very involved, I was invited to attend a retreat with the board of directors at a beach house several hours away from where we lived. I'd heard people joking about how much alcoholic fun they were going to have there, which immediately made me feel unsafe. The facts that I don't drive and would have no way to get away if I felt unsafe, didn't know many of the people involved very well yet, and was the only young person all made me very nervous about the situation, and I expressed my misgivings to a friend who worked at the store. She assured me that there wouldn't be much alcohol, that people wouldn't be getting too drunk, and that if I felt unsafe she would be available for me. With that assurance, I somewhat reluctantly came along.

On Saturday night, two people left to get alcohol, returning with four cases of beer and several bottles of liquor. Everyone except for me was an adult and everyone except for me drank pretty heavily that night, including my friend who said that she would be available for me. I felt very uncomfortable, but I didn't have any way to leave, any idea where I was, or any alternatives for entertainment, so I just sat through it. The next morning we got started with our work hours later than we'd planned to because folks were hung over and wanted to sleep. When we debriefed at the end of the retreat, I mentioned that one thing I would have changed was to have less alcohol, but I didn't feel comfortable enough to express how seriously I felt alienated and unsafe, or ask for ways to hold the group accountable next time. No one discussed it further or followed up with me about my discomfort. I don't know how to breach the subject without putting people on the defensive, and I feel like I'm being selfish, whiny, hypersensitive, a "party pooper," or anti-democratic by expressing how I feel about it. I don't necessarily think that it would be fair to ask the group to completely ban alcohol at the retreat, especially given that every single person but me of a group of fifteen or so enjoys drinking, yet the only alternative seems to be the default of me faking smiles and sitting uncomfortably through situations that make me feel unsafe and alone.

One way to address such a situation for sober folks to feel safe and able to still participate might be to ensure in advance that at least one or two other people will be there who will commit to stay sober for the night (whether or not they usually do). That way, the group could still drink if they chose to do so, while the sober person can still have a way to feel safe with someone, or leave if necessary and not feel totally isolated. I would suggest finding someone you trust a lot and know will be committed to an evening of sobriety, and to be sure to ask them to commit in advance, so that they haven't built intoxication into their expectations for the activity. Other possibilities include asking all of the people involved to make it an alcohol-free occasion, particularly if it's a small group or event, or simply declining to attend and making clear that the presence of drugs and alcohol is the reason why you're not coming. Whatever you decide, it will probably work best to calmly and specifically explain your discomfort, and to take care not to judge or make assumptions about other people's behavior. If people committed to sobriety stop making excuses, staying home, or remaining silent when they feel unsafe, hopefully we can start a dialogue about issues of intoxication in activist communities that will help create social space for substance-free folks.

Story #2

I attended an environmental defense action camp for a week with about 150 kids in the mountains. I was pretty nervous about going out there with no way to get out of the situation and a big crew of rowdy booze-loving primitivists, but I decided it was more important to go and to learn the skills I could learn. Things went surprisingly well for most of the week; half way through there was an alcohol-light campfire sing-along that was a blast. On the last night, there was a big party planned, with all sorts of preparations made for multiple kegs and beer runs and home brew and more. Amazingly, the organizers were really concerned with ensuring that the folks who wanted to remain sober had a safe space, and planned to make a clear community agreement in advance with specific dry zones, etc. The full-group meeting broke off for dinner before the conversation could take place, so a group of fifteen or so folks interested in seeing that sober spaces were secured stayed late and talked through options; even more amazingly, almost all of the group were folks who were planning to drink, but wanted to be allies to the sober folks. After a frustrating and long set of negotiations, a separate campfire area that was to be not only alcohol free, but only for folks who had not had any alcohol that night, was set up, with individuals committing to gather wood and dig the pit. I was pretty thrilled, having never before been in a space where people even acknowledged that sober people had valid needs, let alone worked hard to create a distinct safe space and make it a priority.

So I hung out that evening at the sober campfire... along with about five or six others. We were a pretty low-key bunch, and I for one felt distinctly glum. It was nice to have the company, but I couldn't shake the feeling of being quarantined. We were only a few hundred yards away from the massive drunken bonfire, with over a hundred kids hollering and stomping about, though none of them could come to our fire, and most of us didn't feel remotely comfortable going over to theirs, even though most of our friends and crushes and lovers were over there. After thirty or forty-five minutes, most of us had drifted off to our tents, the screams of the revelers echoing in our ears. I sat morosely by the dwindling embers for a long while, trying to figure out why I felt so dejected. Isn't this what I wanted, our own separate "safe space"? I felt guilty for not sufficiently appreciating what was undoubtedly the most comprehensive effort to address my needs that had ever been made in a radical space. Finally, as the main party in the distance tailed off into isolated voices fighting and cursing or sobbing, I ambled off to bed, feeling as lonely and isolated as ever.

That experience represented a mixture of positives and negatives, and could point towards some constructive solutions. On the plus side, organizers and participants (at least a number of them) did make a substantial effort during the day to plan a sober alternative space that would be safe; on the minus side, the larger group wasn't engaged in that process, and most folks in fact were simply informed that if they planned to drink, they weren't permitted to go in a certain area, reinforcing the absolute sober/not dichotomy which felt isolating to me. On the plus side, many non-sober allies stepped up to make sure that safe spaces were provided, which I think is crucially important; on the minus side, the allies didn't extend their support into actually participating with the sober folks and abstaining themselves, except for one person, and not many of the sober folks for whom the space was being designed actually participated in its planning. On the plus side, the space was created and respected; on the minus side, there were hardly any folks there, and it wasn't much fun, though everyone agreed they were glad it was there. The proximity to the "main" drunken party, the severely disproportionate number of non-sober to sober folks, the lack of actual activities beyond a space and a campfire, the feeling of being quarantined, and the general lack of support among many camp participants (excepting the organizers and wonderful allies) made the reality of the sober space fall far short of the expectations.

To improve the situation in the future, a few things that could be changed:

1. Ensure broader participation in the process of making sober-safe spaces; make it a part of full-group discussion, make a caucus of the folks who actually plan to stay sober a central part of the process, and figure out so me mechanism for accountability to that caucus.

2. When circumstances permit, make the actual space far enough away physically from the drunken ground zero so that it doesn't feel like we're being pushed just outside the "real" fun, and we don't feel the need to defend the territory as our only few square feet of safe space.

3. Plan not just spaces, but activities for sober folks — be creative and flexible, whatever folks think could be interesting and outrageous. Spin the bottle, treasure hunts, hide and seek, twister, bike scavenger hunts, dance parties, anything! The idea is not only to make it more fun for the sober folks, but to make an incentive for some of the not-always-sober folks to commit to being sober for the evening so that they can hang out with the fun group. This can be the best kind of substance-free advocacy — showing that the sober kids can party hardy even better than the drunks!

Conclusion: The Beginning?

Hopefully some of the ideas in this zine have been helpful, or provocative, or maybe showed things in a different light, or gave you some starting points for addressing the concerns of sober folks in your communities. I wouldn't expect most folks to accept or agree with everything I've written, but with luck it'll open a few minds and hearts and start some debates. Also, some of us are thinking towards developing a sober support network to share resources, develop propaganda, start conversations in our communities, identify safe spaces, and support each other when we feel isolated. It's a long way towards a less fucked up world, but with honesty, dialogue, and each other's support we can begin heading that way. Until then,

with love and rage,

Nick Riotfag

Afterword:
Towards a Less Fucked Up World: Five Years and Counting

In the five years since I originally released the zine *Towards a Less Fucked Up World: Sobriety and Anarchist Struggle*, I've had hundreds of conversations with people who read the zine and felt moved by it in one way or another. When I wrote and published it, I never would have expected it to resonate with such a wide range of folks. But the fact that it has shows me that there's a tremendous desire to confront the realities of substance use and intoxication in radical communities. In this short essay I'll talk a bit about how the zine came together and how folks have responded to it, and frame this in the context of other discussions about radical sobriety that have taken place in punk/anarchist spaces. Hopefully tracing this trajectory will provide some context for the potential for radical sobriety within US anarchist resistance through the lens of one zine and its reception.

How it came together

The ideas that eventually coalesced into *Towards a Less Fucked Up World* began to take form when I was seventeen or eighteen and became increasingly involved in broader currents of radical and anarchist activity. Attending conferences, gatherings, mass mobilizations, and countless shows and potlucks, I began to notice patterns of drug and alcohol use that often reinforced rather than challenged oppression. My personal decision to remain drug and alcohol-free crystallized along with my politics; the more certain I felt about circling my "A"s, the more confident I felt in my sobriety. But to my surprise and frustration, my comrades in struggle rarely saw things the same way. The question that always perplexed me most was this: why don't radical folks ask the same kinds of critical and self-critical questions about our alcohol and drug use that we ask about so many other aspects of our lives and behavior? What's so different about intoxication, to the degree where just mentioning it can provoke such intense defensiveness, dismissal, or ridicule?

Coming to understand these reactions meant grappling with the impact of sXe amongst punks, anarchists, and radicals in the US. When I was growing up, I only knew a single self-identified sXe kid. He was a pretty homophobic jerk while he claimed edge, then after about a year washed the X's off his hands and started getting wasted with the rest of the punks. So apart from my interaction with a single (thoroughly unimpressive) sXer, I was never connected to or even aware of sXe

Afterword: Five Years and Counting // **Nick Riotfag**

as a scene or movement — I never even knew there was such a thing as sXe music until I was probably nineteen! I'd only heard the term used as a synonym for sober.

Then as I became more involved in punk and anarchist circles, I started hearing the horror stories about sXe kids who harassed or beat up drinkers or drug users, played out hardcore masculinity to its idiotic extreme, and displayed incredibly judgmental and obnoxious attitudes. When confronted with my decision to be intentionally sober, many people I met lacked any context for a conscious radical sobriety. To them sobriety was solely connected to a violent, cult-like hardcore identity. As I confronted the reputation that sXe had acquired amongst many radicals and anarchists, little by little the defensiveness I encountered became more understandable.

But as I started meeting actual sXe hardcore kids, most of whom were invariably friendly and respectful, I began to doubt how true all the stories were. Were defensive drinkers just creating a sXe straw man onto whom they could project all of their nightmare fantasies of crazed puritanical anti-drug boneheads? Was their emphasis on the myth of the violently judgmental sXe kid really just a means of avoiding a critical look at their own intoxication habits and how they impacted our scene? While I certainly don't deny that some folks have had negative experiences with individual sXe kids, they can't possibly outweigh the innumerable negative experiences all of us have had with the obnoxiously intoxicated.

At the same time, I wondered whether I was starting to embody some of those projected qualities. When I discussed my choices with others, was I conveying them in a way that came across as judgmental, preachy, or confrontational? By labeling my decision to be entirely sober for political as well as personal reasons with the term "sXe," was I placing myself in a trajectory guaranteed to promote defensiveness? Was I shutting down dialogue rather than opening it up?

Although the solidarity I discovered with other individuals who claimed edge provided some sense of support, more often than not I found that using the term to describe myself made it harder rather than easier to connect with the people with whom I really wanted to discuss issues of intoxication culture. As discussion with drinkers and drug users about how to negotiate healthy and mutually respectful community norms became increasingly important to me, I found myself shying away from the sXe label. But I wanted to convey that my sobriety stemmed from my convictions as an anarchist and a feminist, not just from an individual preference, yet without the having to rely on the problematic legacy of sXe to do so.

So I wrote *Towards a Less Fucked Up World* in an effort to pry the discussion about sobriety and intoxication away from the context of sXe and the mythology surrounding it. I wanted to discuss sobriety as a politically motivated lifestyle choice, not simply as a personal preference without collective or political dimensions, while also avoiding making it into an identity or a scene or a polarizing or moralistic thing.

It turned out to be more difficult than I'd expected! Fortunately, the responses I got to the zine showed that most people who read it were able to see past the controversy around sXe to the underlying issues I wanted to address.

Responses and critiques

The most common response I've received from readers has been a feeling of affirmation: folks related that the arguments and stories in the zine resonated with their own thoughts and experiences in ways they'd never heard articulated before. This surprised me on two levels: first, that so many people were thinking about the same issues and feeling similar frustration and alienation; and also that there were so few other people talking or writing about it. Another surprise: most people who've written me about my zine aren't totally sober themselves, but still felt that the zine spoke to them and their experiences. Certainly a number of sober/sXe folks have appreciated its ideas and used it for outreach; but by far and away the majority of the folks who wrote me did so not from that perspective, but from looking critically at their own intoxication and the culture supporting it. In addition to folks from within the young punk/anarchist/activist milieu, I've also gotten mail from mainstream college kids, lonely small-town teenagers, older alcoholics in recovery, and a variety of other folks.

The most vigorous and spot-on critiques I heard dealt with the section I wrote about intoxication and patriarchal masculinity. The section that now appears as "Masculinity, Rape Culture, and Intoxication" looked very different in the initial edition; it contained language that framed sexual and partner violence in simplistic and inaccurately gender-specific terms, represented sex workers in a disrespectful way, and didn't offer any trigger warning to brace folks for my rather abrasive discussion of sensitive issues. After a variety of conversations about the flaws of the original section, I began circulating an insert that addressed the critiques and reworked the section with the zine as I continued to distribute it. The section as it appears in this anthology represents substantial revisions that came out of many difficult and important conversations, to whose initiators I gratefully owe a much more nuanced critique of the connections between intoxication, masculinity, and violence.

Some other miscellaneous critiques: several people suggested that I could have spoken in more depth about the importance of sober spaces for people in recovery from addiction, and about harm reduction ideas and radical recovery models. Some wanted me to elaborate more on how to create sober spaces that weren't just quarantines but could effectively integrate drinkers and non-drinkers into fun alcohol-free environments; they also suggested avoiding the term "safe space" since it implies a fear of drinking rather than an aversion, which polarizes people more than necessary. Others wanted more acknowledgement of home brewing and growing as alternatives to capitalist control of addiction. A few countered my historical examples about sobriety in radical movements by mentioning the ways that intoxication has played into histories of resistance, from drunken workers riots to drug use in 1960s counterculture. Some found my treatment of drinkers and drug users far too judgmental and unlikely to stimulate the kind of dialogue and self-reflection necessary to break out of patterns of denial, blame, and judgment. All of these comments and others I appreciated and thought over; some are reflected in changes in this edition, others I hope to incorporate into future issues of the zine, and a few I decided to leave unchanged with the recognition that the arguments and tone are provocative, intentionally so, and will always provoke criticism.

Fortunately, the zine has provoked much more than criticism — it's inspired dialogue and action, too, as I've heard in stories from people around the US and beyond. In Maine, a group of punks copied and distributed the zine and then hosted a sober potluck to discuss the issues it raised and how they related to the local scene. One group of Canadian anarchists altered the direction of the community radical library and show space they were establishing after reading the zine, deciding to promote the space as an explicitly sober social alternative for radicals. In North Carolina, one reader started a weekly sobriety discussion group at a radical community space. Every other week, the meeting was open to anyone and discussion revolved around the role of intoxication in their town's radical scene and how to create alternative spaces; on the alternate weeks there was a closed meeting for folks in recovery from addiction who wanted to support one another from an explicitly radical perspective. These and a variety of other inspiring stories have convinced me that radicals long to challenge the role of intoxication culture in communities of struggle.

The future of radical sobriety

In the last few years I've also observed shifts in anarchist culture towards breaking the stranglehold of intoxication culture in our scenes — in zines, workshops, discussions, and many other formats, we've spoken out about our complex experiences with drugs, alcohol, addiction, and sobriety individually and collectively.

Since the release of *Towards a Less Fucked Up World*, a variety of zines have emerged in the US addressing different aspects of intoxication, sobriety, and resistance: the following are just some of the ones I've read and enjoyed. *Prescription for Change* offers a personal account of a recovering addict, insightful critiques of the AA model, and a nuanced outsider's take on sXe. *Distress* #1-2 offers crucial harm reduction info and analyses of how intoxication relates to mental health. *Out from the Shadows* #1-2 (successor to *Encuentro* zine) blends a militant vegan sXe and green anarchist perspective on radical sobriety with a passionate love for sXe hardcore, and links struggles against intoxication culture with resistance to civilization. *Stash* describes personal stories of addiction and recovery as well as domestic and sexual violence while discussing the radical community's role in perpetuating or challenging these dynamics. *Twinkle Pig* #3.5 traces one sXer's personal history of exclusion, self-redefinition, and political critiques of intoxication culture. *Total Destruction* #1-4 focuses on anarcho-communist theory, prisoner solidarity, and eco-resistance, from a vegan sXe perspective. *Cuddle Puddles* #1-3 presents a vegan sXe anarchist standpoint on a variety of political and lifestyle issues — #1 addresses the continuing value of sXe. *Ruffsketch* humorously chronicles the animal rights activism and cross-country travels of a vegan sXe hooligan. These and many other zines document the groundswell of thought and action taking place in radical scenes around intoxication and sobriety.

This explosion of discussion of radical sobriety in print has continued face to face at radical gatherings. My first such experience took place just after the publication of *Towards a Less Fucked Up World* in early 2004, at the National Conference on Organized Resistance in Washington, DC, a large yearly anti-authoritarian conference. I presented with three friends a workshop titled "Beyond a Culture of Oblivion" that discussed the potential of radical sobriety contributing to anarchist resistance. To our surprise, the workshop was packed out the door, with well over 100 people attempting to squeeze into a tightly cramped classroom, demonstrating the widespread desire for dialogue around intoxication in radical communities. We presented some basic critiques of intoxication, framed by stories from our experience, discussed the role of sobriety and sober individuals in various radical movements from different times and places, and tried our best to facilitate a discussion about the impact that drug and alcohol use had on the different communities of struggle represented by the folks present. The room included everyone from cranky sXers with "Fuck You for Smoking" hoodies to intransigent drinkers and drug users who defended their choices vehemently, and at times antagonism surfaced. But overall, most participants seemed grateful just to have a space to openly vent their frustrations with both the stranglehold of intoxication culture on their scenes as well as the inadequacy of judgmental, cliquish sXe scenes as viable alternatives. We distributed copies of *Wasted Indeed!* and *Towards a Less Fucked Up World*, and encouraged folks to continue the conversation in their scenes at home. Ultimately, we were surprised by how successfully the workshop had gone and encouraged by the enthusiasm for addressing the issues constructively.

Since then, workshops and discussions about intoxication and sobriety have popped up with increasing frequency at radical gatherings. Folks came together to discuss these issues at events ranging from the Richmond Zine Fair to the CrimethInc. Convergence, from the C.L.I.T. Fest (a feminist punk festival) to the Earth First! rendezvous, and numerous others. I personally helped facilitate workshops at two radical queer/trans gatherings, the Florida United Queers and Trannies conference and the Sweaty Southern Radical Queer and Trans Convergence in North Carolina; the latter operated as an entirely sober gathering, the first queer/trans-specific conference I'd ever heard of doing so, and to our surprise the organizers received almost total support from the participants in respecting the drug/alcohol-free agreement. More and more gatherings create sober spaces for folks who want or need them, encouraging drug- and alcohol-free social events, and including discussions of substance use in broader guidelines around consent and respect. This represents a subtle but important shift in radical culture towards challenging the entrenchment of intoxication culture and opening up space for radical sobriety without imposing it top-down as a norm.

Interestingly, most of these discussions and spaces of which I've been a part haven't used sXe as the primary framework for conceptualizing the choice to be sober. In fact, many folks said things like "I'm not sXe, but…" to describe their choices to be sober or critical of intoxication culture, which indicates the negative associations many US punks and anarchists still hold with sXe. I think it's premature to sound the death knell of sXe, or start talking about "post-edge" radical sobriety — I think this anthology makes clear that sXe still holds power and relevance for a lot of people around the world. But clearly we should embrace a variety of different possible ways to forge radically sober identities, including sXe but not limited by it. In my opinion, whatever one's relationship to the phenomenon of sXe may be, the underlying critiques and positive alternative visions remain as relevant today as they were during the days of Minor Threat. I hope that my zine, this anthology, and all of the conversations that come from them will help us find the tools we need to fight oppression and domination culture tooth and nail while never failing to love and support each other along the way.

Reflections

- **My Edge Is Anything But Straight: Towards a Radical Queer Critique of Intoxication Culture**
  Nick Riotfag

- **"The Only Thing I'm Drunk on Is Cock" (Interview)**
  Lucas

- **Emancypunx (Interview)**
  Jenni Ramme

- **xsisterhoodx (Interview)**
  Kelly (Brother) Leonard

- **When the Edge Turns Crust (Interview)**
  Bull Gervasi

- **Straight Edge, Anarcho-Primitivism, and the Collapse (Interview)**
  Andy Hurley

My Edge Is Anything But Straight:
Towards a Radical Queer Critique of Intoxication Culture
Nick Riotfag

Nick Riotfag is an anarchist, queer, and straight edge activist/writer who lives in North Carolina. He is the author of "Towards a Less Fucked Up World: Sobriety and Anarchist Struggle," also included in this volume.

I've been intentionally sober ever since I first started going to punk shows when I was fourteen or fifteen, and have always thought about my sobriety not just as a personal preference but as a social and political statement. I've always felt ambivalent towards sXe identity, though, a major reason being that I also identify strongly as queer. It's not that I think the two identities are necessarily incompatible, but they seem to have an uncomfortable relationship. On the one hand, I haven't felt much space to be my queer self in most punk/hardcore scenes, and the hyper-masculine reputation of sXe definitely turns me off. On the other hand, I've faced a lot of exclusion within queer scenes for my sobriety. With this article I'm attempting to reconcile these parts of myself, wondering how I might hold on to the edge while leaving behind the straight. I hope that it will provoke conversation and debate about drugs, alcohol, queer communities, sXe, radical politics, and about how we can transform our society.

Is sXe sexy? Straightedge, sexuality, and queer identity

"Life's full of conflicts, we'll face / We'll overcome them, thinking straight"
-Youth of Today, "Thinking Straight"

"The song [Out of Step], really, it resonated with a lot of people... Because I think there were a lot of punk rockers who were straight, and who felt like, finally, here is someone who's straight..."
-Ian MacKaye

The initial "formula" laid out by Minor Threat in their song "Out of Step" — "don't drink / don't smoke / don't fuck / at least I can fuck-

Seeing how this story is going to end, run away to another story.

ing think" — adds sex to drug use and drinking as one of the things that hold kids back from being "straight." As a response to negative trends observed in the punk scene, the song certainly made an important critique by calling out careless and conquest-oriented sexual exploits — often while wasted — as a destructive pattern that brought nothing positive to its participants and served as just another distraction from the deluded bullshit mainstream reality that political punks ought to be actively resisting rather than just mindlessly perpetuating. To be fair, Ian MacKaye has stated clearly that he never intended his message from "Out of Step" to become another dogma to mindlessly follow — to hear it as such would be completely missing the point. Nonetheless, because of the song's huge influence on what became the sXe scene, it's useful to look critically at those lines and to understand how they relate to queer people.[1] For one, our sexual desires definitely prevent us from being "straight" in a very different sense; a kind of straight that many of us, trapped by self-hatred, desperately want to attain. For queer people attempting to break the shackles of internalized homophobia and shame about our sexuality, any framework that positions sex as something to struggle against is not likely to lead us towards liberation. And of course the unfortunate wording of "straight" edge hardly appeals to queer people right off the bat.

Of the three parts of the Out of Step formula, sexual abstinence or restraint has definitely figured far less prominently in most sXer's self-conceptions than abstaining from drugs and alcohol. For the sXers I personally know, sexual ethics have little to do with their sXe identity. From what I've read about other sXe people and scenes, many of the folks who associate sexual restriction with sXe are either Christian or Hare Krishna sXers whose decision to abstain from sex until heterosexual marriage has more to do with God than edge. There are also some who see the sXe contribution to sexual ethics as one of moderation, self-discipline, "waiting for someone special," and chivalrous concepts of hetero masculinity revolving around defending women from the abuses of male heterosexual promiscuity. That's all fine and good, but I have a hard time understanding what directly connects those sexual ethics to abstention from drugs and alcohol; besides, every testimony I've heard or read describes an exclusively

---

1. A note about words: I use "gay" and "queer" more or less interchangeably in this essay. By "gay" I mean people (men or women, though sometimes with a gay male connotation) who experience primarily or exclusively same-sex desire. By "queer" I'm generally referring to people with dissident sexualities for whom same-sex desire forms a significant part of their experience (including gay, bisexual, pansexual, and other same-gender-loving identities). I use "queer communities" in the plural to acknowledge that there are many different ones; we're not homogenous, we don't all identify with each other, and we can't be made into a single entity. By "homophobia" I mean hatred and fear of queer people by individuals and groups; by "heterosexism" I mean the systematic oppression of queer people rooted in institutions.

heterosexual experience. For me, I know that I couldn't get married to my lover even if I thought marriage wasn't bullshit (which I do). And gender-based models of protection don't translate too well to my experience as a man having sex with men. The particular types of pressure that lead to the kinds of heterosexual activity criticized by some sXe bands bear little relation to the types of intense internalized shame impacting queer sex and intoxication. Gay male sexual culture embraces so-called "casual" or promiscuous sex for a variety of reasons, many problematic and others more politically conscious, but all different from the context of heterosexual conquest that MacKaye and other sXers criticized.

Basically, sXe sexual ethics weren't intended for queer people, straight up. But is sXe homophobic? Of course, some elements of so-called hardline sXe incorporated explicitly homophobic conceptions of sexuality and "natural law" into their ideologies. For example, the "Hardline Manifesto" that came with a Vegan Reich 7-inch single read: "Adherents to the hardline... shall live at one with the laws of nature, and not forsake them for the desire of pleasure — from deviant sexual acts and/or abortion." There is also plenty of anecdotal evidence suggesting that many hardcore scenes, sXe or not, are actively hostile to queer people: every queer sXer I've spoken to has experienced some kind of harassment or shit-talking in their scene. In their song "I Wanna Be A Homosexual," Screeching Weasel (not a sXe band!) pokes fun at homophobia in the sXe scene: "Call me a butt loving fudge packing queer / I don't care cause it's the straight in straight edge / That makes me wanna drink a beer." Some sXe bands such as Slapshot used AIDS as an example of how the lack of discipline associated with not "living straight" could lead to one's downfall. On the other hand, a number of well-known bands including Outspoken and Good Clean Fun made an effort to counter the homophobic elements of hardline sXe by speaking out in favor of gay rights at shows or in lyrics and liner notes. None less than Earth Crisis, toughest of the militant sXe bands, criticized anti-gay laws and violence in their 1996 album *Gomorrah's Season Ends*. They declared that sXe should be a weapon against homophobia and that it is necessary...

> *To demonstrate to heterosexuals that gayness is natural and beautiful and that it is not a threat to their existence. To make being openly gay safe and to make the pain of the closet part of a mythical past...*

These statements are certainly positive in challenging homophobic norms. But the way they're phrased indicate that they are a response to a widespread problem within the sXe scene. Furthermore, they are clearly intended more as messages from straights to straights than an acknowledgement of queer kids in the scene. sXe scenes have never made space for queers in any consistent way, so it's no wonder that so few of us have embraced sXe as a framework for critiquing intoxication culture.[2] This is especially understandable since alcohol and drug use impact queer communities differently from punk and hardcore scenes. So let's step out of the pit for a moment and take some time to explore the ways in which intoxication culture plays out in queer culture.

Alcohol use in queer communities[3]

The reason why alcohol plays such a central role in the lives of many queer people is simple: we need to meet each other, it's not safe to meet each other in most places, and the places where we can meet almost all center around alcohol. Depending on where we live and how open we are about ourselves, most queer people in the US will face some combination of the following responses to our sexuality: physical harassment and attacks; hostility, mockery, and bullying in schools; loss of jobs and housing; rejection by family and religious communities; no access to relevant and sensitive health care and other services; refusal to recognize our relationships; lack of positive role models; indifference to our needs by authorities; exclusion from innumerable traditions, rituals, norms, and other major and subtle aspects of social life. In this atmosphere, combating isolation by meeting one another is absolutely crucial, often a matter of life or death; if sober spaces don't exist, we have to find each other where we can. The oppressive social context we live in frequently results in feelings of depression, anxiety, loneliness, shame, and self-hatred, many of which we grapple with our entire lives. It's not hard to understand why many of us turn to intoxication in an effort to alleviate these intense negative emotions.

Nearly all of the major institutions of queer life in the US include alcohol consumption: bars, discos, clubs, bathhouses, drag shows, most film festivals and Pride parades, Radical Faerie and other rural gatherings... the list goes on and on. In nearly all of these spaces, alcohol provides an essential element of the socializing, the means

---

2. By "intoxication culture," I mean the entire set of institutions and behaviors that establish alcohol drinking and drug use as community norms. The term assumes that people's decisions on whether or how much to drink or use are based not just on their individual preferences but also on our collective context of norms around intoxication and community structures that uphold them. I also want to emphasize that an individual's decision around whether and how to drink or use is not a neutral personal choice but has community-wide implications. Within this framework, use and abuse are mutually reinforcing patterns, each equally necessary to maintain the status quo.

3. My experience as a queer guy frames my understanding of alcohol and drug use in queer communities, so my discussion is weighted towards the experiences of gay, bi, and queer men. Lesbian culture differs significantly from gay/bi male culture in terms of social and sexual norms; it is also shaped by sexist oppression. These factors each change queer women's relationships to substance use. I also don't intend this article to generalize the experiences of transgender folks of various sexual orientations, since I neither identify as transgender nor do I understand all of the ways that gender identity and transphobia specifically impact substance use.

through which we relax, come together, and build connections of friendship, romance, and sex. Apart from gay or lesbian AA meetings, very few sober spaces exist for queer people to meet each other. There are a few urban community centers; some gyms; youth groups,[4] in areas lucky enough to have them; political meetings; occasionally coffee shops or game nights — generally all low-key settings distinctly apart from the most popular and widespread nodes of queer social life. I know of an older gay man who struggled with severe alcoholism and entered AA in an attempt to regain control of his life. However, after feeling the painful loss of social affirmation and sexual possibility that resulted from staying away from the bars and parties, he decided that the disconnection from his community was too high a price to pay for sobriety and resumed drinking.

Another part of the reason why alcohol holds such a central role in queer life is because it was the first commodity ever sold to queer people *as* queer people. In seedy, often Mafia-controlled bars, we found the first sellers willing to acknowledge us economically as a market, and thus socially as a people. The role of alcohol as the glue of gay identity originated during days of severe repression and invisibility, yet remains stubbornly persistent today as a primary linking feature of queer life. Long before the days of lesbian cruise lines and rainbow flag bumper stickers, our only link to one another economically was through alcohol, and to this day no other product cements our group identity as cohesively. As the gay liberation struggle increasingly abandoned its radical roots in the 1970s and shifted towards a more single issue gay rights approach, our collective ability to be targeted as a consumer market somehow became conflated with liberation. Ironically, gay participation in the consumer boycott of Coors beer, coordinated by gay politician Harvey Milk in mid/late 1970s San Francisco, demonstrated one of the first successful collective examples of gay consumer power when the company was forced to drop some of their discriminatory anti-gay hiring practices. Nowadays, although Coors is still a major funding force for right-wing and conservative causes, they advertise heavily in gay publications such as *The Advocate*, and they sponsor Pride festivals and LGBT lobbying groups. Is this progress?

No matter how much the alcohol companies may want us to believe that the fact that they advertise in our magazines shows the social progress we've been making,

---

4. The absence of alcohol-free spaces weighs even more heavily on queer youth, who are legally excluded from most of the few venues available for us to meet outside of major cities. Since we're not allowed into most queer spaces until we're eighteen or twenty-one, many of us suffer our most intense isolation during the volatile coming-out years when we most desperately need community support and affirmation. This isolation fuels the astronomical levels of alcohol and drug use among queer youth, patterns which are often solidly in place by the time that we're legally allowed to participate in some aspects of intoxication culture. When we finally obtain access to the mysterious world of the bars and clubs, we more often than not abandon the spaces we've carved out for ourselves with other youth to soak up these new worlds and the possibilities they present.

they themselves know better. They know that so long as we hate ourselves, so long as we feel crippling shame about our desires and identities, we'll keep on drinking whatever they give us to numb these feelings that we can't escape. So long as queer sex feels frightening and shameful we'll need a haze of intoxication to be able to unleash our deepest desires. These corporations have a financial interest in our continued degradation, because they know that if we actually loved ourselves — and one another — without shame, we might not need their anesthesia anymore. With alcohol in queer communities, use and abuse aren't distinct opposites but two sides of the same coin, a coin that goes into the pockets of the alcohol companies. Only when we can imagine ways to connect personally, socially and sexually without relying on alcohol will we move towards liberation.

Sex, intoxication, and internalized homophobia

One of the primary reasons why queer people drink and take drugs is to have sex. Of course, this isn't unique to queer folks — plenty of straight folks can't get confident or relaxed enough to have sex while sober. But it takes on particular significance for queer people in the context of homophobic oppression. From as early as I can remember, queer sex was associated with deviance, disease, sin, ridicule, fear, and shame. As men, we're often told that our desires are disgusting and unnatural; queer women are often told that their sex isn't real or meaningful, except as a fantasy for leering straight men. Until just a few years ago in the US, queer sex was illegal in many states, and there are still hardly any of us who receive useful queer-positive sex education from schools, churches, or parents.

Some of my queer friends have pointed out that if they hadn't been intoxicated during their first same-sex sexual experiences, they likely never would have been able to go through with it. I can't deny that if I hadn't already been sXe when I first became sexually active with men, intoxication might have helped me overcome some of the confusion and shame that racked my early same-sex sexual experiences. But does this mean that alcohol is a sexually liberatory force for queer people? In my opinion, no — our dependence on it merely confirms the extent to which we've internalized our oppression. I feel a lot of compassion for those who make the decision to use in an effort to transcend their negative feelings — just as I feel a lot of compassion for those who, like myself, decide not to use and might subsequently miss out on realizing their desires. Still, by relying on intoxication to overcome the constraints of shyness or shame, we blur lines of consent, avoid rather than tackle the underlying issues of oppression, and frequently make unsafe sexual decisions that grievously hurt our personal and community health.

Drug use in queer communities

In my experience, drug use forms a significant part of shared gay male culture and experience, especially among those into the dancing and partying that are generally seen as the most emblematic gay activities. Lesbian/bi/queer women also use drugs at markedly higher levels than their straight counterparts. It's not hard to compute the reasons why: considering all that's been said above about social marginalization, it's a wonder that any of us escape drug dependency. The social and sexual exclusion we face as drug-free queers can feel so pronounced that I've felt at times as if my sobriety challenged or threatened my queer identity.

The centrality of drug use to gay men in the US dates back to the mid-1970s, when widespread sexuality began to replace political engagement as the key trait characterizing a genuinely liberated gay person. In this context, using drugs to loosen up and enjoy the party, socially and sexually, assumed an unprecedented role as the facilitator of all the things that make us gay: an unquenchable thirst for life to the fullest, fabulosity, the wildest partying, and of course sex. Drug use became so universal among sexually active gay men in urban areas that in the first years of the AIDS epidemic researchers actually theorized that the horrible array of symptoms might somehow be caused by the use of poppers, a popular form of amyl nitrate inhalants. Why? Because their use formed one of the only common behavioral links between the urban gay men who formed the majority of early AIDS cases. Poppers help guys loosen up emotionally enough to let go of sexual shame and anxiety and physically enough for anal sex. But neither the tightness in our hearts nor our assholes can be relaxed through the constant application of a chemical substitute. What we really need to loosen ourselves up is to overthrow the system of heterosexist oppression that keeps us afraid, trapped in hatred for ourselves, our bodies and our desires, and unable to relate to each other while sober.

Unfortunately, the consequences of our collective difficulty to extract sexuality from intoxication can be far graver than a foggy memory the morning after. According to research studies, queer men who reported being intoxicated during sex were also more likely to engage in sexual activities with high risk for HIV transmission. Of course, this doesn't mean that intoxication causes risky sexual behavior, nor should we blame or judge folks who have sex while intoxicated. But it does mean that in order to protect our personal and community health we need to take a careful and critical look at the role that getting intoxicated plays in our sexual decision-making. In an even more frightening trend, HIV prevention workers are now finding that men are not merely getting intoxicated before having unsafe sex that they regret; some men have reported that they get intoxicated *in order* to have risky sex that they would not be comfortable with while being sober. In other words, the sexual "hang-ups" that we're overcoming through intoxication are not just shame and internalized homophobia, but safer sex messages that "hold us back" from having sex in ways that hold high risks for disease transmission. This pattern indicates the grip of intoxication culture on our sexuality and the frightening consequences that may result until we can figure out different ways of sexually connecting to each other.

In the last decade, crystal methamphetamine has surged to the top of the list of drugs integral to gay culture. According to one study, meth use is twenty times as prevalent among men who have sex with men as among men who don't. Why are we such a vulnerable sub-population? Some of the factors involved include the drug's effects, which increase sexual arousal and lower inhibitions, alleviate stress and produce feelings of euphoria; feelings which provide vivid counterpoints to many of the negative emotions that commonly constrain gay men. As a drug counselor at the LA Gay and Lesbian Center said about meth, "It's sort of the perfect gay drug."

Wait, a perfect gay drug is one that allows us a temporary, fleeting escape from anxiety, sexual shame, and depression? What does this say about gay life? Is our gayness so defined by our internalized oppression that the drugs we use to escape it can also come to define us? Of course, many of us refuse as individuals to accept the role drugs have come to play in queer culture and identity. But until we can combine a fierce struggle against shame and queer oppression with a concerted effort to break the stranglehold of intoxication culture over queer life, we'll remain dependent on society's poisons in our attempt to escape the shame that this society has instilled in us. As the frightening correlations between having sex while intoxicated and HIV transmission show, the stakes are nothing less than our lives.

Given this complicated and painful relationship to addiction and substance use, one might expect that queer folks, especially radicals, would have a profound critique of intoxication culture and the political implications of sobriety. However, apart from a substantial movement of LGBT people in AA/NA/recovery, I've encountered few instances of such a critique. For me as a punk and an anarchist, my primary context for political critiques of intoxication culture comes from sXe. So can we queers create a space for ourselves in sXe culture? Can sXe provide a tool for queer people to transform our individual and community-level relationships to substance use?

Queer edge: Bridging the gap between queer culture and sXe

In spite of the lack of space for queer people in sXe, there are examples of individuals and bands who have attempted to forge a "queer edge" identity that blended commitment to sXe ideals with uncompromisingly queer imagery. Hugely popular and influential gay punk group Limp Wrist put out records showing vividly Xed up hands that juxtaposed sXe anthems like "This Ain't No Cross On My Hand" with distinctly queer songs like "I Love Hardcore Boys" and "Cruising at the Show." Zines such as *Total Destruction* #3 drew links between queer oppression and intoxication culture from a militant vegan sXe perspective. There was at one point a queer edge website for queer sXers to link with each other. I've seen rainbow-colored patches circulating at punk shows that said "Taking the Straight out of Straight Edge." Although they're too few and far between for my liking, I'm excited to see hints of a queer edge culture emerging from the overlap between queer culture and sXe punk and hardcore scenes.

I think that sXe and queer culture have a lot to offer one another. From sXe I'd love for queer culture to absorb a sense of commitment to health, self-respect, and intentionality about lifestyle choices, as well as a sense of how individual choices can be meaningful within the context of a broader community. Queer culture can offer sXe a refusal of the machismo and gender rigidity that plagues the scene; a rejection of the false moralism of pseudo-militants; and above all, a fucking sense of humor. I would love to see a thriving queer edge scene full of bands singing righteous pro-queer, pro-sober messages, zines documenting and exploring a culture of sober queer punks, and who knows, maybe even gatherings and festivals? (Yes, this is a challenge!) But I don't know how realistic that is — I mean how many sober queer punks are there? It may be that we're just not visible, but it's also possible that there just aren't a lot of us. So while I want to support the development of an explicitly queer edge scene — both as a pathway to link sobriety with radical queer identity, and also because I'm into gayin' up the punks however possible! — I think we need to go further. In addition to making space for queer people within punk and hardcore scenes, I want to encourage queer communities to radically challenge intoxication culture.

Towards a radical queer critique of intoxication culture

What would it take to transform queer communities towards healthier relationships with drugs, alcohol, and each other? As I see it, creating a radical queer critique of intoxication culture within our communities provides a place from which we can begin answering that question. As a starting point, we can critically examine the past to understand the role of intoxication in our queer communities today. The dominance of drugs and alcohol in our communities has a history — how did it come about, and whose interests did it serve? And what about hidden stories of queer people who have challenged or resisted intoxication culture?[5]

---

5. For example, the largest group marching in the 1982 Gay Freedom Day Parade in San Francisco (that's what Gay Pride parades used to be called— fuck, how times have changed!) was the "Living Sober" contingent. While the AA recovery model doesn't necessarily hold a lot of radical potential, this example demonstrates queers in recovery and other sober allies asserting sobriety as a transformative choice for queer life — and not just in isolation, but in large numbers.

Having examined the past, we can shift our focus to understanding and analyzing how intoxication operates in queer communities and lives today, reinforcing our self-hatred and stifling our ability to challenge oppression. We can't rely on moralistic frameworks, which have always been used by people in power to scapegoat queer people, so this critique must be grounded in compassion and solidarity, aware of the ways that our options are constrained by the social conditions in which we operate. In my opinion, we should focus on harm reduction rather than total abstinence as an imposed norm, on creating space for sobriety as a viable and non-stigmatized choice and on promoting community health. This means setting addiction treatment and recovery as a community priority, while rejecting the individual, depoliticized alcoholism-as-illness framework.[6] Alcohol abuse is neither a moral failure nor an individual pathology; it's a response to a collective reality of oppression and the lack of social alternatives for challenging or coping with that reality. What we need are empowering models that understand addiction as a response to an oppressive society and locate the sickness in that society, not in ourselves. In the spirit of the radical queer ACT-UP activists who helped create the first needle exchange programs, we can develop treatment practices that don't rely on professionals, including supportive counseling, recovery groups, and resources coming from radical perspectives.

In addition to supporting one another in escaping the clutches of intoxication culture, a radical queer critique can also inspire active resistance. A crucial component of this involves examining the economic structure of the alcohol industry and how its tentacles have slithered into the deepest levels of our communities. Refusing to allow alcohol and tobacco corporations to sponsor LGBT events, especially Pride festivals, and protesting them when they are featured, can be a starting point for action and for re-envisioning our relationship to intoxication and consumerism. Promoting community health includes holding accountable the agents of alcohol and drug distribution as well as the addiction profiteers outside and within our communities for the harm that their efforts produce. Realizing that the prison industrial complex offers no path towards freedom for queer people or anyone else, it's up to us to creatively find strategies to impose this accountability without relying on police, courts, and jails. These could include direct action of many kinds, exposing/shaming profiteers, organizing boycotts and divestment, public demonstrations and theatrical symbolic

---

6. Most books and articles about alcohol abuse by queer people frame alcoholism as an individual disease, with no analysis of how the overall structure of queer life makes drinking seem like a necessary part of life for so many of us. Defining alcoholism as an illness of individuals prevents us from accurately diagnosing the illness of intoxication culture that plagues us collectively.

actions, art and "subvertisements" that mock alcohol ads, and whatever other forms of action we can devise.[7]

Along with strategies of resistance that disrupt the functioning of intoxication culture, we can create viable alternatives to the alcohol and drug centered institutions of queer life. We can open up collectively run cafés, performance venues, community centers, and other social spaces that provide us with opportunities to meet without the mediation of alcohol and drugs. At conferences, gatherings, meetings, and performances, we can advocate for events to be alcohol and drug free, or organize our own counter-events and alternative gatherings side by side in order to show solidarity with sober/recovering queers. Although I expect that these efforts will encounter some resistance, especially at first, I think we might be surprised by how receptive queers will be to create alternatives to the drunk, high, or tweaked consensus forced on most queer events and spaces.[8] At two different radical queer & trans gatherings I attended in the southeast US over the past years, workshops discussing the role of substance use and abuse in our communities were very well attended, passionately debated, and widely praised and appreciated. Even just starting conversations about drugs and alcohol can produce positive shifts in our shared queer culture, as we become increasingly aware of the importance of our collective struggles around intoxication.

These struggles are important: transforming our collective relationship to drugs and alcohol forms a crucial component of the struggle for queer liberation and self-determination. In his classic essay "Refugees from Amerika: A Gay Manifesto," Carl Wittman argues, "To be a free territory, we must govern ourselves, set up our own institutions, defend ourselves, and use our won energies to improve our lives." Applying this logic to the appalling rates of addiction and substance abuse in queer communities, I believe that breaking the stranglehold of intoxication culture among

---

7. An example of creative queer resistance to intoxication culture: the radical queer group Gay Shame organized a protest when planners adopted a Budweiser beer slogan, "Be Yourself," as their official theme for the 2002 San Francisco Pride Parade. Mattilda, one of the group's founders, describes their action linking the literal poisoning of our bodies by the beer companies with their poisoning of our community celebrations with commodification and assimilationist politics: "We also created a seven-foot-tall cardboard Budweiser can that read 'Vomit Out Budweiser Pride and the Selling of Queer Identities,' and a large closet, so that people could put their patriotism back where it belonged. Just in case people wouldn't have time to reach the official Budweiser Vomitorium, we also created official Gay Shame vomit bags, which described our three primary targets: the consumerism, blind patriotism and assimilationist agenda of the Pride Parade."

8. At a 2006 radical queer & trans gathering I helped to organize in North Carolina, we made the controversial decision to keep the space for the entire weekend of workshops, meals, and performances completely drug and alcohol free. To our surprise, nearly all of the participants expressed appreciation and mentioned that the atmosphere felt more respectful and less intensely sexualized; many felt safer than they had almost ever in queer spaces before, and found that their perspectives on the role of drugs and alcohol in queer scenes had been radically altered.

queer people is a necessary step towards self-governing and self-defending communities. As xDonx writes in *Total Destruction* #3, "Us queers can never rely on straight people for support or defense, and it's about fucking time we stopped drowning in their poisons."

Framing recovery from addiction, creation of queer sober space, and queer challenges to the status quo of intoxication culture as matters of community self-defense emphasizes the political and not just personal dimensions of intoxication and sobriety. Sobriety is not the same as freedom, nor does substance use equal slavery. However, I do believe that destroying the conditions of oppression that make sobriety difficult to impossible for most queers, and hence making sobriety a viable alternative, is a precondition for our collective freedom.

Above all, a radical queer critique of intoxication culture would insist that nothing short of a fundamental transformation in our society will bring liberation for queer people — and everyone else. It would recognize the ways that intoxication culture impacts queer people differently along lines of gender, race, orientation, class, and other axes of identity. Understanding how our whole selves include multiple overlapping identities, it would recognize how only an active struggle to abolish all forms of oppression can sew the seeds of a world in which we can experience genuine self-determination. Therefore our strategies for confronting intoxication culture must not only challenge homo/transphobia and heterosexism but also white supremacy, capitalism, patriarchy, and the power of the state. Whatever tools we use — punk, sXe, music, direct action, queer sex, etc. — the time to act is now. Breaking the shackles of addiction and dependency can free up our energies for the revolutionary struggles we need to break the shackles of oppression and misery — we've got a long way to go, so let's not waste a moment being wasted!

"The Only Thing I'm Drunk on Is Cock"
Interview with Lucas

Lucas is a twenty-nine year old queer vegan straight edge kid living in Oakland, California. He's been straight edge for a long time and gay even longer. He spends most of his time hanging out, watching *Golden Girls* and *Strangers with Candy* with his roommates, and practicing Danzan Ryu Jujutsu.

What were the major influences on your decision to be sXe?

I started calling myself sXe well before I came out, let alone admitted to myself that I was gay. I have this vivid recollection of having a bunch of friends get into drugs around the end of middle school. I just wasn't interested at all. My best friend, who was getting way into the drug culture, called me up and told me he wasn't my friend anymore. I was devastated; the only difference in our friendship was the introduction of drugs. For a long time after that, I had no friends. Sometime around early high school, my brother started going to punk shows. I began tagging along, and I fell in love with it all. I met a lot of political kids who were into being young and stupid and not doing drugs. Shortly after that, I began calling myself sXe.

My views on sXe have changed over the years. About seven years ago, I dated an alcoholic. I started making connections between his struggle and the struggle of queers, and how we deal with the pressure of living in a hate-filled society. I started seeing how the places in our society where queers go to escape are usually filled with drugs and alcohol, and I don't think that's an accident. One of the weapons used against us are these intoxicating killers. It was awful seeing my friend struggle with these things. That's one of my reasons for still being sXe; it's my active stance against these weapons.

sXe is a personal choice, and all my sXe friends have different reasons for being sXe. I also have many friends who aren't sXe, and as long as their personal choices don't negatively affect our relationships, they can do whatever they want.

Have the sXe scenes you've been a part of been homophobic? If so, in what ways? If not, why do you think sXe has a reputation as homophobic?

The hardcore scene is a microcosm of society at large; all the same hatreds and fears exist. Sometimes it's overt, but usually it's more subtle.

First and foremost, queers, like women and people of color, are vastly under-represented in the hardcore scene and in sXe. For the most part, it's not a welcoming place for these groups of people. This has to do with what the scene doesn't do, more than with what it does do. Basically, there's no attempt to create a welcoming environment. Sure there are bands like Limp Wrist who address issues, but at least in the San Francisco bay area, where I live, they're viewed almost as a spectacle or gimmick by the straight majority, like "I can't believe they're saying those things and wearing those freaky clothes." Like my friend said when we saw Limp Wrist play to a mostly straight crowd at a gay bar, "I never thought I'd be scared of getting gay-bashed at a Limp Wrist show." People definitely don't go to hear a message of queer liberation — fucking bike hipsters!

How have other sXers reacted to your sexuality? Has it been an issue in bands/at shows/in your scene?

It's pretty easy to be sXe and queer in the bay area for me. As a disclaimer, though, I will say that it seems as if most people don't know I'm queer unless I tell them, or it comes up otherwise. I "pass" as straight to most people, in other words. My experiences might be different if this weren't the case. But the scene here is at least outwardly tolerant, as you might expect from the bay area. However, as my last answer stated, it ain't all roses there either.

Where I'm originally from, Indiana, it's a different story altogether. When I came out many of my friends in the sXe scene at the time ostracized me (though there were a few who stood behind me, which I really appreciated). I took a sabbatical from the scene for about two years. I never felt like my safety was threatened; I just didn't feel like participating on their terms. After a while (and a break-up with a boyfriend) I found myself hanging out with some anarchist kids who happened to also be sXe. This time of my life reminded me a lot of my first few years of hardcore; there was a youthful innocence in these kids, and some of them were really hot. I started going to shows again and eventually re-befriended an older kid I had lost contact with. Through him, I eventually re-immersed myself into the sXe scene. Since I was one of the older kids in the scene, the fact that I was gay was never openly an issue. I think I was a lot of those kids' token gay friend. I was definitely the only queer kid. When I left, however, the scene devolved into crews and tough-guy shit.

As far as my involvement in bands, we've always made the conscious decision to play at venues and with other bands we know won't pander to homophobic tough guy bullshit. This means playing in a lot of basements to friends. But I wouldn't want it any other way. Punk rock to me is about those intimate moments of celebration and rage that can only happen in those kinds of settings. Basically, I proactively avoid those parts of the scene that might be a problem. They exist, and they can fucking have their stupid shows (while we have our awesome shows!). My last band, Send 'Em to the Cemetery, had one song with the lyrics, "Suck Dick! Fuck Ass! Blow Shit Up!" Apparently there was a "discussion" on some lame hardcore message board about this song where "faggot" and other such lovely epithets were thrown about. Sometimes that kind of thing brings you back to reality. But nobody this day and age says that shit to your face.

At this point in my life, I get out of the scene what I want, and fuck the rest. I've met some awesome people and been exposed to some awesome ideas through sXe and hardcore, but I really don't hold much importance to it. It is what it is. I find much more meaningful community through other outlets.

What do you think about the sexual ethics of sXe (i.e. "don't drink, don't smoke, don't fuck")? Are your own sexual ethics tied to your sXe beliefs?

sXe has nothing to do with my sexual relations, unless sXe means liking to get it on with cute boys. As I like to say, the only thing I'm drunk on is cock. All in all, I try to be responsible with sex, both emotionally and health-wise. And I think that's what Ian MacKaye was talking about. But I've never let my sXe beliefs dictate my sexual ethics. I do like the boys.

How have other gay/queer folks reacted to your sobriety?

With radical queers, I have never had a problem. In fact, quite a few of the radical queers here are sober or close to it. Live and let live. Ultimately, I don't care what the fuck you do to yourself as long as you're not creating violence or making my community unhealthy or unsafe. There's room for all types in my queer community, as long as we're all fighting towards liberation for us all. That's the most important thing.

Within mainstream society, including mainstream gay society, there is a certain backlash against people who choose radical sobriety; a sort of "you think you're better than me?" reaction. People also get this "you must be a stick in the mud" attitude, until I fuck their "straight" cousin or something. One time, this normal gay wanted me to go to the clubs with him, and I told him I wasn't interested. He told me that I need to "own it," implying that by not being interested in drug and club culture I was somehow not living up to gay standards. That seems to be a pretty common attitude.

Why do you think that is?

Well, if you were to spend Pride weekend in San Francisco, one thing you would immediately notice is the sickening amount of advertisements for alcohol blanketing the city. In fact, I think the whole damn thing is sponsored by Budweiser. I mentioned earlier how bars became a refuge for many queer people. Alcohol seems to have become pretty intrinsic to the make-up of a large portion of the queer community, so much so that it eventually came to represent gay people to the world during Pride. Somewhere the culture becomes the media and vice versa, and they start reinforcing each other. What I'm getting at is when the largest gay event of the year is sponsored by an alcohol company these two things have ultimately become one in the same: drugs and gays. And people within the community reinforce this notion, or else it wouldn't survive. So the attitude prevails within the mainstream gay community that to be gay you have to drink, etc.

And let's be honest, marketing professionals know what they're doing. They put their products where they'll sell, and marginalized communities have always been a favorite place for alcohol companies. The more suffering, the more sales. Capitalism thrives off inequalities and suffering, so abusive substances permeate these communities while the people in charge of this mess turn a blind eye. We also live in a society rooted in religious moralism, where being gay, being transgender, or sometimes being a woman or a person of color, is seen as a sickness. These forces create this perfect shitstorm where it's really fucking hard to survive as a marginalized person, especially a gay person. I don't think it's a coincidence there's an overabundance of drug use in marginalized communities. It serves both capitalism and moralism pretty well.

Do you want to see queer scenes change to be more accessible to sober people?

I've never felt unaccepted by the queer scenes I've been apart of, only by the scenes I don't care to be a part of.

Where do you meet other like-minded gay and queer folks? Are there many other openly queer people in the punk/sXe scenes you've been a part of?

Before I moved to the west coast, I didn't know too many queer folks, especially in the radical and sXe scenes. Since moving out here, I've met a few through hardcore and more through radical politics, etc. As you might imagine, there's quite a large radical scene out here. I've met a very small amount of queer kids who are into hardcore or sXe. For the most part, the radicals queers I hang out with are not really involved in sXe or punk.

Are you connected to much of a "queer edge" scene?

I know queer kids who are in bands, and I know cute queer edge boys, but it's not really any type of unified thing. We're all a bit older and kind of divorced from the silliness. Some of the Limp Wrist guys live out here and I see them every once and awhile. But I don't really see an active scene existing, and I'm not too interested in being active in one.

Do you want to see sXe scenes change to be more accessible for queer folks? How can that happen?

I'm not too worried about the state of the sXe scene. I've never needed a scene to support my beliefs. However, I love meeting other queer folks who are sXe. Like myself, most of them don't need the support or acceptance of a scene. So fuck the scene, unless the cute gay sXe boy population suddenly explodes. Then I'm there. See you in the pit, boys!

As far as how? Like I said, I'm not interested in the reformation of the scene. Sometimes I see myself and other queer kids into hardcore as the antithesis to the normal hardcore kid. We exist in spite of them, and if we ruffle a few feathers or make some dudes uncomfortable, then awesome. If we out their "straight" best friend, even better. We're not trying to be the beacon for change, or any of that bullshit. I'm not gonna run for president of the sXe scene.

Emancypunx
Interview with Jenni Ramme

Emancypunx Records was founded in Warsaw, Poland, in 1997. The project developed out of the city's hardcore and anarchafeminist underground and became an international focal point of feminist and queer politics with straight edge sympathies. In 2003, Emancypunx released *X The Sisterhood X*, a seminal compilation of female straight edge bands spanning three continents.

Jenni Ramme is the founder of Emancypunx, a festival organizer, photo artist, and political activist. She lives in Warsaw and Berlin.

Can you tell us a little about Emancypunx?

It all started with an anarchafeminist group called Women against Discrimination and Violence, which we had with some girls since 1994/1995. This group worked closely together with the already existing antifascist group Youth Against Racism in Europe. After a while we decided to continue as a separate women-only group. We kept on cooperating with the antifascist group, however.

Everyone in the group was into punk, and we were active in the underground scene which was quite big and still united at that time. We didn't organize within main anarchist circles like the Polish Anarchist Federation, because part of the anarchist movement was extremely male dominated, often prejudiced and didn't include women rights in their struggle at all.

Anarchist punks and political oriented HC folks seemed way more open to these issues. Many of them had learned a lot from listening to all kinds of political bands like Crass, Dirt, Nausea, Nations on Fire or ManLiftingBanner which all had a pro-feminist and strongly anti-sexist message. Polish bands also stepped up the plate more and more often, for example Homomilitia, 105 Lux, Cymeon X, Post Regiment or Piekło Kobiet. These bands were quite progressive compared to what was generally going on in Polish society at the time. They also really distinguished themselves from the 1980s Polish punk/HC scene where these issues weren't discussed at all.

So as anarchist feminists we felt better in a punk, hardcore and antifascist environment where we got support. It should also be noted that the Polish feminist movement was not established yet and that the riot grrrl wave that appeared in the US and in some European countries never came to Poland.

Anette of Störenfrieda (Germany), Berlin, 2009 Jenni Ramme

There was basically no internet and access to information was hard to come by. The situation was very different to the one we have today. People were not traveling that much either. Feminist literature was really hard to find. That's why we started to run a distribution in the middle of the 1990s with books, zines, pamphlets and music, and were sending out packages with information about women rights to people from all over the country. This was the beginning of Emancypunx — that was the name we gave the distro. We first did it all as a side project, but it soon turned out to be a great opportunity to spread information and to communicate with people, and we also started organizing stands at shows, gatherings etc. Meeting people face to face and talking to them was important, because at that time you could hear the craziest rumors about what feminists were supposedly like — a lot of people were really scared of feminists even though they had never met one.

The word Emancypunx is a word game and means "emancipation in punk" or "punk suffragettes" since "suffragettes" in Polish means "emancypantki." It was already used at that time as a term to describe feminist punks — girls and boys.

When there were plans to turn Women against Discrimination and Violence into a regular NGO in 1996, Emancypunx also became the name of a new group we founded. Women against Discrimination and Violence eventually ceased to exist.

Throughout the years we, as Emancypunx, organized a lot of protests, rallies, political street performances, radical cheerleading and poster actions. For example, we were very active around Take Back The Night and the 8th of March, the International Women's Day. We raised issues like sexual violence, abortion rights, body image, exploitation and housework, women in Afghanistan and others. We also organized protests against racist border politics, deportations and corporations like Siemens. We were active on many platforms.

Emancypunx the group dissolved around 2002. The end was related to conflicts around a sexist incident that happened within the circles of the Anarchist Federation. The incident was one of many, but this time it was more intense and direct and it was the first time when women from different cities, groups and even countries united and spoke out in public against the sexism in the libertarian movement. They had simply had enough.

A lot of anarchists responded to this with violence and tried to silence us by all possible means. The conflict grew bigger and bigger and I think it had far-reaching consequences for the whole movement. I think it made it difficult for many to even address sexism. The traumatic experience, the huge pressure and the disappointment were too much for many of us. It was really a big factor in our group dissolving. Some of us focused on our activities within the punk scene, some got more involved with the general feminist movement.

Of course there were also personal issues that were involved in the break-up of the group. Not everyone wanted to do the same things anymore and we all went into different directions. However, we all remained politically or culturally active. Some of us are part of a new anarchist feminist group called A-Fe, while others are active in Bildwechsel Warsaw, a zine archive and library, in Fundacja MaMa, a feminist NGO, or in the band Mass Kotki. I would say that most of the girls who were connected with Emancypunx the group are still very active. The name Emancypunx remained as a record label, distribution and organizer for shows or festivals.

I started Emancypunx the label around 1997/98. The first release was a licensed re-release of the all-girl compilation tape "Donna Wetter." The tape was originally released by Rotzgore Records, a small tape-label of the band Re-Sisters from Switzerland. I heard that tape for the first time on an anti-nuclear women's camp in Germany and was totally amazed. It was exciting to see so many new European all-girl bands play really angry punk rock with a radical feminist message. It was finally a loud voice resisting the traditional role of the subordinated, sweet, nice female. At the end of the tape was a melodic girl sugar-punk band and the producers just put a machine gun voice over the whole song. I could identify with that a lot.

After that the label slowly developed and more releases were done in the next years in different formats (CD, vinyl and tape) for international, mostly all-girl and female fronted bands. So far, we've put out about twenty releases, with bands from Europe, North and South America. We also booked shows, tours, and festivals like Noc Walpurgii (Walpurgis Night), the second Straight Edge Fest or the first Open Hardcore Fest.

From 1998 to 2001, Emancypunx was involved in the W-wa Hardcore Force collective. This was created as a joint project of hardcore initiatives from Warsaw in order to organize shows for foreign and local HC bands. Not that many foreign bands were touring in Poland at this time, so we wanted to change that. We also wanted to join forces to develop the scene.

This was a short version of the story around Emancypunx. We tried to be active and visible in order to change the situation of women: in society, in the hardcore punk scene and in radical movements.

How did the label and the anarchafeminist group relate to one another? Was the whole group involved in the label or was it run by just a few?

Emancypunx Records was always pretty much a separate project and never run by the entire group. Of course we had many friends helping out. From the Emancypunx group, Aga was probably involved in the label the longest — well, apart from me.

I still can't say that Emancypunx Records is a collective effort. It would be great if it was a project of more people, which was the original idea. But I have kind of given up on that idea. I made several attempts to involve others, but none of them really worked out. The way a label or a distribution works is very different from the way that an informal group works. A label needs regular work. For an informal political group like Emancypunx, regular work was not necessary. You can sometimes focus intensively on a particular action or campaign, and then take a break or turn to another issue. For a label this would be disastrous. Another thing is that running a label means that you need money to release records. Political activism can be done with almost no money. In my personal experience, the money that you invest in records hardly ever comes back. I think this also keeps many people from getting involved in a label.

How does straight edge play into Emancypunx's intentions and your activism?

In the sense that I'm straight edge and try to promote a straight edge and a drug-free life style. It means that in addition to promoting women and feminism in hardcore punk I mainly release straight edge bands or bands where some members are straight edge. I also organize shows for straight edge bands and promoted straight edge in the zine I did.

Straight edge is not an end in itself for me. I've always seen it as something broader — let's say as a positive opportunity within the DIY punk/hardcore/feminist/anarchist movement. This might sound trivial, but at the time Emancypunx started, straight edge and drug-free living were met with a lot of suspicion in punk circles.

A big part of my feminist and hardcore friends are straight edge. And there are also many who might drink on occasion but who do not use alcohol as the sole means of socializing.

So Emancypunx the group was not necessarily a straight edge project, but Emancypunx the label was — would that be right?

Yes, we can say that, if we consider projects done by straight edge people as straight edge, even if not every single project they do is focused on straight edge.

X The Sisterhood X, a compilation that you brought out in 2003, was a major contribution to female straight edge culture. It featured all-girl straight edge bands from Argentina to Portugal to Serbia to Belarus. How did you get the idea for the compilation?

Hardcore and straight edge always had a strong focus on the idea of brotherhood and of male friends supporting male friends. Women were often seen as separate and not on equal footing with the guys. In fact, I think it was often enough reminiscent of the skinhead movement, which is also very male-dominated and where guys hang out with other guys. In order to achieve equality it is important that men change their attitudes, but it is also important that women are supportive of one another. So if we have brotherhood, we should have sisterhood too.

In the 1990s, straight edge sisterhood groups were formed by girls in Sweden, Germany and Portugal. Michaela Böhm, for example, formed an initiative called the International Straight Edge Sisterhood. I did an interview with her for my zine, but then the initiative disappeared and I lost contact. But I really felt the need to spread the idea of worldwide straight edge sisterhood and to support and unite with other sXe girls.

At the 2000 Ieperfest, a hardcore festival in Belgium, it was the first time that me and Aga, who was also straight edge, got to meet many straight edge girls from different countries and even continents. It was a time when straight edge became more international and when it became easier and easier for people from everywhere to stay in touch. Point of No Return was the first South American straight edge band that came to tour Europe. In this context we got to know girls from Brazil and found out about this great all-female band called Infect. We talked with girls from Belgium, Italy and other countries and thought it would be great to bring straight edge girls together and to do a joint project. This is how I got the idea for a sXe sisterhood compilation.

For many months I searched for everything I could find on girl straight edge activists, zine makers, websites and all-girl straight edge bands — anyone who would like to join the project. I guess the basic intention was to say: "Hey! We are here!" We hoped that this would help us to promote the different activities of women within sXe, to make them more visible, and to inspire other girls to become active. The responses I received were all very positive and in the end we had bands from Brazil, Argentina, the US, Serbia, Belgium, Germany, Poland and Belarus. The compilation was released on 7" vinyl with a thirty-page booklet. It got great feedback and reviews. Today, all the copies are sold.

Are you still in touch with many of the girls who contributed?

With some. For example, a band called Trust from Argentina released a 7" EP on Emancypunx Records, and one of the band members used to play in Venus Genetrixxx, a band that was featured on the compilation. Flopi, who was in the same band, recently came to the Walpurgis Night festival as a D-Jane and organized a workshop together with Laura from Synthesis. Tatiana from Infect was visiting Europe with her other band I Shot Cyrus.

I'm in touch sometimes with other girls from Infect too. Asia Bordowa, who made the drawings for the booklet, now sings in The Fight and does a zine called *Chaos Grrlz*. I also run Bildwechsel Warsaw, the zine library and archive with her. I don't have much contact with Geraldine from Uneven, but she is still involved in music projects. Ljuba is still active in her band Lets Grow and has her own label, Ha-Ko Bastards, in Serbia. Dasha from Belarus was the singer in the country's first sXe band called Jiheart and is now in a band called I Know. Two members of To See You Broken are in a vegan sXe band called This Time Tomorrow, but somehow I lost contact.

Some people are not part of the scene anymore. There have been a lot of general changes and new generations have come. And even if it's relatively easy for us to stay in contact now, it's still not necessarily easy to meet if you're not a constant traveler, as we are from different countries and continents.

> **On your website it says that Emancypunx is both about "cultivating and spreading independent women culture" and "emancipation in punk." I'm wondering whether you focus on one aspect more than on the other. Like, are you focusing more on feminist politics in general, believing that this will necessarily affect the role of women in punk — or are you focusing on the emancipation of women within punk as a contribution to a wider feminist struggle?**

Cultivating independent women culture in general and specifically working for the emancipation of women in punk can go together. What we mean by "independent culture" is a DIY culture with punk ethics. There doesn't necessarily have to be punk music. At the same time, an "independent women culture" is certainly needed within the punk/hardcore scene as well. Although there are obvious connections between the struggle within the scene and outside of it, there are also differences of course; as there are always differences when crossing the line between the underground and the mainstream. While within the underground there are always specific scene aspects you have to address, within mainstream society you address fundamental issues that affect everyone. Emancypunx the group was active on both levels: we fought for internal changes within punk/hardcore, and we were engaged in political activism within mainstream society, also working together with mainstream feminists. As far as my personal focus goes, as a feminist punk I'm mostly interested in forming a counterculture that can avoid integration into the mainstream. Something that remains an oppositional force.

I think we were successful concerning the promotion of women's DIY culture, but not necessarily in the form I had envisioned. In particular, parts of mainstream culture caught on to our ideas and various clubs and organizers started to organize events or dance parties including the word "grrrl" or promoting female performers, DJs etc. The press caught on too and started publishing more and more articles on female artists. We definitely triggered something.

It's a double-edged sword of course. On the one hand, it all appeared more than a fad than anything else often enough, and the political message was left behind almost completely. On the other hand, women are without doubt more present in Polish cul-

The Tangled Lines (Germany), Leisnig/Germany, 2005   Sandra Gärtner (xcirclepitx.com)

ture now than they were fifteen years ago. They are no longer reduced to mere objects but actually have possibilities to create culture by themselves. Their perspectives and ideas are more present.

What I see as the main problem with the mainstream adaptation of our ideas is that the social frames are still intact. Men still make all the important decisions, set up norms and handle profits. Just because we induce some of our ideas into mainstream culture, the system itself will not disappear. I think it is dangerous to believe otherwise. Some people are able to use the creativity and the ideas that come out of DIY culture to make money and establish personal careers. The community aspect is left behind. For me, the willingness to communally create and share a culture that is not for profit is the very base of our movement and the reason why I am a part of it. This is why I consider a division between mainstream culture and a DIY underground culture really important.

Of course such a division is not always easy to maintain. For example, there was a lot of media interest in Emancypunx. How do you deal with that? At first, we tried to stay undercover and ignore them. But that made us even more interesting and they were reporting on us anyway. At one point, there was even a fake interview published in a magazine like *Bravo Girl* or some shit like that. Eventually, some of us "went public" and agreed to do personal interviews and photo shootings. However, this didn't solve our problems either. Now we had girls who were portrayed as "leaders" and a new media-prescribed image: childlike, cute, sexy — with radical and punkish overtones. Our political intentions were completely lost.

All in all, these experiences made me really skeptical of mainstream media and even though I compromise sometimes, I generally think that mainstream newspapers and TV are not the right places to share information about underground culture. People must learn to find out about underground culture in other, more direct ways. Mainstream media will never see underground culture as anything but new, fresh meat to make profits. They are part of a capitalist and consumerist culture of bloodsucking zombies. They take without giving anything back. This is not a base to build radical movements on.

This is also where we differ from mainstream feminists who accept capitalism and make integration into the system their main goal. As anarchafeminists we don't want integration into capitalism or the state, we want to create a space that goes beyond that. I think that it is alright to get involved in mainstream campaigns when it means that our living conditions within the system improve at least a little, but to me it is mandatory to pursue radical social transformation at the same time and to attempt creating utopian societies right here and now.

Another issue that separates us from mainstream feminists is our complete rejection of hierarchies. Mainstream feminists put a lot of effort into making powerful social positions accessible to women. The often hierarchical structure of their organizations reflects this "leader" principle too. This often means that community aspects are lost and that most of the support goes to women who already are relatively privileged and who come from the intellectual upper classes. This is not my idea of equality. Equality must be more than this.

How successful has your work on gender issues been in the punk and hardcore scene?

There has been success, but I also had to realize that no success is forever. The constant flow of people entering and leaving the scene also means that the education about basic issues constantly needs to begin anew. This does not only concern feminism, but also animal rights issues and others. It is tiring to repeat the same things over and over again, but I think it is really necessary.

Of course there are big individual differences. As feminism has become increasingly accepted in Poland, you have access to books, can attend genders studies classes at university, etc. So when people join the punk/hardcore scene with this background, they are already conscious as far as these issues go. But overall, I would actually say that the focus within the scene on music, fashion and parties is stronger than ever today. A lot of people are not interested in anything else.

An example is the Walpurgis Night festival. It used to be a big festival embedded in the DIY punk scene. I think it had a big influence and really helped create a positive atmosphere toward women. But the DIY scene is shrinking and the ones who are really behind this idea are getting older. When there used to be 1000 people attending, now it's barely 500. In the beginning, gender equality and fighting homophobia were really important aspects of the festival. But now the scenes are all split. Everything is fragmentized. It seems like a lot of people can no longer be bothered defending their ideas within certain scenes; when they encounter problems, they just leave the scene and form a new one or do their own thing.

So, all in all, we have seen huge progress on certain levels, but we are also confronted with regressive tendencies because there's a lack of communication between the divided scenes.

I understand that you had to struggle against a very male-dominated punk and hardcore scene. Why do you think that domination is so strong?

I would say that it has a lot to do with general social roles. The way hardcore expresses itself is rather aggressive and powerful. It doesn't take a victim's position, it's more about reclaiming space. The way that hardcore bands perform, their presence, their lyrics etc. are not "feminine" according to general social norms. Women are not expected to be like that. Women are expected to be nice, sweet and obedient. So any female who wants to be part of the scene has to break these rules. Men can to a large degree live out their "manliness" in hardcore culture without making any such step. In fact, many men within hardcore culture are so tied to stereotypical gender roles that they have a problem with women who act like them. They feel uncomfortable when women stage dive, are confrontational, sing with a strong, aggressive voice, or use "bad" words. A lot of guys have a very "romantic" notion about what a girl should be like and they see all these things as a kind of "loss of femininity." That's why you see all these women at hardcore shows taking pictures of guys in the pit or on stage — much more so than you'd see them in the pit or on stage themselves. It's as if their main role is to be shy, silent and good-looking — just like in mainstream society.

It took a while for people to get used to women singing and playing in hardcore bands. I still hear guys saying that they can't stand female voices. I think with the growing amount of women singing in hardcore we can see a clear progress, but women still try not to break too many rules at once. Many retain a very feminine look and make an effort to "behave." It is also still true that most women are involved in the less visible and spectacular parts of the scene, like in organizing shows, making zines, cooking at shows etc. Women certainly provide a lot of the scene's infrastructure.

In terms of overall gender relations within the scene, one also has to make local distinctions of course. It differs from town to town and from country to country. It also differs from genre to genre, if you will. Like modern hardcore, tough guy or metalcore are extremely male-dominated I would say. To the point where it seems really hard to change those patterns. I mean, if you go to a show as a female and you are one out of three women in a crowd of 300 guys, it is simply alienating. Even for me — if I attend a show like that, I simply feel like being at the wrong place and I certainly won't come back. I'm not desperate to belong to a male club.

DIY-oriented punk and hardcore punk scenes, on the other hand, have a fair amount of women involved. For example, here in Warsaw I would say the DIY punk scene is not male-dominated at all. Women are an active part in creating the scene, they are involved in bands, they book shows, run distros, live in squats and form a big part of any audience. As far as I remember, Warsaw has always had a bigger involvement of women than most other Polish towns.

Local and genre differences set aside, however, ridiculous macho attitudes are still prevalent in the hardcore scene. You just have to check our local hardcore forum. This is the only place where people from all the different hardcore scenes get in touch. There you can read stuff where some guys organize "hardcore soccer games," but without women, as "their bodies are different." Of course this example is so pathetic that it's easy to just laugh at it, but I think it also reflects a deeper problem: many guys try to compensate for their lack of confidence and their low position in a male hierarchy by putting down women. It's a common feature in mainstream society and it's frequently reproduced within hardcore culture.

Fortunately enough, there is an increasing number of males who are involved in hardcore who are annoyed by the tough guy bullshit too. Violent dancing has become a much discussed issue, as it's often enough to have two or three disrespectful people in the crowd to spoil the fun for the other seventy or so who are there. It just sucks when some idiots take over the place and start to define rules for everyone else. The values that tough guy wannabes promote are not only oppressing women, they oppress guys too.

I want to say one more thing about the reasons behind the general male dominance of the scene though. I think a big factor is how history is written. A lot depends on the power of definition. Many guys simply ignore or deny the presence of women and their contributions to the scene. This can be very demotivating for women who put a lot of energy into hardcore. It also means that there is a lack of role models for women in the "official" representations of the scene. I mean, look at the movie *American Hardcore*. The first thing I thought after seeing it was that I don't wanna have anything to do with hardcore anymore if it's really all just about guys and for guys. I actually felt ashamed that I had anything to do with hardcore and with the guys who were so excited about the movie. It was an irrational reaction, because the hardcore scene I'm involved in is completely different and really has nothing to do with what was presented in that movie. But it's just that movies — and to a certain degree also discussion forums like the one mentioned before — have such a powerful influence on the images we, and others, have of our scenes. So whether they represent the truth or not, they may still define tomorrow's scene.

You mentioned that an increasing number of guys within the scene get annoyed with the macho elements too. How strong are these changes?

It's difficult to give you a general answer because, as I already said, there isn't just one scene. New scenes are coming and going and there are a lot of trends that are constantly changing.

Again, if we talk about the modern hardcore scene, and parts of the metalcore scene, I have the impression that things are actually getting worse. Not just because there are only few females at the shows, but also because these scenes have moved away further and further from underground and DIY culture. There are parts of the hardcore scene that have become very commercialized. People accept sponsorship, they are obsessed with buying from big corporations like Nike, and they love hyped and neatly packaged festivals like the Vans Warped Tours. Considering the MTV-like character of these scenes, I'm not sure which values we still share. Especially since the consumerist attitude seems to go hand in hand with a lack of awareness concerning human and animal rights.

On the other hand, I do have the impression that the DIY hardcore punk scene is changing for the better — however, I also see it shrink. I hope it will get stronger again; not least because that's where I feel I belong and where I think definite progress has been made with respect to the involvement of women and an understanding of the importance to support women's rights.

How do you see female straight edge today?

Female straight edge has always been very diverse. As I mentioned before, there were groups in Europe who called themselves straight edge sisterhoods in the 1990s. Recently, the Portuguese XsisterhoodX was apparently reactivated. Generally, though, it seems that the concept has disappeared in Europe.

I have the impression that the sXe scene is getting smaller and becoming less important overall. This also means that less girls are involved than a few years ago.

There are almost no all-girl sXe bands left. Like, I think today it'd be almost impossible to do another *X The Sisterhood X* compilation. At the same time, we can see more girls singing or playing in sXe bands. This has definitely become much more accepted and is not sensational or threatening anymore. I can name a number of projects that sXe girls are involved in: the bands Reaching Hand and Together, as well as the zines *X Cute* and *Off The Map* in Portugal; the band Drama and the zine *Strength&Courage* in Spain; bands like The Tangled Lines, Sugar Crash, Lipkick, Ex Best Friends in Germany, Beyond Pink in Sweden, I Know in Belarus, Fight For Fun in Russia; XSpeciesTraitorX is a queeredge band from Finland; in Poland there are the bands The Fight, Audre, Slowa We Krwi, and the zines *Chaos Grrlz, Kiss My Edge* and *In Full Swing*; in the US there are bands like Gather, This Time Tomorrow, Socialized Crucifixion, Kingdom, Sentient or Look Back And Laugh, and there is Kelly's xsisterhoodx website; in South America there is Trust in Argentina, or Justica and Arma Laranja in Brazil; and in Asia you have Choke Cocoi in the Philippines, or Last Minute in Malaysia.

Had you ever planned on doing any follow-up compilations to *X The Sisterhood X*?

Yes, that was always the plan, but, as I said, I'm not sure whether it will work out at this point. It's just become really hard to find any all-female straight edge bands. But if there are any interested bands and possible contributors out there, get in touch! I would definitely love to put out a second volume!

I also wanted to ask you more about "Walpurgis Night." What kind of an event is it?

Together with Robert from Refuse Records we came up with the idea to organize a small show dedicated to the fight against sexism and homophobia. Since we all had a lot of energy to share, the small show turned into a big festival. The first Walpurgis Night was held in 1996, and it remains an annual festival to this day. We invite bands with female members, bands who support the ideas of the festival, and bands that address the issues we want to draw attention too. Every year we have more women participating, as they start to reclaim their space as D-Janes, bands or performers. Our intention was to create an event where punks, gays, lesbians, hardcore kids, queers, feminists and straight edgers would have fun together. It was meant to be a day of celebration for all people who are usually excluded, and for everyone who wants to support them. One of the things we do is to have all-girl bands, feminist male bands and drag queens perform together in order to challenge sexism and homophobia. It hasn't always been easy. There has certainly been a lot of tension at times, and on occasion we had to kick people out who would behave in an offensive way; but all in all I think the mix is working out well. The festival has never been limited to music, by the way. There are also films, workshops and political actions. Over the years the festival has turned into one of the biggest and most important events of the DIY hardcore and anarchist feminist scene.

> **About the pro-queer aspect: I'd be really interested to hear about your activities related to queer-positive messages. That's something that seems terribly neglected in hardcore culture; I mean, there have even been clearly homophobic tendencies, also within certain straight edge scenes.**

Yes, there have been homophobic tendencies if we consider hardliners a part of the movement. There have also been strong pro-life and some religious (Catholic, Islamic, Krishna) tendencies in straight edge, not only in the US but in Poland too. These have fortunately almost all disappeared. On the other hand, there have been very clear anti-homophobic messages from bands like Seein Red, Good Clean Fun or Saidiwas, and there has been the great *Give Me Back* compilation on Ebullition Records. I think that most of the blatant homophobia — or pro-life advocacy — has pretty much been left behind. Or at least people no longer voice such opinions openly. An interesting aspect is of course that an all-male pit with shirtless sweaty guys bumping into each other can easily have the air of a gay event, so I think it's great when bands like Limp Wrist expose this by taking it to the extreme and turning the macho attitudes against themselves.

In general, though, I think that queer messages are too much for most straight edgers and hardcore scenesters. Most of them just can't relate to the concept. Of course there exist bands where queer and straight edge elements mingle, like in the already mentioned Limp Wrist or XSpeciesTraitorX, the US band GO!, or the girl band Stoerenfrieda and the hip-hop act C.B.A. from Germany. I guess Beyond Pink could be mentioned here as well. But, all in all, combining straight edge with queer-core or homocore is really rare.

I would say that Walpurgis Night is a pretty unique event in that sense, even though we have recently been able to bring together hardcore punk and queer culture at other events too, for example at Klir Szyft — which kinda translates as "Queer Shift" into English — a four-day queer festival we've started to organize in Warsaw. Unfortunately, the queer and hardcore projects at these events often co-exist more than they'd actually overlap, but I think it's a step in the right direction. Over the last two years I've also been involved in establishing a queer cultural center. I'm not active right now, but after I had organized some hardcore shows there, other people from the hardcore scene started to do the same, and they feel comfortable in the space, which is cool.

All in all, though, most of my queer activism is not really related to hardcore or straight edge. It's difficult to create more links, although I'd love to. Drugs and "partying" play a big role in queer culture, and musically a lot revolves around electronic or pop music, disco, and maybe hip-hop. Although I like these genres and think that a DIY scene should be as diverse as possible, the truth is that my heart beats faster when I hear hardcore punk!

What are your future plans with Emancypunx?

Things are going slowly as running a label is not easy nowadays and I don't have that much time anymore because of work. But I'm still at it and there is always something happening. I remain committed to supporting bands that I like and that fit into the label's philosophy. As far as the future goes, I think it's best not to talk about plans too much but to make things happen! Maybe when I'm eighty years old, though, and arthritis won't be too much of a problem, I'll fulfill my dream and play drums in a straight edge, grandma positive power violence band!

xsisterhoodx
Interview with Kelly (Brother) Leonard

xsisterhoodx.com is an online magazine and community devoted to the women of the straight edge and hardcore scenes. It has been administered by Kelly (Brother) Leonard since the 1990s, and has been essential in forming an international network of politically conscious and engaged straight edge women. Kelly works as a Marketing Web Manager and lives in East Haven, Connecticut, with her husband and daughter.

For those who are not familiar with it, please tell us about xsisterhoodx.

xsisterhoodx.com is an on-line community and zine dedicated to the girls/women of the hardcore and straight edge scenes. Founded in the early nineties as a small e-mail discussion group, xsisterhoodx has evolved into a worldwide on-line community of over 10,000 people of both sexes. xsisterhoodx strives — though we are not always 100 percent successful — to be a positive force in the scene by encouraging positive discussion and involvement.

It seems hard to deny that the hardcore and straight edge scenes are extremely male-dominated, and that this in turn renders them unattractive to many women. What is it that still draws you and other women to it, and what are your experiences from being involved in one of the major projects dedicated to strengthening the position of women within the scene?

I don't think the fact that hardcore is male-dominated is what makes the scene unattractive to many women. For some, it may be a big reason why they are attracted to it. From an outsider's perspective, male or female, hardcore might be viewed as violent, extreme, and dangerous. The music is aggressive, the shows are intense, and the people involved in the scene tend to band together in tight-knit cliques. People, not just women, may find those factors intimidating.

When you say that the male dominance of the scene is not what makes the scene unattractive to many women, then what is it? Or asked differently: why is the scene so male-dominated?

I think it's a combination of factors. The first being exposure. It has been my observation that little girls are taught to shy away from the more aggressive aspects of life, where little boys are encouraged to seek them out. Younger boys find out from older friends and relatives about hardcore. They tag along and go to shows. Girls on the other hand tend to not have that older friend or sister exposing them to the scene. On top of the exposure factor, younger girls may have a hard time convincing their parents to let them go to shows. I know I had a hell of time convincing my mom I would be safe. For years she was convinced that if I went to a show in Newburgh, NY, I would get stabbed. Even now, at almost thirty years old, my mom still worries about me going to shows. It's nutty.

So how did you find your way into the scene then? And how did you deal with the male dominance?

Growing up I was a typical tomboy. Most of my friends were guys. I was never much of a girly girl. So, when I first stumbled upon hardcore the fact that it was male-dominated didn't strike me as an issue. Before my first hardcore show my dad had taken me to see a few bands in arena settings. My first hardcore show was somewhat of an awakening. No stadium seating or large screens. It was so much more intimate, more visceral. I was drawn in by the passion and excitement of the shows. I think those feelings are what attracts people to hardcore. Now almost fifteen years later I still feel that excitement when I go to a show. That is what keeps me involved.

What were the reactions when you started xsisterhoodx?

My experiences from being involved with xsisterhoodx have run the gamut from being intensely rewarding to mind-numbingly frustrating. Every once in a while I'll get an e-mail from a young girl thanking me for xsisterhoodx. They all have incredible stories, and they're all looking for the same thing: a place where they can feel accepted. It's an awesome feeling, when someone validates all the time and effort I have put into xsisterhoodx. It truly is a labor of love. But for every positive, there is a negative. I've received tons of hate mail, mostly misogynistic rhetoric, and obscenities. There are people who hate me, hate xsisterhoodx, and really have no understanding of who I am, and what xsisterhoodx is about. There are women who at their core do not believe that women belong in hardcore, who try to talk me down. People try to involve xsisterhoodx in their own agendas, be it to promote their lifestyle, movement, or ideas. But, I have no intention of letting that happen.

It sometimes seems that the male dominance in the scene perpetuates itself in the form of a self-fulfilling prophecy: like, it's

been a reality for so long that one doesn't even notice developments challenging it. Do you think that women in the scene are sometimes simply overlooked or not taken seriously?

I'm not sure if the women of the scene are being overlooked. A lot of attention has been being paid to the numbers of girls who are going to shows, and even more attention is being paid to what they are wearing and how they choose to conduct their personal affairs. If you do a quick search on MySpace you'll find page after page of groups that exist to eliminate "sluts" in the scene. Slogans like "slut free" and "girls with self respect" are smattered across personal profiles as badges of honor. Women are not being overlooked, they are being scrutinized. And it's not just the men and boys who are leading the charge, it's other women and girls. Women have turned on each other. Calling each other out and fighting over who is really hardcore and who belongs in the scene.

Now I'm all for people having self-respect. But, when a group uses a term like that to promote a moral agenda I have a major problem. Frankly, I don't care who sleeps with who in the hardcore scene, and if Jill Hardcore wants to sleep with all the members of her favorite band, it's none of my business, and it certainly is not the hardcore scene's business. It seems to me that a girl or woman who truly has self-respect will respect other people and refrain from using judgmental terms like slut.

People like to say girls don't get respect in the scene and are not taken seriously because they "sleep around" or are seen as social climbers. These thoughts and ideas are not unique to the hardcore scene and are pervasive throughout society. One would think that a progressive sub-culture/scene could get beyond such thinking.

I find it very interesting that you see women in the scene scrutinized rather than overlooked. But let me specify my question from before then: are women's contributions to the scene — as artists, promoters, zine editors, etc. — often disregarded?

I don't think that they are so much disregarded but marginalized. There are so many more girls who are active in the scene than when I first got involved that it would be hard to overlook what women as a group have been able to accomplish. However, rather than given credit for their accomplishments, they are brushed aside, and treated as jokes. I can't tell you how many times kids have called xsisterhoodx a joke. The comments aren't based on what xsisterhoodx is about, or our politics, but simply on the fact that we are a group of girls and women who want to support one another. How many times has a female guitarist gotten on stage only to hear "show me your boobs" or an equally objectifying comment? Granted, I don't see it as much as I used to at shows, but the objectifying and marginalization of women in the hardcore scene is alive and well on message boards all over the internet.

What about international networking? Is this a big aspect of xsisterhoodx?

xsisterhoodx has members from around the world. Though most of the members who participate regularly are from the States. It's definitely a goal to get more women/girls from around the world to participate and network with each other.

At the risk of making gross generalizations: Do you think that women in the straight edge movement are often more politically conscious and active than many of the men?

Straight edge is a funny thing. At its core it's just a few simple statements that a person agrees to live by. And that's it. There are no moral or ethical strings attached. The basic clean-living principals of straight edge fit neatly into a lot of religious and conservative values, so, making the leap between straight edge and conservatism, be it religious or social, is not really a leap but a small step to the right.

In my experience living on the east coast, and growing up in liberal states, the straight edge girls that I have known personally have been politically conscious and active in a progressive manner. They tend to be more aware of women's rights issues, fighting for equality, and voting on such matters. On the other hand, I have had many on-line encounters with girls/women from the bread basket states who are just as politically conscious, but could hardly be described as progressive. I've talked to quite a few women who believe that women should not work, and who willingly give up their rights and freedoms to their husbands, and boyfriends.

Now back to your question. No, I don't think that women in the scene are any more active than the guys. I haven't seen too much activity, at least politically, in the hardcore/straight edge scene for a long time. I can remember going to shows when I was a teenager where the walls would be lined with tables of people who were involved in anti-racist movements, political movements, and animal liberation. It has been a long time since I've seen anything like that.

Not exactly an encouraging sign...

No, it isn't.

How do you see the connections between straight edge and feminist politics? Can the two support each other? Do they?

Like I said earlier, straight edge is simply a set of statements that a person agrees to live by. I see no reason why straight edge and feminist politics wouldn't support each other. Feminism is about being able to make your own choices, and in a way so is straight edge. I made the decision long ago to abstain from alcohol, not because I believe alcohol to be morally wrong, but because I feel that I do not want any substance that will inhibit my ability to make good choices for myself.

One of the aspects of the straight edge hardline scene in the 1990s that drove me nuts was the militant anti-abortion stance that developed in certain circles. Like, some zines looked like youth propaganda material for Operation Rescue. I never understood how such attitudes could enter a scene that claimed to be progressive, rebellious, even revolutionary. What's your take on that?

I started to get into this a bit in one of my previous responses. It's pretty easy for me to see how someone who is socially and/or religiously conservative, or in hardline's case fanatical, can find out about straight edge and feel like it really fits into their life. Without the context of the hardcore scene, straight edge is really just a few, and I have to admit, conservative rules, that fit very nicely into a lot of core religious and conservative lifestyles. When you add the hardcore element, and one remembers when, where, and why straight edge came about; that's when the progressive, rebellious, and revolutionary aspects come to light. I think people have always understood music's ability to spread a message or an agenda, and the hardline movement recognized that and took advantage of the power and passion of music, just as the more progressive movements did.

Kinda related to this: I have to admit that I was very happy to read that you distanced yourself from the views of Bring Back Prohibition, a group that was featured with an interview and an article on your site. To be honest, to me their self-righteousness and militancy represents just about everything that's wrong with straight edge politics. Calling hardline "beautiful and as close to perfection as mortal people can get" sounds really frightening to me. And then there's the troubling suggestion that we shall rely on the government and laws for positive social change. Can I ask you how their views even ended up on your site?

There are a lot of views that appear on xsisterhoodx that I do not agree with. However, even though I disagree with the views of Bring Back Prohibition, they are a part of the straight edge world and just because I don't agree with them does not mean that they do not exist. The article that was written for xsisterhoodx served as a catalyst for a lot of positive discussion. Good questions were raised and people for the most part behaved in a respectful manner. I am not one for censorship, and I believe that people have the right to express their beliefs, even if those beliefs contradict my own.

However, I will not publish works of hatred on xsisterhoodx. I know that sounds a bit contradictory, but I will not allow xsisterhoodx to become a soapbox for hate. I do want xsisterhoodx to be a place where people can go and and feel that they can express their opinions and beliefs.

I am in complete agreement with you that we should not rely on the government and laws for positive social change. I also believe that we should never give the government the power which Bring Back Prohibition suggests. I think the vast majority of xsisterhoodx readers feel the same way and it was evident in their response to the article.

You already suggested that it's a hard line to draw — but can you give us any indication of where "hatred" would start for you?

Hatred starts where respect ends. When it comes to a difference of opinion, as long as the conversation is respectful who am I to censor it? Sometimes the best way to make positive change is to have respectful dialog about the very ideas you wish to challenge. We can't just put our hands over our eyes and ears every time someone has a difference of opinion.

Let me quote the xsisterhoodx mission: "xsisterhoodx strives to be a positive force in a scene divided. Our goal is to create balance and eliminate the biases which exist in today's global scene. As a community we encourage and support positive discussion and involvement without the negativity and posturing often found on the web. We stand against violence and elitism and do not tolerate bigotry, racism, sexism, or discrimination in any form." Have you come closer to this goal? Have you been able to build a community that lives up to these ideals?

I believe I've built the foundation for a community that can one day live up to all those ideals. It's up to the individual members to really make that mission statement a reality. Some things we are better at than others. One of our biggest challenges has been managing expectations. Some people read "support positive discussions..." and assume that when they make a post everyone will agree with them and no one will challenge them. Such is not the case. And when said person is challenged they get very upset and claim that the site is not positive. The biggest challenge by far is getting people involved. People like to say they're a part of xsisterhoodx, but only a small percentage write for the site, or post on the boards.

I think that's often the case — you know, that the core group of those who are really active is rather small. Let me ask you about the men who are part of the xsisterhoodx community: Is there a rough percentage you could give us? And are some of them amongst your more active contributors?

We have quite a few male supporters, and surprisingly a fair amount of our contributors and regular posters are male.

What are your feelings about where xsisterhoodx is at right now?

Right now xsisterhoodx is in a bit of a lull. I gave birth to my daughter seven months ago and have had to learn to juggle her needs, work, my family, and xsisterhoodx. I have been working on a new version of the site with updated functionality and new content. Once the new site is launched I hope to be able to keep the momentum going.

Sounds like you are still motivated to put a lot of effort into the site/zine. On a personal level, what would you say is the most rewarding aspect of the work?

To create an environment where girls/women, and the people who support them, can feel comfortable expressing their opinions and ideas. Furthermore, to promote and highlight people who are really taking what xsisterhoodx has written in our mission statement and making it a reality. I also think it is important to cover the straight edge and hardcore scenes from a media perspective.

Final question: What are your future visions for xsisterhoodx? And for the straight edge scene — and its politics — as a whole?

My vision for xsisterhoodx is to keep making it bigger and better. I would like to see us grow and make more meaningful connections with one another. By grow I don't necessarily mean in numbers. Grow, evolve, however it is phrased. I want to see xsisterhoodx take it to the next level. I would also like to see a lot more girls getting involved and contributing to the website.

As for the straight edge scene, I'd like to see it remain as a positive force in young people's lives. I prefer the politics of the scene be geared toward positive change, not moral or religious agendas.

When the Edge Turns Crust
Interview with Bull Gervasi

The band R.A.M.B.O. was founded in Philadelphia in 1999. Famed for its eclecticism, self-irony, extensive touring, and anarchist politics, R.A.M.B.O. was one of the few bands that earned itself both the attributes "crust" and "straight edge." The band dissolved in 2007.

Bull Gervasi, formerly of Policy Of Three (1989-95) and Four Hundred Years (1997-2000), was R.A.M.B.O.'s bass player. He lives in Philly and is a member of the Mariposa Food Co-op managing collective.

Many folks seemed bewildered at my idea of including something on crust and straight edge in this book. Apparently, this is still seen by many as a contradiction in terms. What's your take on this? Do people just think in stereotypes, or is drug-free living really so alien to most crust kids?

Unfortunately, I do think it's a foreign concept to most crust punks. There seems to be this segment in the scene that just can't let go of the '77 style "get fucked up and fuck shit up" stereotype. I've gotten shit from people for not wanting to drink or smoke weed with them.

The crust punk scene is commonly perceived as more political than the hardcore punk scene. How come straight edge has made few inroads?

It is true that there are many political bands within the crust punk scene, but only a very small contingent of straight edge bands. I find it hard to say why that is. For me personally there always seemed to be a natural connection to straight edge — especially with part of the scene coming from the "peace punk" scene of the 80s. Also within a radical political context it just makes so much sense. I don't take issue with punks who drink on occasion or brew their own beer. I think folks should do to themselves whatever they want. However, I do take issue with drunk punks following a tired stereotype or with political punks supporting corporate alcohol/tobacco companies that target "at risk" populations and profit from people's addictions. I think it's unfortunate that the crust scene is still so dominated by the drunk punk image. That's exactly how "The Man" wants us to act!

Bull Gervasi, Philadelphia, 2006 Joshua Peach (joshuapeach.com)

As far as US straight edge is concerned, I think it's rarely synonymous with politics or activism these days, other than a few small scenes. That doesn't make it particularly attractive to political crust punks either.

The most common criticism I hear from straight edge crust kids with respect to straight edge hardcore culture is that the latter has become way too commercialized. This turns into an argument for crust being closer to the "original" straight edge spirit in terms of anti-consumerism, DIY ethics, rejection of mainstream society etc. Does this resonate with you?

As far as commercialization goes, I think that this goes for any aspect of punk at this point. Look at the expensive and elaborate uniforms that many punks have regardless of the particular scene they count themselves in. Maybe some of them are less commercialized than others, but a lot are highly stylized and expensive nonetheless. There's also the fetishization of record collecting.

For me, the straight edge hardcore scene has lost most of its connection to punk at this point, so it barely even registers for me as something to consider. So, yes, on that level the criticism certainly resonates with me. Straight edge has never been a style for me. I've never been one to "X up" or wear straight edge shirts. But I can absolutely get behind a movement that promotes personal responsibility and accountability.

Felix von Havoc, with Neil Robinson of Tribal War Records maybe the most prominent straight edge crust punker, once wrote in a HeartattaCk column that when he first got into hardcore "charged hair and studded jackets didn't clash with X'd hands." Do you also remember such times? If so, when did the studded jackets and the X's start clashing? I assume this would tell us a lot about the history of straight edge...

When I first started going to shows in the late 80s, the straight edge scene was just starting to become popular in Philadelphia. At that point there were just punk shows, period. Everyone played together, all the distros sold all sorts of bands' records, and the only real division was between the punks and the nazi skins.

We put on shows in New Jersey at the Harwan Theater through the early 90s and it was the same thing. It wasn't until the straight edge hardcore scene started to get violent and apolitical that the division occurred. It was about 1993 around here. The straight edge scene in the north eastern part of the US was very dominated by the New York hardcore scene. Once that scene started to go more mainstream it really went downhill. The shows started to be full of the meathead assholes I hated from high school. It had little resemblance to the punk scene I knew and loved.

That was when my friends and I all left that scene to start doing our own thing, which became part of the mid-90s DIY punk scene. That scene was very political, predominately straight edge and a musical mix similar to my earlier days at shows. We started a group called the Cabbage Collective where we put on shows with crust, emo, riot grrl, pop punk bands and whatever else we could come up with. We never had a problem. Well, except for the Citizen Fish and Spitboy show were some crusty train hoppers broke beer bottles outside and tagged the bathrooms. Then we got kicked out of that space.

Why did that happen?

The crusty train hopper scene in the US has little to do with the actual crust punk scene. "Train hopping" refers to boarding freight trains illegally as a mode of transportation. It became popular in the US during the Great Depression as a way to get from one place to another while looking for work. Sometime in the 1990s, a subculture with ties to the punk scene developed around using freight trains as a means of free transport. It consists mostly of homeless and often violent and addicted youths that would hop trains from city to city. They often squat in northeast or northwest towns during the warmer months, then hop south for the winter. They are often hostile towards punks that aren't part of their scene, especially straight edge folks. Quite often they would just turn up at shows and expect to get in for free. They were more interested in a meeting place than in the actual show and would usually cause trouble whether you let them in or not. That particular night, we wouldn't let them in for free, so they hung out outside, drank, and broke bottles before tagging the bathroom as well as the outside of the venue.

You said that you and your friends left the violent and apolitical straight edge hardcore scene in the early 90s to do your own thing. Does this mean that you set yourself apart from the Victory scene? Did it ever come to any serious conflicts?

Victory was still coming up at that point, but yes, we very intentionally set ourselves apart. No serious conflicts though. The overall scene in the US was big enough to sustain smaller scenes. We just found our own venue, picked who we wanted to support, and asked them to play, read, or table at our shows. We felt strongly about providing a drug, alcohol, and smoke free space, but we figured that style and attitude ought not to be more important than substance.

Forming R.A.M.B.O. was directly related to that. R.A.M.B.O. was basically a reaction to how increasingly violent the scene had become leading up to 2000. We wanted to play heavy music, but we wanted to have a safe environment for whoever wanted to come. It's funny to think that, given the ways things had developed, this seemed like a novel concept.

How were your experiences with R.A.M.B.O.? Did you have a strong straight edge following? Or was being straight edge rather "tolerated" by mostly non-straight edge fans?

R.A.M.B.O. came out of a love for crust and hardcore, a strong set of beliefs, and a love of fun. At the time R.A.M.B.O. started, the hardcore scene here in Philly was dominated by violent assholes. We wanted to create a safe space for punks of all sorts to enjoy crust music with hardcore breakdowns played by straight edge vegan anarchists. I think that's why people caught on to us. We brought together certain ideas at a time when that wasn't really done, and people got what they wanted from it. Some marginalized groups within the punk scene felt safer at our shows, some people were excited about our politics, some liked the music we played, some were into the props, and some dug all of it. We did have a lot of straight edge fans, but not so much in the traditional hardcore scene sense. We mostly attracted the punk rock misfits that didn't fit into all the neatly defined scenes of recent years — into which we didn't fit either. I'm very thankful to the punk scene for everything we were able to do. Our experiences were phenomenal — except for the broken foot, the broken leg, and the typhoid fever, but that's another story...

Speaking of typhoid fever: R.A.M.B.O. was well known for touring extensively and in far-flung places where not many Western punk/hardcore bands venture, Cambodia and Borneo included. What were your experiences playing there? How were you received as a crust punk band? And how did people react to you being straight edge?

There is such a huge crust punk/grindcore scene in Southeast Asia! Both our tours there were incredible. I'm so thankful that we had the opportunity to meet so many great folks and play in so many places that most Westerners will never go. It was all possible because of the global DIY punk network. We met a handful of straight edge crust punks there, but everyone showed us incredible kindness and was genuinely interested in what we were about.

The scenes in each country are quite different and only a few of them are strongly linked. When we went to Indonesia, some folks from Malaysia and Singapore came with us to create a stronger DIY network in the region. Things like that were quite inspiring. We planned the tour in such a way that we would have several days in each place to hang out with the punks outside of playing shows. This really enriched the whole experience. We got to see their favorite places, eat with them, see nature, and we were able to really get to know each other.

You said that R.A.M.B.O. "brought together certain ideas at a time when that wasn't really done." This reminds me of a number of labels that the band has been associated with: crust, straight edge, vegan, environmentalist, anarcho-syndicalist. The name of the band is an acronym for "Revolutionary Anarchist Mosh Bike Overthrow." How did all these ideas come together for you?

First off, the name was a joke suggested by a friend of Tony's because Sylvester Stallone went to his High School in North-East Philly. It became an acronym to pay homage to the Japanese band G.I.S.M. whose name was kind of nonsensical too.

As far as the labels go, you covered most of them. We wanted things to be spelled out very clearly for those who were interested: we believed in these things, we sang about them, we had information about them on our table and in our records, and we literally beat you over the head with them, in a fun way of course. I felt really good about our overt politics as a way to try to introduce people to new ideas or spark conversation. At the bottom of it all, we were four or five individuals with similar politics and a love of punk and fun.

For me it was also really important to give back to the punk scene because it had provided me with so much guidance early on. Bands like Conflict, 7 Seconds, Youth of Today, and Discharge allowed me to escape into a different world, but more importantly, provided the framework for me to become who I am today.

R.A.M.B.O. disbanded in 2007. What happened?

The rest of our lives became more of a priority. We all had a lot happening and it just felt like it was time to move on. As you said, we had been touring quite a bit and I personally felt like I couldn't devote enough time to either my home life or the band. I was and still am a manager at our neighborhood food co-op and I was also working on an old communal house. Tony was planning to move to Arizona for school and a relationship, Andy was beginning to work more on films, Dave was moving to Pittsburgh to relocate his vegetable oil vehicle conversion company, and Mick was just starting school to be an electrician.

We had a great run as a DIY band. We managed to accomplish quite a bit. As a band we were always trying to push things to the next level, and I feel that this is how we try to live our lives too.

You mentioned dedicating a lot of time to the Mariposa Food Co-op. Now we all need to know: do you sell organic wine?

Lucky for us it is illegal in Pennsylvania for alcohol to be sold outside of state-run liquor stores. I do spend a lot of time at the co-op. It is a great example of a democratically run business that adheres to most of my anarchist principles. There are over a thousand people that are members/owners of the business, I'm part of a small staff collective that manages the storefront, we make decisions by consensus, everyone works and everyone pays the same prices, we have direct relationships with about twenty local farmers who grow organic produce, 90 percent of our members live within a few blocks of the store, and we provide access to high quality food at reasonable prices in an underserved neighborhood.

Apart from the co-op, what are you up to?

I live in a communal house with five others. The house was purchased in 1989 with the intention of providing affordable housing for anarchists/activists. It was built in the 1890s and maintenance requires a lot of time and energy. It's a huge eight-bedroom, four-story Victorian style twin that was bought for $7000 because there had been a fire in it. In 1999, a few friends and I took over responsibility. This past year we started on some serious structural projects to insure the house's longevity.

I love traveling and nature, and so I try to get out of the city as much as possible, either for a bike camping trip or to help friends maple sugaring, seaweed harvesting, bird watching, mushroom hunting, or something like that. My partner and I have been trying to teach ourselves how to garden the past few years. We maintain a guerrilla garden in an abandoned lot near my house. I like to be as self-sufficient as possible. So I'm always trying to learn new skills.

Are you still involved in punk/hardcore?

Since I was twelve I've been involved in the punk scene. It's part of me like an appendage. It has influenced every aspect of my life and will always be with me. After R.A.M.B.O. I was pretty burnt on playing music and needed a break from it. I needed some time to focus on the other aspects of my life. So I haven't been playing much music since, other than in a handful of cover bands — Minor Threat, 7 Seconds, The Misfits, Iron Maiden — for our annual Halloween events.

Where do you think the punk/hardcore movement — and straight edge specifically — is headed politically?

It seems to be cyclical and I think we're due for a resurgence of politically charged straight edge punk! I think it's a perfect time for a new crop of punks with a righteous analysis to evolve from the ashes of the outdated crust punk/straight edge hardcore stereotypes. There's plenty of lyrical fodder these days, that's for sure. Look at the state of the world and the political climate. The youth are also inundated with advertising at a level unlike any other in history. Much of this is coming from alcohol, tobacco, and pharmaceutical companies that sure as hell don't have our health or well-being at heart. I'm optimistic.

Andy Hurley, Milwaukee, 2008   Mac self-portrait

Straight Edge, Anarcho-Primitivism, and the Collapse
Interview with Andy Hurley

Andy Hurley, known as a vegan straight edge anarcho-primitivist, has been a drummer for various punk bands, including Racetraitor (1995-99), Killtheslavemaster (1996 to present), and Fall Out Boy (2001 to present). He lives with four of his best friends in Milwaukee, Wisconsin.

"Andy Hurley, the anarcho-primitivist vegan straight edge drummer of Fall Out Boy" — you hear and read a lot about that label, but it's usually never backed up by any substantial stories. Do you wanna clear some of this up for us? Maybe tell us a little about how you became politically aware and encountered anarcho-primitivism?

Well, I was into punk rock as a kid, and Rage Against the Machine had a huge impact on me. *Evil Empire* had all those books on the cover, and I tracked down every single one of them. I didn't read them all, and in hindsight I'm probably happy because a lot of them are about things that I'm not into anymore. But I read a bunch, and that set me on my path to be politicized. Other influences were Public Enemy and Paris. At the time, I didn't get into that stuff because it was political, I didn't know that then. But I think getting into the music so young and then realizing what they were talking about definitely opened me up more to ideas that weren't so prevalent in the white suburbs I grew up in. So this was kind of the first phase.

Then, fast-forwarding a few years, I joined Racetraitor. That was the second phase. That was the kind of sharpening of my political life, I would say. The other guys in the band were much older and much more politicized, and they had also been doing a lot more activism. So joining that band I started doing stuff with the National People's Democratic Uhuru Movement and different kinds of socialist-communist groups like that.

Can you tell us a little more about Racetraitor? It always seemed to me that it was a really unique band that didn't really fit into any particular scene. Would you agree with that?

I definitely think so, yes, for a lot of reasons. There were a lot of things that were unique. I mean, even on a very basic level, having a dude who was Iranian shook things up; even though he was from the suburbs too, but still. And then just the whole approach, like getting the audience engaged in all these discussions. The first time I ever saw Racetraitor — so this is before I joined the band — 90 percent of the show was them arguing with people. As a result, we definitely didn't fully fit in anywhere. Definitely not with Earth Crisis and all the vegan straight edge bands from that scene. But not with *Punk Planet* or *Maximumrocknroll* either — though we were on the covers of both, I think.

Again, I believe what really set Racetraitor apart was the nature of the shows and just how argumentative they were. Obviously this was a tactic to make people think. I mean, if people are talking, at least they're talking, you know? And it certainly helped my politics too. If you argue, you get better at understanding what it is that you are arguing.

I think by the end of it we started to fit in a little more. We definitely felt connected to bands like Extinction 'cause they were from Chicago, and we sort of came up with them and were friends. And in hindsight there were other bands too. But we didn't feel very connected to any scene for quite some time.

One thing I always wondered and never found out was whether the band's name was connected to the *Race Traitor* journal?

No, the name came from Dan Binaei whose family is from the South. One time he had this discussion with some folks about what he was into, and someone said, "So, you're one of those racetraitors?" And Dan kinda took that name like the early straight edge kids took the X's on their hands: he was like, "Ya, I'm a racetraitor, and I'm proud of it!"

Let us get back to your political history: you said that Racetraitor sort of marked phase two...

Yes. Even though I forgot to mention Earth Crisis. They were definitely a big influence too. Firstly for veganism, but also for a more political understanding of straight edge.

Did you get into straight edge through Earth Crisis, or were you already straight edge before that?

No, I became straight edge around that time — like, when I was fifteen. Before that I drank and smoked pot. But I knew straight edge from a lot of rad bands, like Youth of Today, and Bold, and Gorilla Biscuits — those were all bands that I listened to and liked. Straight edge made sense to me, also with the situation at home, like how me smoking pot was affecting my mom, but I didn't know anyone who was straight edge and it all remained a bit distant to me.

But then Earth Crisis came along, and they made it so much cooler. To begin with, they were the heaviest hardcore band I had ever heard. And they made the whole thing just so much more political. It felt like the approach that Rage Against the Machine had too: they were explaining their beliefs. That just spoke to me a lot. So that was probably the biggest reason why I became straight edge — and definitely vegan.

So when did anarcho-primitivism enter the picture?

I would say that this would be like the third phase. It was when I quit Racetraitor to do more Killtheslavemaster 'cause they were starting to play more shows and such. My anarcho-primitivist leanings come from that time, because early on we read *Ishmael*, the Daniel Quinn book, and that was how I got started on the anti-civ [anti-civilization] politics. I think that was even before the big wave of *Ishmael*-inspired hardcore, so before Undying and bands like that. Eventually, there was a kind of split in the scene, where a lot of the Milwaukee kids, including me, got into the anti-civ stuff, and a lot of the Chicago kids, including some of the Racetraitor dudes, remained dedicated to what they had already been doing, like human rights, anti-racism, anti-imperialism, anti-colonialism.

I still believe in all that too, but I got more and more into anti-civ. From *Ishmael* I went to Derrick Jensen 'cause he's sort of the next step. I really liked him 'cause his stuff was kind of a melding of anti-civ, *Ishmael* type ideas with the theories of the likes of Howard Zinn and anti-imperialist, anti-colonialist stuff. Then I went to John Zerzan, and now I'm really good friends with Kevin Tucker. I think he is one of the biggest thinkers and speakers in anarcho-primitivism. It's kind of funny too, because I knew about *Species Traitor*, Kevin's zine, even when I was in Racetraitor, and now it's become this thing that I'm really into.

How do you see the relationship between Jensen and Zerzan? It seems that while a lot of people on the left remain open to Jensen and see him as someone who is able to build bridges, Zerzan is seen as more of a pariah with his radical anti-leftist critique.

Overall I would tend to agree more with Zerzan. I'm also really into the anthropological aspect, which seems to be more important to Zerzan and Tucker than to Jensen. But I already said how important it is to have dudes like Jensen and books like *Ishmael* because these are such good starting points for people who are new to all these things. I also think that it is really important to have guys who can kinda bridge the gap.

But, ultimately, I think the Zerzan school, or more so even the Tucker school, is really central. I agree with their anti-leftist critique. All those things are part of civilization, obviously: communism or socialism aren't at all dealing with what the problem is.

So what do you say to people who, for example, spend a lot of time trying to secure health care for folks who don't have any, or who try to organize unions for unprotected workers — are they just wasting their time?

That's a really difficult issue. It's certainly not that I'm totally opposed to these things. I mean, as a dude who came from a lot of human rights stuff with Racetraitor, I definitely still care about that struggle. It's important to ease suffering. Besides, I'm against oppression, and that means oppression on all fronts. And I do believe in justice. Since civilization is not gonna end tomorrow, it's important to fight all these fights, and that goes for each stage of the struggle. I think in the end it's all a matter of perception, perspective, and relevance.

For example, I just saw *Che*, the movie about Che Guevara, and I really got excited for the dude who came from a wealthy background and was a doctor and went on this trip and was like, "Fuck, I need to do something!" And, you know, I think for the time he did a lot of awesome things. The problem is that in the end there was still an authoritarian system that was set up, and people are still being ground under it, and there is still industry, and people are still working, and all the alienating aspects of abstract culture and symbolic thought are still there — all those things that Zerzan would talk about and I definitely agree with him. But it is really inspiring that there was this guy who was just a regular guy, and then he did something and it actually worked, and it changed the world. I think this is something that anyone with radical ideas, including anarcho-primitivists, can relate too.

I guess one of the arguments you hear from anarcho-primitivist circles is that all the mentioned struggles just help to make civilization more bearable and hence delay its collapse.

That's the thing that's so hard to say. I mean, in general I agree with that. Fixing a lot within the system helps to sustain it. The worse things get, the readier people become to hear and to learn and to change things. At the same time, people are being oppressed and I'm against oppression. I think this is a really hard question, and I think it's really hard to give a definitive answer. Luckily, I'm no spokesperson for anarcho-primitivism and don't claim to have the gospel truth.

I do believe the following though: ultimately, people need to see that, no matter what happens, no matter how much you change about the health care system or workers' rights, it's the fact that we are working, it's the fact that there are hierarchical systems in place, it's the fact that you have to appeal to people in charge, that's what's fucked! The whole system is fucked from the get-go. We shouldn't even have to worry about that stuff when there is a way of life that humans have lived for millions of years where none of this was a problem, where there was no division of labor, no hierarchy, none of the things that we have now.

Let me confront you with another common criticism of anarcho-primitivism: all that stuff that you are critiquing, the fact that we have to work, symbolic thought etc. can only be critiqued by people who have no real pressing struggles in their own life — they don't need to struggle to send their kids to school or get enough to eat or a job that pays the bills. In other words, anarcho-primitivism as a Western middle-class phenomenon.

Oh, I totally understand that. I totally understand that there are situations and contexts that people are living in where they don't have the luxury of thinking about things like that; where it's really abstract and doesn't apply to their situation. However, when we really wanna speak about the ultimate causes of what's wrong with the world, I don't think there is any way around anarcho-primitivism. These causes aren't based on class or race or some specific situation that you are in. But, as I said before, I understand that people need to be doing certain things in these specific situations. People are working, people are suffering, and things need to be changed on all levels.

Ultimately, though, I think civilization needs to come down one way or another.

And hopefully it will happen sooner than later because the loss of life will be more the longer we wait. And I think that's really the crucial thing: continuing to eek out civilization's existence is only gonna kill more life: human and otherwise.

That's an interesting take, because people often say that if we all lived like Zerzan or Tucker would want us to live, the world population would be down to a fraction of what it is now.

Yes, I totally understand that too. However, obviously the ideology or philosophy of anarcho-primitivism is not calling for the mass murder of anyone. But the reality of the situation is that the earth can't support this many people, only civilization can. And this civilization will come down some day, just as every civilization has in history. The explosion of population stems from the advent of civilization, particularly industrial civilization. The population explosion that the latter caused was just insane. Civilization is not sustainable and it will end — whether we will end it ourselves, or whether the myriad things we are doing to the earth will destroy it, something will happen and it's all gonna be over, and a lot of people will die.

So what are anarchists supposed to do? Prepare themselves for the downfall, which is partly Kevin Tucker's approach, I guess? Or do we actively contribute to it, because the sooner it all comes down the better? If so, how do we do that?

I would say all of those things. First, I definitely agree with Tucker, and I've been trying to learn as many wilderness skills as I can. I think that's important for anyone, no matter what, because we are humans, and these are the skills we're actually supposed to be learning as opposed to math and science. Besides, I think it's something that's cool and fun and really satisfying at a deep level. To have that kind of skill-set leaves you feeling something more. So I do think that's crucial. But I also think that it's crucial to bring about the collapse as soon as possible, because, as I said, every day is — how many? — 200, 300, 400 species of life lost? How much longer can the planet afford this in its well-being?

As for how to do that, I can't really say. A lot of the means available are not really open to me because I'm in a public position where it'd be pretty stupid to get engaged in them or to have connections and networks like that. It would be dangerous and compromising. But there's a lot of information out there, and there are a lot of groups that are doing good things. ALF and ELF are the obvious, and there are others.

Armed struggle is an option?

I think that armed struggle is an important facet of how change needs to happen. Going back to Che, one of the things I find most inspiring are his theories about armed struggle. Now I don't think that the political ramifications of what Che did were for the best, but I can really relate to the reason behind it: like, when he was asked about the meaning of armed struggle and revolution, his answer was: love. I agree with that, I think that it's all about love: love of humanity, love of the world, love of all species of life.

So you're open to all sorts of means?

Oh, yes, I think it needs a variety of means. And, like we were saying, there remain situations where people need to change things within the context that we are living in today. So it needs a variety of struggles too.

Since this is a book about straight edge we have to start talking about that... How does straight edge play into your politics?

One of the reasons why straight edge became important to me is because I'm an addict. Whatever things I embrace, I have the tendency to go to the extreme, so straight edge was kind of my salvation with regard to that. I couldn't do anything within moderation.

That being said, in joining Racetraitor, and in being politicized more solidly, straight edge became entirely political to me because of all the things that the industry of drugs and alcohol have been used for in the pacification and criminalization of different groups of people. It was a big part of COINTELPRO, the counterintelligence program in the 60s, and the CIA used it against the Black Panthers, the American Indian Movement, and other radical groups that were setting out to change things for the better.

It's well documented that crack was flooded into impoverished neighborhoods, which a) apathizes people, and b) criminalizes them. In turn, this sets up the new slave trade, which is the prison-industrial complex — you can see in the make-up of the prison population what that's all about.

Alcohol has been used to destroy indigenous communities all over the world, in Australia, America etc. So these are the reasons why, just on a moral level, I can't support any of these industries. Besides, in the end, it always goes back to Earth Crisis: it's about the purity of mind.

In my experience with anarcho-primitivist circles, straight edge is not exactly a hot thing. What are your experiences?

My connections to anarcho-primitivist circles are not that deep really. I know Jensen, I know Zerzan, who I've met a couple of times, and I'm friends with Tucker. And Tucker is straight edge. Or "feral edge," as he calls it: the anarcho-primitivist version of it. It's a big part of what he's into. I think he has a great analysis of drugs and straight edge and of how it connects to anarcho-primitivism. He has this shirt that says *Feral Edge — anything less would be civilized*. I think that sums it up pretty well.

It's a big thing for me, too. A lot of drug use comes with sedentism, which is one of the initial things that lead to civilized living since it causes dominionism and domestication. I think drug use and its social implications are big factors in civilization because we have become so socially retarded, so stunted in our social growth. We have no real social connection and alcohol serves as the big social lubricant. I think it's so obvious how drug use is prevalent in civilized societies and why it's a bad thing for so many different reasons.

How about veganism? That's another thing that doesn't appear so hot in anarcho-primitivist circles these days. It seems hard to find an anarcho-primitivist zine without roadkill recipes...

That's a big one for me as well. It's been really hard to wrap my head around this. I know that Tucker was vegan for a long time and now he does roadkill and stuff. I always understood that in a better way of living, in the way of living that humanity is supposed to live, I wouldn't be vegan. There is just a different connection, a different relationship. There's a relationship between predator and prey that has nothing to do with the relationship that civilization has to the animals it uses in the meat and dairy industry, in factory farming etc. So I definitely don't agree with the analysis that veganism saves the world. Not at all, because the whole question is still about civilization, and about farming and agriculture. However, having been vegan for so many years makes it really hard to just jump back in. Besides, within civilization veganism is important to me because, again, I'm against oppression and this applies to the meat and dairy industry and all that, and so that's another thing I just can't support. But I've been planning on buying some land up north in Wisconsin, to at least have something that can never be clear-cut and used for timber, and to have a place that's wild, a place that I can utilize natural survival skills on. And then maybe one day I'll start looking for roadkill, start fishing in natural ways and stuff. I don't know when I'll get to that bridge and when I'll cross it, but I assume it will happen. As I said, I've been struggling with this for a while now and have had lots of talks with Tucker about it. It's become kind of a running joke.

Let's go back to your connections to the 1990s vegan straight edge scene. You talked about how important Earth Crisis was. To be honest, I consciously did not approach too many people from that era as contributors for this book because, politically, it all seemed to become so ambiguous, not least with the very puritan tendencies. Does that make any sense to you, or do you think that's just "overly p.c." or whatever the verdicts are?

No, I totally understand that. I mean, different people would draw different lines, I guess, but I understand the concerns. And I think especially the puritan aspect of straight edge can be a real problem, not least with respect to anarcho-primitivism. I mean, as I've tried to explain, in the context of my life right now straight edge makes a lot of sense, but it can take on very problematic forms. I had my falling outs with people from that era too.

Quite a few people from the Uprising circles, where Racetraitor and the early Fall Out Boy stuff came out, turned towards Islam. How did you experience these developments?

Well, that also marked the beginning of the end of Racetraitor. Some turned towards Islam, others didn't, I was kinda young and mixed. I remember some of the guys explaining to me why Islam was *the* revolutionary way, and I was like, "Yeah, I can see that," but, I mean, I still couldn't fit it in into other things I knew and believed.

And you still can't, obviously?

Exactly. I mean, when I read *Ishmael* it became really clear how religion comes from civilization and is part of the problem. Not that I have a problem with spirituality! But the way it exists within civilized living is totally different to how it exists in the natural world.

I guess the natural world is an important reference point for you?

That, for me, defines anarcho-primitivism: I'm an anarchist because I don't believe in systems of authority and because I don't believe that anyone is there to rule us; and I'm a primitivist because I think we have lost our way and we belong into the system that has been around forever, and that's the natural world.

You said before that humans have lived for millions of years without the problems of hierarchy etc. So you agree with Zerzan's analysis that life in hunter-gatherer societies was egalitarian, had no well established authorities and so on?

Yes, definitely. I mean obviously there were a lot of different groups of hunters and gatherers, or band societies, which differed from one another in their social set-up. So there is no blanket way to explain them, but on the whole, yes, band society is a society that is comprised of much less people than any town, or village even, and obviously it works better: you know everyone, it's more egalitarian, it's more benefiting to the group. It's totally different from anything we know. And it's definitely better.

Alright, one more common criticism: band societies have no place for disabled or even physically weak people.

I think it all comes down to civilized living. We have a medical system that's been set up to extend our lives — disabled or not — so unnaturally that it's insane. Besides, civilization is the reason for most diseases we have. So, what will happen after the collapse? I don't think anyone can say that, but I think it's not gonna be pretty by any stretch of the imagination. And the further we go down this road, the uglier it will get. But I think eventually a certain balance will be reached.

Aren't you working on a comic book about what's gonna happen after the collapse?

I have been. I mean, I still am, I just don't have a lot of time. I'm also really scared sometimes that I suck at writing a comic. The idea comes from me loving comics and movies — a contradiction since they are part of civilization, I know — and especially zombie type post-apocalyptic stories. I really think there is a reason why they are so present in popular culture right now. I think it's because people kinda know what's gonna happen, they sense that things are changing and that things are getting bad. And so they are really interested in the question of what people would do when it all ends. But with comics and movies, they usually end up dealing with it in a really fantastical setting. There have been some recent comics, though — comics I really loved, like *The Walking Dead* or *Y: The Last Man* — that made me think that it should be possible to do a different sort of story about the aftermath of the collapse. First I just thought, "Man, that'd be something I'd be really interested in reading!" — and then I thought, "Okay, so why don't I write it?"

I guess the idea is to put some thoughts out there using a comic book, like not hitting people over the head with it, but being like, "Think about this resource running out, think about how bad it will get, think about how this will affect us all!" It's not anything I'm having any big commercial plans with; in fact, I was thinking of doing it DIY maybe. It's just something I've always wanted to do, and if there are a couple of kids out there who care, great!

You mentioned being into comics and movies as a contradiction since they are part of civilization. I guess anarcho-primitivists get to hear a lot of these arguments.

Sure. Also with Zerzan or Tucker, there is always the obvious, "Okay, so why don't you go and live it?" But I think these people need to continue writing about it because others need to hear their ideas and understand them and see what's, in my opinion, wrong with the world. Even if reading and writing are obviously contradictions too...

It seems to me that no one can escape contradictions anyway, and I guess everyone has to find a balance between their beliefs and reality. How does this play out with respect to you being in a commercially successful rock band? This must certainly imply many contradictions too?

There are huge contradictions. I fly a lot, I use a lot of fuels, we play shows for corporations that I don't agree with, we meet people I don't like — stuff like that. But, in fact, I think the whole experience has really galvanized my beliefs and my feelings, and I think it has got me to where I am today, to how radical I've become in my thinking.

I went through a pretty rough phase, where I was really bummed and lost, and I felt really hopeless, just wishing for the collapse. But the recent years and the experience with the band have made me stronger again. Maybe also because I've seen so many people mellow out, or sell out, or stop being straight edge or whatever. And seeing a lot of my friends fall on the wayside, within the band or outside, it just galvanized my beliefs and my convictions.

In being anarcho-primitivist?

In being anti-civilization and anarcho-primitivist, yes; and also in being straight edge and vegan within the context of civilization.

Does this not create problems within the band?

No, not at all. For example, the other guys did a lot of stuff for the election. But whenever we did interviews, I just wouldn't talk. They know what I think, they know that I'm not into it. Sometimes there'd be an interview when one of the reporters would direct a question specifically at me, and I'd be like, "Look, I'm an anarcho-primitivist, which means that I'm an anarchist, and so this is what I think about that... That being said, I think one of these two dudes is gonna be elected, and even though I think the difference is really minimal because either will be the head of the same shitty system, I guess it'd be better for Obama to win 'cause it'd be kinda cool from a historical standpoint." And I mean, there were other things to consider, like Sarah Palin could have been pretty damaging for women, lots of things like that. In the end, I just think it goes back to what we were talking about before: there are things that still need to be done in the situation we are living in now.

What about the social settings you find yourself in with the band? I assume you meet quite a few corporate executives and such.

257

For the most part I just avoid these situations. I hate that shit. But there are others in the band who can take care of that. I don't have to be there. When we're at shows and label people come, I just go somewhere else. And it's helped, 'cause it's kept the reason I'm doing the band pure.

Just one more general comment on the contradictions of being in this band: I think there are contradictions in any fucking job. So at least I can play music with some of my best friends, guys who I have been friends with for years. And I love music, I've always played music, and I love the music we play.

Do you feel that you can also use the public position you are in to inspire others? You know, like you said that Rage Against the Machine had a big impact on you...

Definitely. I think that's one of the best things about it. It's the same with Jensen who has some kind of mainstream appeal and is getting bigger. And I think he's so important because of that, because he does get out to people who others don't get to. And I have probably even bigger mainstream appeal and can get out to even more people. I might affect less people than he does because most of the people he'll get already have some kind of radical interests. But I can at least bring up something that someone's never heard and thought about before — and it might lead to them changing. That's why I think Rage was so good. I understand all the criticism that they got, and I understand all the criticism of myself and the band I'm in — and the band I'm in is not even a political band. But that's not the point, I guess. Anyway, I understand all that, but I think it's just so important to educate and to use the opportunity I have. So anytime I can, I talk about stuff.

I also have a website now with a forum and a message board, *fuckcity.com*, and I'm on it a lot, talking to kids, you know, fans of the band or whatever. The main thread I'm on is the one about collapse and anti-civ ideas. Just getting these kids to think about all this stuff has been pretty crazy. It's just a couple of hundred people, but these are kids who had never heard about any of this before, and it's pretty uplifting. It's a really cool thing to see.

I'm using the site to talk whenever I can, and I wish I could do more. I strive to do as much as possible. Sadly, in the media I'm kinda pushed to the side a lot. Like, we recently did this article with *Blender*, and they just made me look like a total survivalist crazy dude. I think that tends to happen when I talk about stuff — but they won't get me to stop talking.

Perspectives

- **Hardcore Networks (Interview)**
  Federico Gomez

- **Between Culture and Politics: Straight Edge as Intuitive Resistance**
  Santiago Gomez

- **Queen of the PC Police**
  Laura Synthesis

- **Why I'm Still Straight Edge**
  Ross Haenfler

- **Building Bridges, Not Barriers: Positive Force DC, Straight Edge, and Revolution**
  Mark Andersen

Hardcore Networks
Interview with Federico Gomez

Federico Gomez is an Argentinean-Israeli-Swedish hardcore punk rocker who has fronted the influential Israeli hardcore bands Nekhei Naatza (1990-97), Dir Yassin (1998-2001), and Smartut Kahol Lavan (2002-06). Together with his brother Santiago he was a driving force in the development of a radical hardcore punk/straight edge underground in Israel in the 1990s. Today he lives in Falun, Sweden.

You were born in Argentina but moved to Israel as a kid. This was a direct consequence of Argentina's politics at the time. How old were you?

I was eleven. The reason we — my mother, brother and I — moved to Israel was that my father was kidnapped and killed by the military regime. My mother thought about starting a new life with another person in a different environment. But we were never Zionists and our criticism towards the country began already in our teens, a bit after the Intifada broke out — which was around the same time we discovered punk.

Jonathan Pollack from Anarchists Against the Wall talks in this volume about the rather unique Israeli punk and hardcore scene and how it has both really strong straight edge and anarchist streaks. I understand that you and your brother Santiago — who is also contributing to this reader — were very central figures in developing the scene in the 1990s. How did straight edge and anarchism get to merge in the small kibbutz near the Lebanese border where you grew up?

To be honest, although I really liked the idea of straight edge as one of the possibilities/philosophies of hardcore punk, I never felt "committed" to it, even after technically becoming straight edge. I was never too interested in smoking and doing drugs. I did drink a bit during high school and the couple of years following my graduation. However, I stopped when it became clear that I didn't need to go to pubs anymore to have a social life: the Israeli punk scene took off and I made friends with people who I shared more than just a space, cigarette smoke and liquids with. Another factor for not drinking anymore was probably my disgust with the apathetic, drunk punk losers that the scene had a fair share of.

I think that my interest in punk/hardcore came from two different sources. One, a love for loud rock music. Two, an interest in various

I Shot Cyrus (Brazil), São Paulo, 2009   Daigo Oliva

socio-political issues. During my early teenage years, I began exploring pop music and then rock. My discovery of punk came when I was looking for a rawer and more honest type of rock, so punk/hardcore seemed tailor-made for me. Its contradictions and ambiguities just made it more interesting and appealing, while some of the more political bands such as Conflict and Dead Kennedys had a really big impact on my thinking.

Concerning politics in general, I grew up in a family of political activists and was interested in politics and social change since a very early age. The anarchism that punk fanzines talked about made much more sense to me than the radical left-wing ideas I had previously been exposed to. The more I learned about the development of punk, its different scenes and the ideas of the people involved in it, the more I considered it to be one of the best and definitely most interesting possible expressions of anarchism. Regardless of whether you had a circle-A painted on your pants or whether you were in a group objecting to radical politics, I saw punk at least as a healthy anarchic injection of political and social criticism, solidarity, iconoclasm and artistic nihilism into the tradition of rock'n'roll, emphasizing this tradition's DIY aspect. I never thought that punk/hardcore (or any kind of music, for that matter) will change the world, but I always thought that it can serve as a network for those who, among other things, want radical political and social change.

When I found out about straight edge, it totally made sense for me as an extension of personal responsibility and social critique — themes that many punk/hardcore bands were singing about in different contexts. When I read zines from the late 1980s — the time when my brother, a friend and myself got into punk/hardcore — and the early 1990s, the criticism against straight edge seemed so idiotic (which surprised me since they were mostly coming from "political" punks) that I probably began developing a sympathy for it just because of the sheer idiocy of its detractors. The fact that some of the best hardcore bands at the time were either straight edge or labeled as such (I'm obviously referring to the early Revelation stuff) made me even more interested in finding out about this sub-genre of hardcore punk.

However, looking back at it, I think that what we understood as straight edge, based on the bits and pieces of information we had, was more sophisticated than what the bands — or the odd sXe zine we managed to get — had to say about it. It became apparent pretty soon that the "youth crew" bands and their scene had removed themselves from "punk" in the sense that they had dropped the sarcasm, contradictions and idiosyncrasies for a "healthy lifestyle for the youth." Although I liked the music of Judge, Chain of Strength, Wide Awake, Youth of Today, Gorilla Biscuits and many others, I thought that their lyrics and attitudes were lacking much of what I saw as interesting, important and defining in punk.

As a result, I would say that my personal understanding of straight edge was not the one you encountered in the straight edge scene. There were merely partial overlaps. My perspective focused on personal responsibility, freedom and control, and not on some kind of dogma to follow. I'm not saying that the vast majority of the people involved in the straight edge movement, or the vast majority of the people who define themselves as straight edge, were simple-minded bigots. In fact, most people I have met who identify as straight edge or have sympathies for it are among the most inspiring and nicest people I have ever met. Furthermore, most stories about "idiotic straight edge guys who beat up drinkers" are urban legends invented by conformist and boring punk kids.

Still, a movement of sorts emerged where people *did* actually spend hours debating whether to drink coffee or to eat liquor-filled candy made you lose "the edge." A lot of the implications of this scene were ridiculous to me: all the religious and millenarian metaphors, the focus on single issues that were disconnected from any wider perspective, the self-involvement of Western upper class kids and how seriously they took everything — at least for some months until they moved to the newer fad.

Sure, I thought it was fun sometimes to use sXe sloganeering as a means to piss off drunken losers and glue sniffers, but for the most part I had lost interest in what straight edge had to offer by the mid-90s. Musically and aesthetically, I had always been much more impressed by the rage and fucked-upness of early 80s hardcore —

and the nihilistic fun of 70s punk — than by the "clean-cut youth" image that most sXe bands chose. And then, when sXe bands began to play metal instead of angry hardcore and when most of them became derivative and lacked any sense of urgency, I simply began to ignore the straight edge scene altogether. Well, that's maybe not entirely true. But if I followed some of what was going on, then more as a phenomenon than as something I felt inspired by — the hardline stuff is a good example for that.

In general, during the 1990s I was much more into listening to early 1980s straight edge bands like Minor Threat, SSD, DYS, 7 Seconds, Uniform Choice and others, and to the early Revelation/late 1980s youth crew stuff; I hardly listened to anything that came out of Upstate New York or Cleveland. There were some good 1990s sXe bands, such as ManLiftingBanner, Nations on Fire, Refused, Sairaat Mielet in Finland, Personal Choice in Brazil, and a few more, but I guess it is pretty safe to say that they all felt out of place or marginalized within the wider sXe scene.

What is your approach to "drug-free living" now?

After having lived for several years in Sweden, I find the "night culture" and the drinking even more repulsive and destructive than before. My tolerance for drunken people has become very low and I try to avoid being around them as much as I can. But this does not mean that I see alcohol as an "evil substance" in a religious/taboo sense. Again, arguments about whether straight edgers can use wine for cooking or whether it is "allowed" to taste a cocktail still only amuse me. As I said before, I never cared for cigarettes or drugs, and while I will never support moves to prohibit them, I'm still glad that my right to breathe less polluted air has been recognized. It took me a while to go from being a vegetarian (which I started during my last year in high school) to being a vegan (which I have been for over seven years now) but I'm happy and proud to live a life rejecting animal exploitation as much as I can.

When we first met in 1996 I came to visit because I was curious to see who was behind the "Upper Galilee Anarchist Brigade" — I believe that I didn't even know that you were straight edge at the time. Can you tell us a little more about how you thought that anarchism informed straight edge — and vice versa?

The "Upper Galilee Anarchist Brigade" was a name we first used jokingly to sign anti-racist letters we sent to a mainstream youth magazine. However, somehow it stuck and we continued using it for publishing zines, booklets and tapes. How did straight edge relate to it? Given my non-militant brand of sXe, I guess it just struck a strong personal chord with me and I adapted and integrated it into my life — and that means my political life as well. But I usually didn't see any point in discussing it unless provoked.

To be a little more concrete, I think that the issue of personal responsibility was particular important and this was also something I discussed in different contexts, for example in the band I was in. However, I never attempted to win "members" for the "sXe movement," or claimed that sXe would be a solution for all personal and social problems and dilemmas.

Even though you spent most of your youth in Israel and now live in Sweden, you always remained connected to Argentina. Can you tell us a little about the straight edge scene there?

I think that it would be unfair to talk too much about a scene which I never really took active part in and don't even know so well. It is true that I was always very interested in the Argentine punk/hardcore scene and that the articles about it in the Argentine political newspapers that were sent to my mom were crucial in developing my interest in punk in general. But save some exceptions — N.D.I.'s *Extremo Sur* for example — I could never get into the Argentine straight edge scene because I saw it as too influenced by the metallic, New York, early 1990s type of sXe hardcore that I never really cared too much for. I'm sure though that my prejudice made me miss some good stuff and that I will eventually catch up with it; but in general terms, I think that compared to the interesting 1980s punk/hardcore scene, the 1990s weren't such a great time for the Argentine scene.

This seems to confirm what Frederico from Point of No Return told me. He said that there was a strong shift in Buenos Aires in the 1990s to the Victory and New Age style.

Yes, that was exactly my impression and the reason why I was not really interested in that whole scene. Unfortunately, I haven't really kept up with the developments since, so I'm not sure what's happening right now.

A few years ago you also went on a longer trip through South America, staying with many people you knew or had been in contact with through the hardcore scene. What were your impressions?

I was in touch with Pedro from — among other bands — I Shot Cyrus through the internet and thanks to him and Frederico from Point of No Return, I managed to get contacts in Brazil, Uruguay and Chile, and ended up meeting lots of people there. I have to say that I was very impressed with what I saw. I also learned a lot about the social and political situation, having access to various different perspectives that many travelers may not have. The hardcore/punk/straight edge scene in Brazil was one of the best, if not the best, scene I ever visited, in every possible aspect one can think of. Basically all the people I had the pleasure of talking to seemed very interested in socio-political issues, and the majority were politically active in various forms — without ever limiting themselves to mere catchphrases. There also seemed to be a lot of solidarity within the scene(s) as well as with other political groups and organizations. Both the bands and the audiences I experienced were enthusiastic and fun, and despite the economic hardships that many scenesters have to struggle with — or perhaps because of them — things appeared really well organized.

Even though the circumstances of your life have somewhat changed in recent years and you are not immediately tied into a hardcore scene at the moment, I know that hardcore, straight edge and anarchism all remain important to you. Share some more thoughts with us before we end this: how do you see the straight edge hardcore scene developing politically and what are the potentials it still holds?

Alternatives to both the mainstream entertainment industry and capitalist or authoritarian politics are vital for our survival as free individuals and I think that punk/hardcore/straight edge movements can serve as networks to discuss, develop and implement these.

There have been a lot of changes concerning the place and role of so-called subcultures. Many of them have been co-opted and with respect to punk/hardcore it sometimes seems as it has turned into a "timeless bubble, where all vanishes in one big, consumer friendly blur," to quote from Erich Megawimp's blog. I hope this tendency will diminish, as there is still much to gain from the continuation of punk/hardcore. In any case, networks for people to challenge the status quo and to share honest, non-commercial forms of art will certainly continue to exist, no matter what they are called.

I believe that the experiences of the people involved in punk/hardcore/straight edge during the first decades of these movements may serve as an inspiration and a strong critical basis necessary for the development of anti-authoritarian currents; hopefully this book will make a contribution to that.

Between Culture and Politics:
Straight Edge as Intuitive Resistance
Santiago Gomez

Santiago Gomez is an anarchist, animal rights activist, and zine maker. His writings and DIY publications — many of which are documented in the volume *It's All Lies* (2002, edited by David Massey) — have been highly influential on the development of both Israeli straight edge culture and the contemporary Israeli anarchist movement. He has played bass or guitar in a number of Israeli hardcore punk bands, including Nekhei Naatza, the notoriously sardonic UxSxFx (Urban Skate Fanatics) (1996/97), and the anarchist vegan straight edge outfit Sleep Furious (2002/03). Santiago alternates between living in Tel Aviv and some place far from Israel.

"'We act by virtue of what we recognize as useful,' observed Bazarov. 'At the present time, negation is the most useful of all—and we deny—'
'Everything?'
'Everything!'
'What, not only art and poetry ... but even ... horrible to say ...'
'Everything,' repeated Bazarov, with indescribable composure."
Fathers and Sons, Ivan Turgenev

> "I'm just a spoke in the wheel
> Just a part of the puzzle
> A part of the game
> I'm being framed
> Innocent until I'm proven guilty
> Deny everything
> Deny everything
> Deny everything
> Deny everything!"
> **"Deny Everything," Circle Jerks**

Sometimes, it seems, it really *is* a question of "location, location, location!" — or perhaps of seeing poetry where there is none. So there we were, setting up our gear on that tiny, rundown stage with almost anti-gravitational speed: five kids, each from a different corner of the world, finding ourselves living here behind London's copper-tinted windows — and then of course finding each

Opposite: Discarga (Brazil), Steenwijk/The Netherlands, 2008 Mateus Mondini

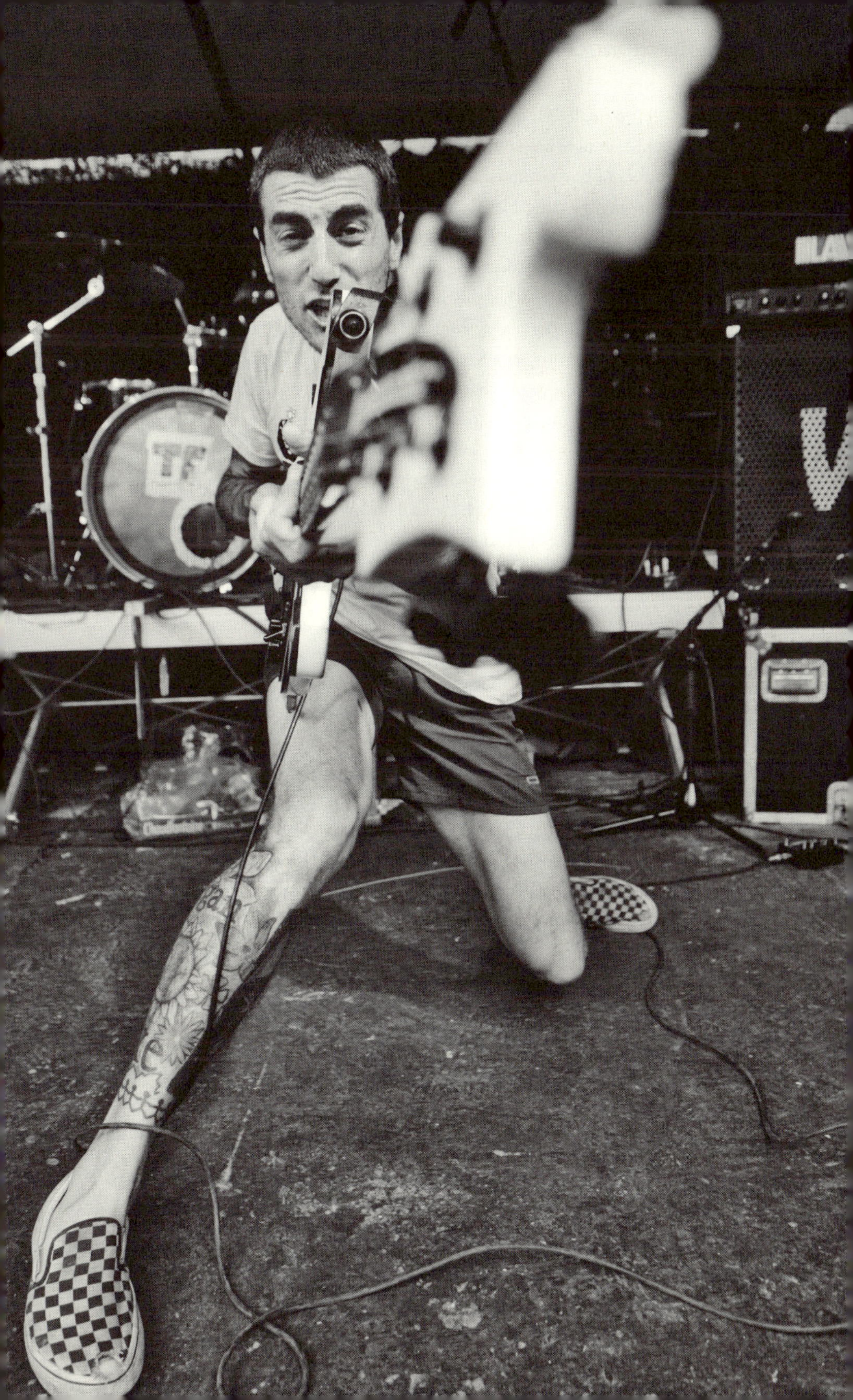
TF

other as well (no small feat, mind you). Five exceptions that negate the rule, all of us vegan, anarchist, straight edge punk rockers, tuning down to D to become tonight's entertainment for our boozed-up brethren in this squatted former Islamic girls' school.[1]

As I am untangling the cables slithering beneath my feet, a drunken woman who has obviously noticed our *Drug Free* insignia stumbles towards me and, with the help of some choice colorful British colloquialisms ("tossers," "wankers," "bollocks," etc.) slurs her disagreement with what she thinks we are all about.

Now, I'll admit I'm not a very confrontational person, I'm usually taken aback when sandbagged like this, so a few seconds pass before I finally lean forward and shout in her ear, well above the chatter and the bottle clinks, that she ought to wash her mouth with a shotgun. But in those few seconds — between red flashes of nano-fantasies where I bury my elbow deep in her nose bridge — I had a sudden, equally deep realization. Well, actually, not so much a "realization," but, y'know, words came to me, sentences fully formed, which I jotted down once we finished our set; and that is what you're about to read, more or less.[2]

x X x

It seems almost Monty Pythonish that oh-so many years ago someone could sing about the frustrations of feeling alienated from his peers and their preferences, throwing in a couple of examples to illustrate his point, and thousands upon thousands of benchwarmers would then choose to fixate on those specific examples, forging coats-of-arms outta them, getting bogged down in ridiculous discussions about how theine, speed-dating or toad-licking relate to their petty definitions...

—*"Let us, like Him, hold up one shoe and let the other be upon our foot, for this is His sign, that all who follow Him shall do likewise.*

—*No, no, no. The shoe is a sign that we must gather shoes together in abundance.*

—*No, no! It is a sign that, like Him, we must think not of the things of the body, but of the face and head!*

—*Cast off the shoes! Follow the Gourd!*

—*Hold up the sandal, as He has commanded us!*

—*It is a shoe! It is a shoe!*

—*It's a sandal!*

—*No, it isn't!*

—*Cast it away!"*

---

1. I am referring here to the band Hello Bastards, in which I play bass, and to an unofficial anarchist Bookfair after-party we played at East London's RampART squat in October 2008 (a benefit gig for the Hunt Sabs).

2. Among the words I scribbled in my little notebook that evening are also bizarre, broken lines that make no sense. For example: "I used to think all drunks were idiots, but I don't anymore; I've changed my mind about idiots." Huh?

Just like in what science geeks know as "quantum decoherence," I believe it is impossible to understand what straight edge initially aspired to be, as well as what it actually was; impossible to either define or describe it, while squinting through "code of conduct" lists, broken down into three or four sections, fissures really, that collapse the whole damn thing by reduction. The often-forgotten fact that the X's originally marked the spot that was youth — not sobriety — is just the tip of the iceberg.[3]

I maintain it is impossible to understand straight edge with such strict, shallow coordinates, not because of the conventional punk wisdom that "rules are stupid" — which may or may not be true — but because narrowing this phenomenon down to specific herbs, beverages or chemicals draws our focus away from the epicenter, from the fire, the raison d'être of straight edge, which is basically an unapologetic, take-no-shit reaction to social estrangement, something it shares with (and inherited from) punk rock.

Indeed, if punk is to be broadly understood as teenage angst dogged by exclusion and alienation, as kids getting bored or fed up with their immediate surroundings and lashing out at them — then what is straight edge but the exact same sentiments resurfacing once more, directed inwards, punk's thesis-antithesis-synthesis, its chickens coming home to roost?[4] Remember Ahab's choice of words as a typhoon threatens his beloved ship in Melville's novel, clutching his harpoon, spitting at the electrical storm: *"Oh, thou clear spirit, of fire thou madest me, and like a true child of fire, I breathe it back to thee."*

The need to emphasize this continuity — readily acknowledged in musical/historical contexts but rarely in the context of *spirit* — stems from a tendency among mainstream media, as well as more overtly reactionary elements, to portray straight edge as a sort of clean, non-threatening heretical divergence from punk, at times even juxtaposing the two as near-inversions. I actually remember seeing an article in some Israeli magazine from the 90s titled "Straight Edge, a Fashion Your Mother Could Love!"

Of course, since music and history have just been mentioned, it's worth noting that to extrapolate punk rebelliousness from straight edge on those terms you'd have to dig a bit deeper than Minor Threat: to the band Teen Idles, whose lyrics, rife with classic punk motifs of youth and boredom, give a more engaged sense of straight edge's primordial soup than even the very song titled "Straight Edge" can. Moreover, I would argue that Susie J. Horgan's achromatic photographs alone, as presented in

---

3. A similar sort of confusion, which again says more about the mentality of the misrepresenters than the misrepresented, occurred a couple of years earlier with fellow punk rocker Richard Hell, whose most famous lyrics were meant to read "I belong to the _____ generation" (with readers filling in the blank), but instead become known simply as "Blank Generation."

4. I'd like to think that perhaps, on a somewhat subconscious level, this is what the straight edge-affiliated fanzine *HeartattaCk* meant to convey when it chose the slogan "Hardcore for the Hardcore"...

the 2007 book *Punk Love*, contain a more vivid and instructive insight into what the essence of straight edge and its true genealogy were (*and for many, myself included, still are*), than any of the scholarly books or articles I've come across.[5] It's all about the spirit of things, the crystalline ethos — the heart.

x X x

"Okay, fine," you may sigh, "dully noted; but why drive this 700-word point home like a mental patient with power-steering?" Well, as a Jew I'm tempted to answer this question with another question (for example "why not?"), but I'll try and stay concise. Beneath the attempt at reconciling straight edge with punk[6] lies the suggestion that if indeed the same sensitivities and undisciplined energies run through their veins, perhaps they could share something else — a shapeless and unmalleable interpretation that transcends categorical by-the-book definitions.

Punk has some general, widely recognizable characteristics, true, but I think we can all agree it is basically something to be painted in bold, impressionistic strokes only. You could dress like a Jamaican hippie, help old ladies across the road, use non-conventional instruments, sing happy, harmonious songs or play slower than a herd of snails traveling through peanut butter — and *still* be punk. Because, in a way, being punk is very much like being in love: there are no rules, no specifics, no rhyme nor reason and no real "definition" except a tautological concept of nearness and identification. And that's the way we damn well like it.

Sure, this vagueness has its downsides, for instance when people fling feces at their audiences or host MTV segments in the name of punk, while we are powerless to disassociate ourselves from them. But overall I think having a serpentine rather than rectilinear definition has not been a problem, and although what is and what isn't punk still constitutes a hot topic (*no pun intended*), I haven't heard many specific complaints about the lack of clear-cut boundaries. In fact, quite the contrary: it seems that in the last thirty odd years many of us, especially those who treasure punk the most, have worked to expand it and blur its features, reshaping it from a sort of exclusive narrative into a more inclusive, crazy one — whistling solos an' everything.

Taking into account the two points I just made — about the nature of both punk *and* the punk/straight edge continuum of spirit — I guess my next question is so obvious it practically poses itself: if the cultural phenomenon known as punk can be loose, associative, amorphous and defined intuitively, and still retain its strength and

---

5. Including, of course, this one.

6. In this (nonmusical) context, "punk" differs from "hardcore" mainly in terms of associations and inferred meanings. One could even claim this as an attempt at recolonization i.e. at bringing back the British Mandate — particularly by highlighting the direct yet unspoken bond between "Never Minding the Bollocks" and feeling "Out of Step."

relevance to our lives — then why can't straight edge? Why purposely keep straight edge in this self-induced, silver-jubilee coma?

The reason straight edge was watered down from a P.M.A.[7] into today's three-rule nonsense[8] is interesting, but it is essentially a sociological question, and sociology is too cold for me; I prefer the warmth of nonsensical honest-to-blog rants. Either way, the heart of the matter is not a question of what "real" straight edge is (although I believe I could lay claim to that as well), but simply of which approach works best within a punk frame, i.e. which attitude kicks the most ass. And in that respect, I think straight edge as "punks who don't take no shit, not even that of the other punks" is by far our safest bet.

x X x

"Here's to the confusion of our enemies!"
Frank Sinatra's favorite drunken toast

I can sense your impatience all the way from here... So what is all this vague, amorphous talk really about? What am I *actually* saying? Is it that straight edge means more than just abstaining from alcohol, tobacco and drugs — something that, let's face it, has been said countless times before[9] — or am I perhaps going as far as suggesting that the aforementioned substances have no inherent relevance to what I think straight edge is, and that someone could even — gasp! — ingest them and *still* be straight edge? Well, in one word: yes. Lucky for us, though, there's no need to limit ourselves to monosyllabic answers, so we can elaborate.

To paraphrase a slogan made popular in the 90s by a certain Louisville, KY, band, *Straight Edge is a Non-Bullshit Movement*. That's it basically, end of story. As we all know painfully well, drinking, smoking and doing drugs make up a sizable slice of punk shows' bullshit pie-chart, and that — as opposed to puritanical notions of "clean living" — is the only reason straight edge has anything to say about them; they relate to straight edge's definition in a purely circumstantial and extrinsic manner, not as something integral. If we ever reach a state where, say, novelty ringtones become a major nuisance in the punk scene that escalates violence significantly, makes people act like irresponsible morons, gets venues shut down or minors turned away at the

---

7. *Positive Mental Attitude* — popularized in hardcore culture by the Washington, DC, band Bad Brains.

8. A watering-down accompanied by the telling compression of "straight edge" (two words) into "straightedge" (one word).

9. Most notably by the concerned individuals of the 90s hardline movement.

door, stinks up the atmosphere (literally as well as metaphorically!) in the name of "coolness," etcetera, then I certainly think that "the straight edge thing to do" would be to raise a collective middle-finger to novelty ringtones, and thus novelty ringtones would become one of the things straight edgers "abstain from" in social settings. Hell, maybe we should start doing that anyway... (But I digress.)

Much like with the issue of veganism,[10] when it comes to straight edge I am not the least interested in what people inhale, inject, beer-bong, snort or otherwise put into their bodies per se (it simply isn't my business), but rather with the wider, cumulative social aspect of it all — specifically with the consequences it has on the punk scene as a whole. Before he used that trigger finger to shoot himself in the heart, Guy Debord put his finger on the heart of this matter when he wrote that "the spectacle is not a collection of images; it is a social relation between people that is mediated by images."[11] That is to say, straight edge, as I see it, is not concerned with how this or that substance affects your liver, lungs or webbed toes — *what are we, the freakin' FDA?!?* — but with how it affects social interaction, how it "mediates between people." Especially when those people are us punks.

I mean, is there really someone out there who needs me to spell out the negative, disastrous consequences drugs and booze have had on our scene lo, these many years?!? What Al-Qaeda cave have you been hiding in?

It is possible to smoke, drink or do drugs on an individual basis, without exacerbating the social problem that these substances constitute within our scene. In fact, there are plenty of people who do so.[12] I'm talking about those good souls who, for example, will not make our closed spaces unbreathable with cigarette smoke; who will not get so liquored-up that they ruin things for those around them; who will not pump themselves so full of drugs that they become liabilities or threats; and, most importantly, those who realize that these habits are not and should not be central to what being into punk is all about. Such people, who are often as annoyed as we are by infantile, irresponsible social behavior, I would be very happy to count within our ranks. Moreover, I genuinely feel they are closer to the spirit of straight edge than many who simply abstain from drinking, smoking or doing drugs due to some sort of disinterested, myopic personal preference.

---

10. Okay, let it be known that I had originally promised myself not to mention veganism or animal rights here *at all*, because I am fanatical enough about the issues to get considerably sidetracked, and there's really no need to complicate things further by tossing that into the mix, right?

11. *Society of the Spectacle* (1967), thesis 4.

12. I cannot help but mention the curious and ludicrous incident in which Ray Cappo had a glass of wine with his meal in some Italian village while touring with Better Than a Thousand some years back, before being forced to "issue a statement" about it! I mean, you couldn't *make* that shit up...

Perhaps the notion of a straight edge person taking the occasional swig or puff strikes you as being a few clowns short of a circus. In that case, let me refresh your memory: remember that band Minor Threat, for example, who everyone — including all you Answers.com know-nothing know-it-alls — agrees were the head honcho straight edge band? Well then, it might interest you to know that all of Minor Threat's members except one were precisely that — kids who, while being straight edge, would occasionally drink a beer or smoke pot, because straight edge to them wasn't a straight-jacket, nor a quasi-religious identity. Actually, if you go through old fanzines, you almost get the feeling that those guys spent the entire time between 1981 and 1983 explaining this basic premise to anyone who would listen. They even re-recorded one of their songs and included a spoken disclaimer about this very issue for God's sake![13]

Another seminal straight edge band worth mentioning here — this one from the second wave — is Chain of Strength, who not only left us with the age-old riddle "Has the edge gone dull?" and the ultimate tattoo promise "True till death," but also offered a challenging wider approach: *"In an interview, we stated that we occasionally had a drink. We made that comment and a lot of people lost their minds over it. We explained that straight edge doesn't mean never. It's your own set of rules. Straight edge is turning into 'don't do this, don't do that.' Everybody is living by everyone else's rules. When straight edge started, it was your own set of rules."*[14]

I don't want this to deteriorate into a list of examples, but believe me, there were plenty of other straight edge bands with similar attitudes, who based their outlook on the *crucial (again, no pun intended)* difference between the "use" and "abuse" of substances.

So whaddaya say: do we now bumrush their Wikipedia entries and "expose" them for the vile fakes they were — so disgusting they would make Caligula nauseous — or do we get a fuckin' clue instead?

x X x

"The purpose is within yourself
The movement is within yourself
Your emotions are nothing but politics
So get control"

"No More Pain," Embrace

---

13. "Listen," explains Ian MacKaye in the second recording of "Out of Step," "this is no set of rules. I'm not telling you what to do, all I'm saying is, I'm bringing up three things that are, like, so important to the whole world, I don't identify as much importance in. Because of these things — whether they're fucking or whether they're playing golf — because of that I feel... I can't keep up! Can't keep up! Can't keep up! Out of step with the world!" Could you be any clearer than this?!?

14. From an interview with singer Curt Canales right after the band's break-up, *Long Shot* fanzine, 1991.

Having saved the best for last, we now come to the million dollar question: *Is straight edge political*? The sensible answer would of course be "it depends," but sensibility is not our forte, and we don't like one-size-fits-all answers anyway. The straight edge record label Catalyst, for example, answered this question with a thousand t-shirts worth of a resounding Yes!, but although I strongly sympathize, I'd be careful of going into Warp Drive with this. You see, on the face of it, the question presents a marvelous opportunity to redefine straight edge; however, I would suggest that it offers an opportunity to redefine "politics" instead — at least what *we* mean by it.

Back in the day I was involved in an Israeli anarcho-punk project, the aptly-named IsraHell Collective, which among other things published a fanzine called *War of Words*. The fifth issue, dedicated entirely to the militarist stranglehold on Israeli society, was radical and controversial enough to make national headlines. Anyway, one night while working on the editing, I remember an interesting discussion around the issue of young people's refusal to be soldiers.[15]

Conscientious objectors — which all of us were, basically — are of course politically motivated. But we know for a fact that for every one of us, for every pinko "Refusnik," there are numerous young people in Israel engaged in what is known as "grey refusal;" people who resolve to place their own wishes and their own plans above anything the state might try to coerce them into. Now, I wouldn't dream of dressing up this silent absenteeism in radical or anti-establishment garments; and yet, when people make choices in their personal lives which are diametrically opposed to societal norms and expectations — not to mention legal obligations — you have to admit that such individualism carries, somewhere within it, certain indefinable political intimations.[16]

The only way in which I can perceive straight edge as being organically and inherently "political" is in a similar fashion: by proxy, so to speak, *intuitively*.

Throughout the years, several interested parties have attempted to pimp straight edge out to this or that belief-system in order to fill their own political coffers. Most famous perhaps are the religious elements — Krishna, Muslim or Christian — who built their wobbly bridges out of notions of "cleanliness" and moralistic mumbo-jumbo. In Europe there have been both Dutch communists — note the "drug free" Lenin quote in Manliftingbanner's 10-inch — as well as the more recent Russian National Socialists — note the Aryan Wear shirt with the X'ed-up Hitler that reads "The Original Straight Edge"! (technically speaking, though, the Führer *did* abstain from alcohol, smoking and drugs...)

---

15. Military service in Israel is mandatory for Jewish (and Druze) men and women. Men serve three years, women two.

16. The German anarchist Max Stirner dealt with this concept, which he termed "ethical egoism," at length in his 1844 book *The Ego and Its Own*. Unfortunately, I find this work too boring to recommend.

Anarchists and other free radicals — the only ones I'm really interested in discussing here, to be honest — are equally guilty of trying to appropriate straight edge via superficial parlor-tricks, with occasional denunciations dug up or faint resemblances extolled to create the illusion of likeness. Whether traveling a hundred years back to the lifestyles of the Bonnot Gang or simply across the border to liberated EZLN territory (in which alcohol and drugs have been banned by a collective decision), these supposed similarities never manage to go beyond poor photomontages of (mostly) out-of-context anecdotes, like for example from Nestor Makhno's biographer about his subject's "aversion for wine and alcohol," or perhaps the most famous of all, from Tolstoy's "Government is Violence": *"All government, without exception, conceal from the people everything that might further their emancipation, and encourage all that degrades and demoralizes them [...] all manner of amusements of the senses [...] even physical means of stupefaction, such as tobacco and alcohol, the tax on which constitutes one of the chief revenues of the state."*[17]

Alternately, there are bands, zines and soap-box aficionados who have labored long and hard to "politicize" straight edge through anti-capitalist and/or animal liberation aspects, emphasizing the corporate greed that drives tobacco, alcohol and drug industries, as well as the cruel animal-testing that the commercial manufacture of these substances entails. However, as I have said earlier, I feel that as much as I sympathize with the aims, these linkages are simply too crude, propagandish and superficial to be meaningful; they seem arbitrary — even capricious. The realities of both capitalism and vivisection offer no empirical basis whatsoever for singling out tobacco, alcohol and (particularly) illegal drugs for special treatment. Simply put, *every single product we purchase*, be it tofu, Star Wars figurines, non-alcoholic beer or Marlboro Lights, entails wide-scale environmental destruction, the death of countless animals (in fields, testing facilities, or both) and continued support for the machinations of capitalist exploitation.

Arithmetically speaking, when it comes to straight edge and politics, too many people confuse "1+1" with "1=1."

x X x

"To treat political ideas as the offspring of pure reason would be to assign them a parentage about as mythological as that of Pallas Athene [...] What matters most are the underlying emotions, the music, to which ideas are a mere libretto, too often of a very inferior quality."

British historian Lewis Namier

---

17. I would like to point out that an example of a more successful marriage between straight edge and anarchism — perhaps the most successful so far — is to be found in CrimethInc.'s excellent *Wasted Indeed!* pamphlet.

So, after this long, arduous process of elimination, I'd like to finally answer the question of whether or not straight edge is political, by replacing it with the question "does straight edge have something in common with anarchism?" To this, my answer would be, perhaps surprisingly, an empathic *yes*. I do not wish to get lost in repetition, though, and since basically all of this alludes pretty clearly to things I've already said (regarding the punk/straight edge continuum, *the spirit*), I'll try my best to keep it short and kinda sweet:

There's no denying that anarchism, particularly in its incubatory, "scientific socialism" phase, has/is realpolitik. Anarchists of all creeds have formed think-tanks and armed cells and workers' unions, published analyses and detailed platforms and concrete demands, involved themselves in a myriad of issues ranging from labor organizing and national liberation to ecological preservation or racial discrimination, and so forth; from philosophy through reformism to street-fighting, and back again.[18] However — and many "serious" anarchists might strongly resent what I am about to say — beneath all of the above, underlying the seriousness and the realpolitik of decades past, I seem to sense something else emanating from the anarchist movement — no, from the anarchists themselves, from the real flesh-and-blood people who this movement's politics attract: a kind of intuitive rebelliousness that transcends, perhaps even overshadows, rational argumentation; an ever-present anti-authoritarian impulse; a tendency to identify with the underdog and "the other" that borders on the reflexive.

I have a gnawing suspicion that, political rationale aside, we the anarchists are and have always been the aliens, the misfits, the marginalized, the born-rebels who have been "out of step with the world" since time immemorial.[19]

This is not to say that our ideological positions were never coherent or well-thought-out — they certainly were, they certainly *are*. At least as much as the rest of 'em. But by and large, there is something setting us anarchists apart that is not to be found in political philosophy or economic tracts. You may sometimes catch a glimpse of it in the writings of certain classic figures,[20] but mostly it is to be found in how we are and how we live, rather than in phrases and wordings. For example, to understand

---

18. In recent years (2003) I have had the privilege of being peripherally involved in the early stages of Anarchists Against the Wall, an Israeli direct action group that works alongside Palestinians in a joint, non-violent struggle against the Israeli occupation in general, and specifically against the Apartheid wall that is being built on Palestinian land in the West Bank.

19. Within modern anarchism, a good "justification" of such suspicions can be found in the vocabulary prevalent in its post-leftist variety — particularly among the insurrectionists drawing on Alfredo M. Bonanno's writings.

20. For example in the famous catechism of Pierre-Joseph Proudhon — usually a very reserved, analytical author — where he suddenly goes on a vitriolic and emotionally draining tirade about what it means "to be governed."

the political difference between Mikhail Bakunin and Karl Marx, the grand arch-rivals in the great anarchist-communist feud, only in terms of the question of the Dictatorship of the Proletariat, is to be completely oblivious to a paratext which can at times reveal more than any prima facie.[21] And the same can be said about the lives led by enough prominent anarchists to prove that this is more than a mere historical coincidence. *(Malatesta's first arrest at the age of fourteen, Berkman's inhuman perseverance through fourteen nightmarish years of prison, Goldman's visionary free spirit, et al. — we don't really need more namedropping here, do we?)*

Many 70s politicos went out on a limb by claiming punk was essentially anarchist. They were right. Now I would like to return the favor by proclaiming anarchism essentially punk. And, moreover, by testifying that straight edge has been pierced by the same magic bullet theory and bleeds the same rich dark blood of intuitive resistance. We are all allergic to bullshit, and we are all out of step with the world...

One spirit, one fire.

Anarchist punks: one more effort to become XRevolutionariesX!

---

21. Both might have been sickly and poor in adulthood, but while Bakunin's life was a brutal rollercoaster of travel, deportations, plots, jails, work camps and insurrections, Marx could spend his days in the British Library and even treat his family to occasional bourgeois luxuries in their London house, supported by monies from Engels' family business, his wife's inheritances and his newspaper correspondent job.

Queen of the PC Police

Laura Synthesis

Laura Synthesis has been editing *Synthesis* zine and running a zine distro under the same name since 1995, organized gigs for a couple of years as the XdotXcottonX girls crew, helped open the vegan co-operative Pogo Cafe in 2004, and has been involved in the London Social Centres Network and some of London's anarchist women's collectives. She lives in a veganXstraightedge fortress with her long-term boyfriend and their vegan dog, Coco. Her plans for the future include starting an eco village in South London including green roofs with guinea pigs and a screamo salon.

"How does it feel to be Queen of the PC Police?" an old friend said to me recently one late night in Paris, "and how does it feel to have lost?" He was referring to the 90s, of course — that era when the hardcore scene was a battleground and straightedge spanned the conflict. On one extreme were the orcs of machismo, violence, commercialism, patriarchal religion and occasional cigar-chomping poses. On the other extreme were anarchist/socialist, atheist, DIY, 'PC' peacepunk feminists against violent dancing. Both extremes shared a few things — veganism, a love of metal (typically, though not in my case), and a straightedge lifestyle. My friend was right in a way; we did lose. We were always in the minority. It would take a hugely popular band that was very explicitly critical of profiteering and machismo to get the majority of those mid-range kids to re-examine their values, and a Catharsis was always going to be outnumbered by the American bands backed by PR companies and hugely commercial non-stop tours through Europe.

Then again, how do we define winners and losers? 99 percent of those kids aren't even into hardcore anymore, much less straightedge. The ones who were tripping off a macho fantasy had a superficial involvement and drifted through the scene and straight out again, carrying with them their 'true 'til death' vegan sXe tattoos. A surprising number of my comrades are still around because our lifestyles, values and beliefs were an integrated whole and we could find more to talk about with each other than gigs and record-collecting. So, are the losers the ones who moved on or the ones who are still involved in a youth counterculture in their thirties?

What could be more ridiculous than sticking to a youth counterculture when you spend all day with proper grownups at a full-time job and can't collect records because you have babies to support? In Europe, 92 percent of straightedgers drop out at by the age of twenty-six (I just made that up, but it's not far off). Now in my mid-thirties, I can inform those edgebreakers that staying true would have gotten no easier at the age of twenty-seven.

I think we all know that most people who temporarily call themselves 'straight-edgers' do so for self-esteem, peer pressure or social status reasons. These are also the main reasons people drop the edge and indeed leave the hardcore scene altogether. Social pressure in adulthood is more insidious than when we were youths. Life gets more complex and destructive life choices have more niches and cracks to insinuate themselves into. For those who feel tempted, it's worth stepping back from time to time to examine the societal effects of intoxication and addiction. Speaking personally, peer pressure to drink has no effect on me whatsoever, but I do feel the social repercussions.

I live in the famously sozzled United Kingdom, a society so alcoholic that drink isn't just the facilitator or basis of all social interaction, but its proxy.

"What are you doing this weekend?"

"I'm going out drinking/getting pissed."

If you don't drink, it can be assumed that you aren't interested in socialising at all. I'll present a couple of scenarios to demonstrate how difficult it can be to extract alcohol from everyday life.

Scenario 1:

The English way of starting a sexual relationship is to snog an acquaintance when both parties are drunk. There is simply no language for approaching the physical/emotional hurdle that people in this society are prepared to use.

Scenario 2:

People do notice, and comment, if one drinks non-alcohol at the pub or a party, no matter how low-key one is about it. Misery loves company and drinkers may feel anything from discomfort to anger around someone more sober than they are. They know it puts them at a disadvantage.

If anything, situations like these become more common after thirty as everyone's lives become so boring they can't do anything together but sullenly sip pints.

One of my sXe contemporaries is certain that by not drinking socially during one's late teens and early twenties, one ends up a 'cranky old loner' with no friends. When I think of the straightedgers my age who do have tight bonds of friendship, it is with other straightedgers (whether or not they call themselves this). On the other hand, I just as often see straightedge adults who hate each other and have been talking shit since the 90s.

It can be positive that many sorts of people are attracted to the sober lifestyle, or repelled by the drunk lifestyle, but it's not much of a basis for friendship in itself. On the contrary, and I am guilty of this, one can be more annoyed by straightedgers who are, for example, anti-abortion / support profiteering in hardcore / evangelical christians / all of the above, than by non-sober hardcore folks with these beliefs. Nevertheless, I wish we could find more common ground. When a friend loses the edge, I don't feel stabbed in the back. It's when a straightedger is too cool to want to know me that I feel real betrayal. When I meet a straightedger who is also an anarchist and into screamo, I almost can't believe my luck, though I know from experience that this is no guarantee of an ongoing relationship. Hardcore kids can be such social fuckups. Dammit people, shared understanding and values, even over something as superficial as straightedge, is a precious thing and these connections need nurturing and maintaining.

From reflecting on these things, I've gained a greater appreciation for the idea of 'straightedge sisterhood' — a term that never has amounted to much and is pathetically rarely associated with feminism. I've had great experiences of fun, mutual support, friendship and empowerment with women through the punk/anarchist scene, but sometimes it seems the explicitly sXe corners of the scene bring out the worst in insecure girldom (eg. popularity competitions and shit-talking). Nevertheless, the phantom of an idea like a sisterhood based on soberness in a world infected by drunk/drugged male violence has potential.

Let's have a posi, postmodern revival of the straightedge crew. Just because the '88 crew has the tinge of cultish, macho chauvinism about it, it's not like we can't reclaim and redefine it in the 21st century. Social solidarity is healthy — it gives us roots and comradeship in an atomised world and can be a base for building or co-operating for social change. When I meet a fellow punk, sober or otherwise, I'll keep trying to build those bridges because we all need each other and the better world we can create together.

We have potential as a counterculture because when we grew up we brought the scene up with us, developing it well beyond a youth movement. The radical straightedgers, I'll call us, saw that straightedge was a dead end for any progressive politics other than animal rights. Fortunately, by the end of the 90s, the punk/hardcore movement had evolved its activist aspects to such an extent that there were practical and exciting ways of putting punk values into practice — the direct action movement.

I'll admit even I'm surprised to meet a fellow anarchist/anticapitalist who is also sXe. These beliefs never gained much of a foothold in the main currents of sXe for various complex reasons — perhaps vegan consumerism had a significant part to play.

Nevertheless, we are out there. Some don't use the term 'straightedge' in order to distance themselves ('drug free adult', anyone?). Some, like me, long ago stopped going to typical straightedge gigs since they had nothing to offer that one couldn't get from a violent mugging by an anti-abortionist. Some have contributed to making the world a better place, and this points to one of my pet arguments for teetotalism — that it frees up our minds and bodies for more good works. Pace, all those drunk activists who do so much — I'd still like to see what you'd achieve if you were sober.

So we see from history that the hardcore scene developed a DIY strand and a commercial strand and a lot of blurriness in between. We neither succeeded in winning over the greedy bastards nor in kicking them out. On the contrary, various aspects of our beloved hardcore were sold to the highest bidder, at least for a few years until they went out of fad. Looking back though, doesn't the DIY stuff look, sound, feel, and generally stand up better than all those lame copycat products cranked out by certain Belgians and Americans? That, my friends, is because it was sincere and deeply felt when it was created and distributed with love by a network of friends.

I won't admit, therefore, that the 'PC police' lost. History always throws up the defeated as the moral victors and the Great Powers as deserving of scorn. Our strain of good works and good lives will shine through. And that's just in the hardcore scene. The progressive punks, including an influential contingent of sXe folks, can claim a global movement for human liberation at least partially their own.

By the way, I wasn't the most active womyn among radical straightedgers (stand up, the Emancypunx girls, among many others). I was perhaps just the one in Europe with the biggest mouth. Hardcore would have collapsed long ago without the unsung and unrecognised work of us wimmin behind the scene's scenes. So there.

Why I'm Still Straight Edge

Ross Haenfler

Ross Haenfler is the author of *Straight Edge: Clean-Living Youth, Hardcore Punk, and Social Change* (2006), the first extensive sociological study of the straight edge movement. He has been involved in straight edge hardcore for about two decades and works as an assistant professor of sociology at the University of Mississippi, where he teaches courses on social movements, political sociology, men and masculinities, and youth subcultures. He has been part of the anti-sweatshop, LGBTQ, animal rights, peace, and human rights movements.

In 1989, at the age of fifteen, I made a decision that would last a lifetime. I decided that I was tired of trying to prove my manhood to my peers by chugging beer or swigging booze. I made a decision to defy my society, through my actions, attitudes, and values. I determined I would never succumb to alcoholism as others close to me had done and I decided that tobacco companies would never profit by slowly killing me. I made a commitment that I would not treat women as objects and sexual conquests to be notched upon my bedpost. The thought of a fifteen-year-old making a lifelong commitment of any sort is laughable — many have trouble deciding between Facebook or MySpace, Xbox or Playstation, Vans or Converse. Yet here I am, twenty years later, still sXe. Or maybe just still stubborn. The old adage "true 'till twenty-one" isn't as true as many people think. Sure, most sXe kids will move on, growing up and out of the scene. But there are a lot of us for whom sXe still means a great deal.

Someone asked me once, Why, after all these years, would I still identify with sXe? After all, I'm not really part of a scene — I'm a university professor! Really, what's so bad about having a glass of champagne at a wedding or a bit of wine to celebrate an anniversary? And even if I wanted to abstain from drugs, alcohol, and tobacco, why claim sXe instead of simply living a drug free life? In fact, isn't it a little sad to hang on to an identity held mainly by adolescent boys and young men with whom I have only little in common? It seems almost ... undignified!

As they get older, many kids eventually give sXe up out of sheer frustration with the petty drama and the hypermasculine tough guy chest thumping that goes along with any scene — even though positive sXe

Cinder (Spain), Barcelona, 2008   Mateus Mondini

kids far outweigh the dogmatic, militant, holier-than-thou types. Others eventually tire of playing dress up, listening to the latest variation of hardcore, and comparing tattoos with twenty-year-olds. Some simply grow out of sXe as it seems less relevant, necessary, or important compared to a job, family, and other aspects of "adult" life.

    I guess none of these reasons ever really resonated with me. While I don't think there is anything wrong with occasional moderate drinking, I learned long ago how to relax, have fun, be social, unwind, get silly, be creative, feel good, deal with my problems, and so on *without* drugs and alcohol — so why start now? As for the macho atmosphere and sporadic violence, I would feel like I was giving in to the meatheads if I let them drive me away from something I love. And while there's nothing wrong with cool clothes and tattoos, that's not what attracted me to hardcore. I suppose I remain sXe for many of my initial motivations: I dislike the assumption that alcohol must be a part of nearly any social occasion; I believe young people face unfair pressures to use at a time when fitting in with one's peers matters a great deal; I think alcohol and tobacco companies profit from people's suffering; I believe that regardless of companies' intentions, drugs and booze are among the many things that keep us pacified and complacent in a world crying out for resistance. Which speaks to a deeper issue…

    Straight edge is more than music.

    Ironically, a number of *bands* have insisted on this all along. DYS sang, "More than X's on my hand / More than being in a straightedge band." Insted inspired me to think about my responsibility to the world, screaming, "We'll make the difference!" Youth of Today encouraged me to examine my priorities and "Make a change" to benefit others. Strife believed we could be a "Force of Change" and Bane sang that "Reasons not words" make us strong. Trial called attention to government repression and political prisoners, proclaiming, "you can't kill an idea and we will not be ruled by fear." Good Clean Fun saw the possibilities of positive change beyond the scene in "Today the Scene, Tomorrow the World." Vitamin X demanded that we "See Thru Their Lies" and "Fight" against "the corporate rich" and "their cruel politics." Limp Wrist challenges homophobia and oppression while Nueva Etica declares "El Tiempo Es Ahora" (the time is now) to defy a government complicit in the drug trade. For Have Heart sXe is "Something More Than Ink," while Verse encourages us to fight against apathy and "Set fire to this fucked up Empire."

With this as my soundtrack, how can I not be moved?

Perhaps the greatest reason I am still committed to sXe is an unfailing belief that sXe is more than music, that it can be a force of change. I believe in the power of sXe as a bridge to social change, as an opportunity to create a more just and sustainable world. Some might call me idealistic or even naïve. Rest assured, I am under no illusions that sXe kids will be the vanguard of some massive revolution, but neither am I so cynical to think that sXe can't be transformative for individuals, scenes, and communities. In researching my book, *Straight Edge*, I discovered that *many* kids credited sXe with opening their minds to new ideas beyond resisting drugs and alcohol. A majority became vegetarian or vegan as a result of sXe — and often went on to influence many people outside the scene. Some began considering environmental or human rights issues, while others questioned their own homophobia. Still others viewed sXe in part as a challenge to a soulless, corporate consumer culture based upon selfishness and greed. Straight edge women told me how being sober helped them feel more safe and in control of their bodies as well as freeing them, in part, from the straightjacket of mainstream femininity. Straight edge kids have long professed the virtues of having a "clear mind," for personal reasons but also to help see through society's illusions. It's up to us to use that clear mind to create a more progressive world.

Still, one could argue that any of these strides towards change can happen outside of sXe. Indeed, straight edge isn't the *only* path to an engaged life; it's simply *one* path, a path that has worked for many others and myself. So again, why still sXe? Several reasons come to my mind.

For one thing, I find value in keeping a commitment to ideals I find meaningful. We are forced to compromise our values so often in life that many of us abandon our efforts to live with some sort of personal integrity. Refusing drugs, alcohol, and tobacco may seem trivial in the big scheme of things, but for many it is *symbolic* of a larger resistance and a vow to live life on one's own terms rather than following a predetermined path to mediocrity.

I also feel we need a space, for young people especially, to escape and challenge a social culture centered on drinking. As adults, it's sometimes easy to forget the power of peer pressure and the hardships of feeling different, isolated, or even ostracized. Critics have often accused sXe kids, regardless of their actions, of being too "preachy" and self-righteous. Some are. Yet a few underground bands and some kids sporting Xs form just a small line of defense against the "preaching" of alcohol and tobacco companies, peer groups, and even, sometimes, parents. Having a place to belong, a second "family" in sXe, provides a lifeline for kids who reject the drinking-popularity game and who may face alcohol and physical abuse at home. As for me, I don't think it hurts to have a few "older" sXe people setting an example that regardless of what you do with your life you can live it drug free.

Finally, sXe serves as the foundation of an incredible worldwide community. There is something special about an underground scene spreading around the world, transcending cultural and language barriers to unite kids in a shared set of principles. I have corresponded with kids in Japan, Germany, Australia, Guatemala, Argentina, Iceland, Mexico, the U.K., Brazil, the Philippines and many other countries. I may not go to so many shows as I used to and I may only hang out with sXe kids a few times a year, but when I *do* go to a show I feel instantly at home — despite the fact that I may be twice as old as many of the kids there! Nearly *all* of my best friends, now scattered around the country, I met through the hardcore scene, some of them well over ten years ago. Many are still sXe; some are not. Regardless, we've shared many "times to remember" and I know I can count on them.

When I decided to claim sXe for life I did not decide to listen exclusively to hardcore, to wear a certain kind of clothing, to collect sXe tattoos, to attend shows twice a week, or to be a pretentious, judgmental jerk. Straight edge, at its core, is none of these things. The image of sXe as an obnoxious, sweaty, muscle-bound eighteen-year-old guy throwing down in a mosh pit leaves out the thousands of "kids" who have left behind the sXe pose in the process of posing an actual threat. Straight edge's flaws are many, including ongoing sexism, machoism, and occasional thuggery; the movement has a long way to go to live up to what I see as its true potential. Yet for all its contradictions, sXe has inspired tens of thousands of kids to live intentional lives and I, for one, have never regretted that decision I made so long ago.

Building Bridges, Not Barriers:
Positive Force DC, Straight Edge, and Revolution
Mark Andersen

Mark Andersen has done outreach, advocacy, and organizing in inner-city DC since the mid-1980s. He was a co-founder of the punk activist collective Positive Force DC in 1985, and is the author (with Mark Jenkins) of *Dance of Days: Two Decades of Punk in the Nation's Capital* (2001) and of *All The Power: Revolution Without Illusion* (2004). He lives with his beloved Tulin Ozdeger and their three cats in the Columbia Heights neighborhood of Washington, DC.

> "The rain of tears is over. The slums will soon be a memory, we will turn our prisons into factories, our jails into storehouses and corn cribs, our men will walk upright. Now women will smile, children will laugh, hell will be for rent."
>
> **Billy Sunday, 1919,**
> **shortly before the passing of Prohibition**

> "Everyone seems to be striving for utopia in the underground scene, but there are so many factions and they're so segregated that it's impossible. If you can't get the underground movement to band together and stop bickering about unnecessary little things, then how the fuck do you expect to have an effect on the mass level?"
>
> **Kurt Cobain, 1992,**
> **shortly after "Smells Like Teen Spirit" went Top Ten**

A skeptical interviewer once asked if I really expected everyone to stop drinking and eating meat, if that was what my "revolution" looked like. My response was to laugh quietly, smile, and say something like, "No, my revolution would look like each of us reaching toward the best of who we really are, while also looking out for and standing up for each other, past our many differences."

Her more pointed — and interesting — follow-up question was simple: "Well, how do you expect to make that happen?" Ah, but isn't that the million dollar question!

Mark Andersen, Washington, DC, ca. 1990   Karland Killian

There is no simple answer to this query, and I am not going to pretend otherwise here. Instead, I am going to suggest one possible response by telling the story of a dance. Both very personal and deeply political, this is the dance between three partners: the idea called "straight edge," and two interrelated — but distinct — concepts, "personal empowerment" and "movement/community building."

The choreography here is not simple. As someone involved in punk since the mid-70s, it is easy to recall a myriad of ways that I have been empowered as a result. Moreover, I've seen literally hundreds of other people find purpose and liberation from the punk world, including through straight edge, of course.

However, as the above quotation from Kurt Cobain suggests, personal empowerment is no magic wand that automatically brings about anything approaching "revolution" in a broader sense. And, contrary to the utopian vision of Prohibitionist Billy Sunday, neither does our own freedom from addiction, chemical abuse, or other mind-clouding, obsessive behaviors.

No matter how developed or strong our own individual sense of direction or power, we human beings tend to divide into small tribes, with often arcane and exclusive rules. Our feeling of power can come not from inclusion, but from exclusion, drawing a clear line between "us" and "them," the "bad" people and the "good" ones. Straight edge has too often been an example of this dynamic.

This approach is seductive, but ultimately futile, at least to the extent that it cuts us off from a more profound source of power: *people standing together.*

In many ways, individual empowerment is far easier than bringing folks together, much less keeping them united for some common cause, i.e., building a movement. Still more difficult is to build truly just, caring, and inclusive community, where we lift each other up towards our best possibilities, and look out for each other, past our differences, simply as a matter of course.

Yet, it is these less self-congratulatory, more self-demanding goals that we really need to aspire towards, past our own life drama and soul-search, at least if we hope to contribute to something as ambitious as revolution.

As I argued at length in *All The Power: Revolution Without Illusion*, while I truly believe that "revolution can start now with you," I also know that there is no one-person revolution. Personal empowerment and a certain degree of balance, sobriety, and clarity are pre-conditions, yes; but they are only the beginning of a life-long process that, in the end, has to involve broad, diverse masses of other people to be worthy of the over-used and often devalued word "revolution."

It is easy to say, but not so easy to do: real revolution means people together, becoming ever stronger, standing up consistently for a new vision of life, love, and liberation. In order to do this, *we need each other... and not just the people within our little group, who already agree with us, but the broader populace, filled with challenging but powerful diversity.*

Honestly, this can be a special challenge for those of us committed to straight edge. Given that most people (at least in our North American society) are deeply wedded to a way of life that includes alcohol and other drugs, as well as meat, how can we expect to find common cause without fundamental compromises? After all, straight edge is unique in that it is an anti-drug philosophy that comes from a largely secular radical counter-culture. That unusual balance of apparent opposites is what gives straight edge much of its power as an idea.

But let's set aside mainstream society for a moment, and return to Cobain's quote: sad to say, few concepts *within the punk community* have been as divisive as the simple, smart idea that we might have an edge on fighting the system, being ourselves, and uncovering truth if we didn't befog ourselves with drugs or other obsessive, addictive behaviors. To some degree, this simply shows how radical that notion is — but it also suggests the shortcomings of straight edge supporters.

As a co-founder of Positive Force DC, the first organized political voice from within the DC punk scene — birthplace of straight edge — I have necessarily had to wrestle with the complications of mixing an anti-drug philosophy with an effort at political mobilization... and I know that to strike the proper balance is not easy.

In fact, it has been tough enough to suggest perhaps the most unsettling question of all for those of us simultaneously committed to straight edge and the pursuit of fundamental transformation: *could it be that straight edge is actually counter-revolutionary, a barrier that keeps people apart, divided?*

The short, honest answer is yes, straight edge can be a barrier — but it doesn't have to be. If we do the dance in the right way, straight edge can help empower us, and provide a bridge to other communities… and, thus, to revolution.

x X x

> "Without community, there is no liberation, only the most vulnerable and temporary armistice between an individual and her oppression."
> **Audre Lorde, Sister Outsider**

For me, the process of reclaiming straight edge as a friend to revolution begins by simply remembering the community I came from: a rural, largely Scandinavian immigrant population rooted somewhat uneasily on and adjacent to the Fort Peck Indian Reservation in Sheridan County, Montana.

My initial punk rebellion was against what I saw as the "twin temples" of the rural working class: the church and the bar. This is to say that alcohol — and the community that grew up around consuming it — assumed an almost religious significance in my home county, as in other working class communities around the country.

As far as I could tell as a teenager, this faith was no liberation, but, rather, a tyranny. Perhaps even more than organized religion, alcohol seemed to be "opium for the masses" that kept people enslaved to a corporate-dominated, dead-end system, where one's life was literally consumed by work, tedious back-breaking labor that mostly benefited rich people far from northeastern Montana. On the reservation, the ugliness was even more obvious, as alcoholism was a plague in the native population, nearly completing the genocide begun by the guns, treachery, and territorial expansion of white people a century before.

For reasons I still don't fully understand, from the outset, I rejected drinking, smoking, and casual sex. In part, a dim awareness of alcohol-related domestic violence in a nearby native family (whose kids were my closest friends and play mates) must have had an impact. Also, learning about the drug-related deaths of early inspirations like Janis Joplin, Jimi Hendrix, and Jim Morrison surely helped turn me against that aspect of the 60s counter-culture.

New insights arrived as I grew older and struggled with the harsh grind of manual labor. I became outraged at the role of alcohol and other drugs in preparing my peers for a life of conformity and toil by providing an outlet for frustration, a way to dispel — temporarily and often at great cost — boredom and lack of meaning.

Finally, my critique was hardened by peer pressure to "fit in" by drinking or drugging. Embittered by the push to conform, I vowed to follow my own conscience, and sacrifice the social support of my peer group.

In these days before there was a movement called "straight edge," I was lucky to have encouragement in my otherwise lonely stand — doubly isolated, given my estrangement from the church — from the likes of Ted Nugent, Jonathan Richman of the Modern Lovers, and early west coast punks, the Dils. Nugent's crazed Detroit rock, Richman's gawky, vulnerable-yet-defiant anthem "I'm Straight," and the Dils' idea of punk as a rebirth of personal integrity, rejecting clichés of sex, drugs and rock'n'roll — these were the life-preservers I held to my chest in the stormy seas of teenage life.

This history is precious to me, and the sense of personal power I discovered was truly life-saving. Yet, it holds darker lessons as well.

Ted Nugent's steady slide to the far right over the past three decades suggests that simply not consuming drugs is hardly a guarantee of progressive — much less revolutionary — politics. Indeed, those back home who shared my anti-drug stance tended to be conservative religious folk, who generally would have been horrified by my other opinions. At the same time, my outspokenly self-righteous stance tended to create an immense distance from my peer group, as well as most of my home county.

At the time, this hardly concerned me, as I was, in effect, saying "goodbye and good riddance to it all!" In short, my struggle was all about "me," not really at all about any sort of "we," any sense of commitment to collective action.

At the time — as with most disaffected teens — it probably couldn't have been any other way. I was seeking identity, personal purpose, and power; without this foundation, I was just an alienated, verging-on-suicidal kid. However, as I exited Sheridan County at the end of the 1970s, settling into college life in western Montana, I began to shift from a solitary rebel pose to a broader activism.

At college, drugs and alcohol were, if anything, even more ubiquitous. Nonetheless, I began to connect to other students — neo-hippie types, church-goers, even a tiny number of other punks — on the basis of shared activist goals.

I heard about "straight edge" and the DC punk scene for the first time there in 1981. I adopted the label, and the knowledge of this broader movement strengthened my own personal position. Still, that stance started to retreat in importance in comparison to my activism, my deepening education, and my broader connection to punk. I studied radical ideologies like Marxism, anarchism, feminism, gay liberation, and deep ecology, reveling in the connections I discovered to the ideas in my favorite punk songs.

My imagination was captured by a new idea: a potentially revolutionary movement of misfits and throwaways celebrated by Tom Robinson Band (TRB) in their anthem "Power in the Darkness." TRB didn't want a solitary, purist stand; they wanted to bring the outsiders — punks, gays and lesbians, hippies, poor folks, labor unionists, racial minorities, immigrants — together to take over and remake society in a fundamentally more just and inclusive way: revolution.

For me, this was a huge step forward. Not only did this vision make sense ideologically, but it suggested, in principle, how to organize; i.e. broadly, not in a narrow, exclusive counter-cultural sense. While I could try to uphold a drug- and illusion-free lifestyle, my politics required straight edge as such to be, at best, the firm foundation underlying my engagement with other issues, issues that could provide common ground for collective action.

In fact, as I grew in my political consciousness, it became apparent that this meant that I had to make peace with Sheridan County and its people. Why? Well, simply because they were part of the people the revolution was for, the ones who were needed to build the movement, part of the power needed to make it real!

Moreover, the actual positive aspects of the bar (and church) scenes, as places where people met, became friends, and laughed and worshipped and shared their truths, however imperfectly, became increasingly clear. It seems ridiculous to have to say this, but say it I will: I came to recognize that not everyone in the "twin temples" was addicted, deluded, or a hypocrite; in retrospect, many led lives of admirable character and insight.

The dilemma for me as a would-be revolutionary became ever more apparent. While my personal integrity (sense of righteous superiority?) was intact, where was my community? After all, as the trailblazing African-American lesbian feminist writer/activist Audre Lorde argued, without community — a broader mass of people standing together — there is no real liberation.

Also left unanswered was the question of how to bring this broader mobilization about, especially for someone like me, who had survived as a solitary misfit, cut off from people at large. I was supposed to now be a "people-person," an organizer, a community-builder? Bit by bit, in group after group, with issue after issue, I tried to stretch to fill this new role.

My dance had taken me from personal empowerment to my first efforts at collective action. However, the ongoing challenge to grow implied by straight edge as much as by revolution was bringing me to a cross roads, caught between seeking a countercultural enclave or trying to help build a mass movement.

x X x

Building Bridges, Not Barriers // Mark Andersen

> "Isolation is the biggest barrier to change."
>
> Chumbawamba, 1984

In 1984, I left Montana and said hello to Washington, DC, and its renowned punk scene. In the two years after my arrival, I helped to co-found Positive Force DC (PF), left behind my academic studies, and immersed myself in the DC underground. This was, I would come to realize, both a step forward, but also potentially a detour into counter-cultural illusions, with straight edge playing a significant — but not always positive — role in this volatile mix.

PF's original statement of purpose borrowed the above phrase from a young Crass-inspired band with an odd name: Chumbawamba. Simple but telling, the quote suggests that, from its very beginning, PF sought to break down barriers, at least within the punk scene, to lessen the divisions that kept people apart. The reasoning was simple, inarguable: even as society's misfits, *we need each other*.

This was true even if we were simply seeking our power as individuals — but it was even more necessary in order to discover the far greater power we could have together. We helped each other to be powerful; simply by getting punks in the same room together, speaking the dreams of our hearts to others, perhaps for the first time, PF helped to bring those dreams closer to realization.

This was even more true given that the dream we were stretching toward was not simply personal empowerment, or some general social change, but revolution itself: a broader, deeper social transformation, "radical" in the sense of going to the roots of our terrible social divides and economic injustice.

This was powerful for me, as for the first time I found myself within an activist group that was at least trying to ask the fundamental questions — including around drugs and youth culture — and grope towards some answers.

At the same time, another version of "radical" was left largely unexamined: how to go to the roots of power relations, to build the power necessary to address these issues by drawing a mass of people together. By creating a group so clearly based in a punk underground, even as we were able to ask deeper and broader questions, in a way I was regressing from my earlier, more diverse community engagement, moving — ironically enough — towards a more isolated context.

In college town Montana, there had been no punk subculture to embrace in the early 1980s. Illusions of a "pure" punk counter-cultural enclave were ludicrous, as there were so few punks around — and misfits of every stripe tended to flock together as a result, to build our own bit of "power in the darkness." In DC, however, punk and other radical communities were large enough to survive on their own, to go their own way, and the resulting distance between different groups could be immense. The shortcomings — and irony — of this approach would soon become obvious.

As for straight edge, from the beginning PF sought to strike a balance that mixed both principled and practical concerns. Although our original statement of purpose rejected the idea of "excessive drugs and drinking as the only means of rebellion or escape," this anti-drug critique was neither absolutist — in that it didn't require complete abstinence — or exclusive, in that it was only one element of many in the mix of ideas that made up our group. In any case, being straight edge was never a requirement for PF membership.

Still, this was an advance in certain regards, as no other activist group I had been a part of even raised the issue. To be fair, some 60s radical groups such as the Black Panthers or the Progressive Labor faction of Students for a Democratic Society (SDS) had explicitly anti-drug stands, at least at points in their history.

Now, as then, however, most were under the sway of the siren song of "drugs-as-liberation," the romantic idea of chemically-assisted rebellion that stretched back to Bohemia, absinthe, and drunken gutter poets; an image cemented by the Beat Generation and offered up for mass consumption by the hippie movement.

Even if most counter-cultural groups that were effective at all quickly moderated their chemical excess, the idea was still left out there festering, the idea that recreational drug use was progressive, even liberating. Again, to be fair, perhaps drugs could play this role in certain limited circumstances, but the danger of crippling addictions and chemical-fueled illusions surely outweighed the benefits. In addition, as many a rueful 60s radical came to recognize, the romance of chemicals could lead to distracting wrangles with the law.

PF was attempting to provide a counter to this wrong-headed history. Our alliance with the Dischord Records community during "Revolution Summer" of 1985 helped to advance our work within the limited confines of the underground. Our meetings were a vibrant, diverse — if often chaotic — brew of generic leftism, heavily tinged with anarchism as well as a dash of revolutionary communism. Ideology was never our forte, but *action* on issues like nuclear war, Central America, South Africa, homelessness, hunger, and animal rights. In all of this, we went far beyond simple straight edge dogma.

When PF started its own communal house in January of 1987, straight edge was a fundamental part of its operation, as drugs and meat were explicitly banned from the premises. In part, this was a principled matter — taking the anti-drug idea a couple steps further — but there was also a strong practical aspect to it as well. After all, we were trying to create a free space for radical political work that would inevitably involve many teenagers, not of legal age to drink. To allow drinking or other drug use in that context was to invite issues with the police, and on terms that were highly disadvantageous to us as a group.

The wisdom of this approach was soon vindicated, as the infamous Meese Is A Pig poster campaign (largely coordinated from the Dischord and PF houses) brought scrutiny from not only local police but the FBI as well. As it happened, the illegal actions of the authorities soon boomeranged on them; the subsequent press firestorm proved embarrassing in the extreme to both Meese (who soon resigned as Attorney General) and the FBI who abruptly pulled back from its harassment.

Over the years, the drug-free aspect of PF House was sometimes debated — and occasionally flouted in various ways — but despite ongoing attention from the authorities over the fourteen years of its existence, our work was never significantly disrupted. Moreover, by creating a space that encouraged a certain anti-drug stance while never regulating what people did away from the house and the work, an equilibrium was created where all parts of the scene could work together on shared causes without a divide between straight edge adherents and drug-takers becoming significant. The relatively high profile of the group in the DC area also provided a clear example of how straight edge ideas could co-exist with collective political action, offering a quite different version of youth rebellion than Sixties — or Sid Vicious-related-punk — clichés.

In other words, PF had successfully danced around the limitations of straight edge as a barrier to collective action. But was this revolution? Yes, in certain ways. However, in other, deeper aspects? No, it wasn't, not yet, not really — because we were running the risk of trapping ourselves in the underground.

x X x

"Most of the murders in DC are not 'drug-killings' but 'money killings.' It's capitalism at its best. Drugs should be legalized. I'm not into any dope, I think it's stupid shit, but I know about economics, I know about people who are poor and I know about people wanting money quick. It's the American Way, isn't it?"

Ian MacKaye, 1990

The shortcomings of PF's counter-cultural approach were highlighted by our attempt to step outside the underground, through our engagement in the crisis of poverty, violence, and drugs erupting in DC's inner city. By the end of the 1980s, DC was the "murder capital of America," facing an unprecedented spike in killings and other violence generated by the arrival of a new drug — crack cocaine — in a desperate and despairing urban environment.

By this time, I had begun to do outreach and advocacy work with low-income seniors in areas of DC that were ground zero in not only the "war on drugs" but this exploding "drug war." I was not alone in this; numerous DC punks had begun to step towards direct engagement with these issues so close to home.

Straight edge would appear to have a lot to contribute to this discussion, at least for those who were willing to look past the surface, to not let our approach to drug policy be impaired by our dislike for drugs. As a group, PF didn't support drug use as a group, of course, but neither did we support the counter-productive laws that were sending thousands of inner-city youth to jail.

This stance was expressed not only in our direct service work, but also by a series of benefit shows headlined by Fugazi, including a "Freeze the Drug War" event with Sonic Youth, an inner-city fundraiser with Chumbawamba, and an anti-drug-war rally in Malcolm X Park, near — as were most of our benefits — to areas in Columbia Heights and Shaw where the violence was raging.

As the above words of Fugazi's Ian MacKaye suggest, our version of straight edge did not simply amount to counseling abstinence. We tried to look deeper, ask the uncomfortable questions of ourselves and of the system. The answers were not reassuring; to us, it seemed almost as if the system was set up to kill or criminalize an entire generation of inner city African-American youth.

This was not news to many inner city residents, some of whom muttered darkly that drugs were a form of genocide; rap superstars Public Enemy spoke of "One Million Bottle Bags" in a 1991 anti-drug rant.

Still, with shoddy schools, scant economic opportunity, and a sense of despair and abandonment in their neighborhoods, the only way for many of these kids towards the "American Dream" of material success was through illegal drugs. Indeed, it was the major economy in parts of the areas where I worked, and where PF was increasingly engaged delivering groceries, visiting seniors, handing out safe needle kits, and helping with tutoring programs for school kids.

As this suggests, PF had an ambivalent and reasonably humble stance, informed by our intimate engagement in such communities. Not all straight edge-related voices spoke with this tone, however. In the song "Firestorm," influential band Earth Crisis railed against the "poison" flooding the inner city, calling down righteous, almost biblical wrath on such communities: "a firestorm to purify the bane that society drowns in."

The rage expressed in "Firestorm" — and by other straight edge voices in less dramatic but just as real forms at the time — was well-intended and surely understandable. The social costs exacted by drugs were truly immense, with the inner city bearing the burden of being the dope market for the broader metro area. Seeing the cost up close and personal, I was bereft, straining at the edge of reason, almost lost in a sense of the terrible waste of drugs and the drug war.

At the same time, however, there was a certain lack of understanding in this knee-jerk straight edge response. This was not simply a moral question; powerful economic forces were driving youth to the street corners to sell drugs. There was a pathology at work, yes, but not simply of the inner city, but of our unequal, drug-demanding, money-mad society as a whole.

Clearly, jailing thousands upon thousands of inner city kids was not going to solve this problem; nor was a self-righteous call for "total war." In 1919, Billy Sunday had touted the revolutionary transformation that Prohibition was supposed to bring about. However, in the end, revolution was hard to find; the rise of bootlegging and organized crime was a more obvious result.

While Earth Crisis plainly wanted to "take back" the inner city, rising to the call of the immense suffering there, their approach ran the risk of simply fanning the flames of police repression and rampant incarceration without touching the root causes of the tragedy.

At the same time, for all our engagement with these issues close up, and our resultant more nuanced stance, PF had no real strategy to do anything but provide a bit of fuel for organizations serving the front line communities, and to make a largely rhetorical statement against the drug war.

This effort was not without value. Our experiences could help transform us and those whose lives we touched. But we were just band-aids, unable to shift the broader social forces of the Reagan-Bush-Clinton years, forces that were shredding "safety net" programs and initiatives of social uplift. How could we actually "turn the tide" (to use the words of Earth Crisis) and bring about the fundamental change needed?

The answer: we couldn't, not simply from one relatively insular community, reaching out from underground. The immensity of the forces we were engaged with, compared to the tools at our command, suggested a cosmic mismatch. Quite simply, we were just not up for the task... not alone, anyway.

Comfortable but all-too-contained in our underground circles, we had little hope of rallying the massive cross-class, cross-race movement necessary to shift the equation of economic inequality and racism, to turn the tide of inner city abandonment and tragic human waste.

This showed the flimsy nature of our "revolution." We were correct in recognizing this shortfall, but were perhaps not as willing to acknowledge its lesson: our desire to engage in a constructive, comprehensive way was bound to push us further out of our tidy subcultural nook into a tricky dance with broader society, with those different from us, even with the mainstream we disdained.

x X x

> *"Advocating the mere tolerance of difference is the grossest reformism. It is a total denial of the creative function of difference in our lives. Difference must be not merely tolerated, but seen as a fund of necessary polarities between which our creativity can spark like a dialectic... Community must not mean a shedding of our differences, nor the pathetic pretense that these differences do not exist... It is learning how to take our differences and make them strengths."*
>
> **Audre Lorde, Sister Outsider**

My growing understanding of the limits of the underground roughly coincided with punk's post-"Smells like Teen Spirit" explosion into the rock mainstream and, through that, into mainstream society in general.

It was in this context that Kurt Cobain made the insightful comment quoted at the outset of this essay. If perhaps a bit self-justifying, the truth of Cobain's words can't be denied: if we were serious about anything approaching revolution, how could we remain so divided, even within our little tribe?

I consciously chose the Cobain quote to press this issue, partly because — for obvious reasons — he is not highly regarded in straight edge circles. The truth is the truth, however, no matter the source. As always, we need to be careful, lest we listen to a far too narrow set of voices and find ourselves caught in an echo chamber that communicates little more than our own self-satisfaction.

This is a danger inherent in this very collection, as something as narrow as "hardcore punk" naturally limits the reach of the ideas contained in these pages, in this very essay. That self-limitation can be overcome only with sustained, thoughtful engagement outside our comfort zones, in open-ended conversation and mobilization with broader communities.

I have written an entire book about this challenge — *All The Power* — so won't tarry with it much here, except to focus once again on this critical point: if we are not careful, straight edge — or any other counter-cultural fixation — becomes a barrier to effective coalition and community building. While I still try to live a drug- and illusion-free life, I recognize that *how* we do something can be almost as important as *what* we do.

Put plainly, if we approach straight edge as something that makes us better than others, rather than as an aid to being fully aware and engaged in dialogue with other people and communities in order to be more effective in our learning and our work, we have lost the game. *Quite simply, we need to live in a way that doesn't cut us off from others, as without each other, revolution is impossible.*

This doesn't mean that we should turn away from our ideals or deny the obvious value of straight edge... but it does mean that we try to live this idea, to preach our gospel — as it were — with our actions, and not with self-righteous rhetoric.

A possible answer begins by clarifying what we do ourselves, and why we do it, while clearly distinguishing that from what we require of others. We need to explore our own reasons for being straight edge, and make sure they are sound, coming from a place of honest self-challenge rather than intoxicating self-righteousness.

Nor is just not taking drugs or not eating meat enough to qualify as "straight edge." No, we need to look more deeply, to see how other things can become addictive, blinding us to reality, shrouding us in illusions that keep us self-satisfied but ineffective. If straight edge is to be anything real in a revolutionary sense, at base *it is a commitment to truth, to being willing to grow.*

This is simple to say, and awfully hard to do — but if we don't build from the right foundation, heading toward the proper goal, how can we ever succeed? Straight edge helps us to have this foundation... but it can't end there.

Taken in this way, *straight edge is the delicate, demanding ballet that allows us to truly connect to others, the exact attitude that we will need in order to stay true to the process of revolution.*

This essay is a story of that dance, the process of opening up to life, to growth. If we are committed to revolution, we need to judge our activism, our straight edge lifestyles on whether they are effective in connecting us to build power together with other people. If they are not doing this, if they are just successful at making us feel superior, better than others, they are an enemy of transformation.

The revolutionary call of straight edge, then, as of punk, is that of a place to start, not an ending in itself. Its promise and possibility is to make us strong to go out into other communities, able to listen, learn, and grow, even as we try to bring broader social change. This is a process that is profoundly aided by the clarity and health that drug-free, meat-free lifestyles can bring — but it is not the victory itself.

From a solid base, however, we can hope to see how to be able to harness our personal power to connect with, touch, and build transforming community with other people, while taking them as they are. This is a path not towards purity, but balance; a way for straight edge to not be a barrier, but a *bridge* to community — and thus to revolution.

If we take straight edge in this best, most self-challenging, and open way, we can be present for the critical, creative spark which Audre Lorde rightly claims that the meeting of differences can bring. If we are really aware and attentive, we can do much a better job of reaching out, befriending those quite different from us, slowly building a broad, mass, majority movement for fundamental change from diverse, unexpected elements.

For me, this is the essence of what Positive Force DC — and its close ally, the We Are Family senior outreach network — now tries to do. Relationships are key, and particularly building them with people quite different from us. Let me repeat that: *relationships are key*. In the end, we absolutely, positively need each other.

Our differences can be our greatest strength, as Lorde says. If we are awake enough to be truly present for this moment and for each other, we will find much to learn as well as to teach.

In the end, we will discover that together — and *only together* — we can overcome.

About the Editor:

Gabriel Kuhn (born in Innsbruck, Austria, 1972) lives as an independent author and translator in Stockholm, Sweden. He received a Ph.D. in philosophy from the University of Innsbruck in 1996. His publications in German include the award-winning *'Neuer Anarchismus' in den USA: Seattle und die Folgen* (2008). His publications with PM Press include *Life Under the Jolly Roger: Reflections on Golden Age Piracy* (2010), *Sober Living for the Revolution: Hardcore Punk, Straight Edge, and Radical Politics* (editor, 2010), *Gustav Landauer: Revolution and Other Writings* (editor/translator, 2010), *Soccer vs. The State: Tackling Football And Radical Politics* (2011) and *Erich Mühsam: Liberating Society from the State and Other Writings* (editor/translator, 2011)

About PM Press:

PM Press was founded at the end of 2007 by a small collection of folks with decades of publishing, media, and organizing experience. PM co-founder Ramsey Kanaan started AK Press as a young teenager in Scotland almost 30 years ago and, together with his fellow PM Press co-conspirators, has published and distributed hundreds of books, pamphlets, CDs, and DVDs. Members of PM have founded enduring book fairs, spearheaded victorious tenant organizing campaigns, and worked closely with bookstores, academic conferences, and even rock bands to deliver political and challenging ideas to all walks of life. We're old enough to know what we're doing and young enough to know what's at stake.

We seek to create radical and stimulating fiction and non-fiction books, pamphlets, t-shirts, visual and audio materials to entertain, educate and inspire you. We aim to distribute these through every available channel with every available technology - whether that means you are seeing anarchist classics at our bookfair stalls; reading our latest vegan cookbook at the café; downloading geeky fiction e-books; or digging new music and timely videos from our website.

PM Press is always on the lookout for talented and skilled volunteers, artists, activists and writers to work with. If you have a great idea for a project or can contribute in some way, please get in touch.

PM Press
PO Box 23912
Oakland, CA 94623
www.pmpress.org

Friends of PM

These are indisputably momentous times – the financial system is melting down globally and the Empire is stumbling. Now more than ever there is a vital need for radical ideas.

In the year since its founding – and on a mere shoestring – PM Press has risen to the formidable challenge of publishing and distributing knowledge and entertainment for the struggles ahead. With over 75 releases to date, we have published an impressive and stimulating array of literature, art, music, politics, and culture. Using every available medium, we've succeeded in connecting those hungry for ideas and information to those putting them into practice.

Friends of PM allows you to directly help impact, amplify, and revitalize the discourse and actions of radical writers, filmmakers, and artists. It provides us with a stable foundation from which we can build upon our early successes and provides a much-needed subsidy for the materials that can't necessarily pay their own way. You can help make that happen--and receive every new title automatically delivered to your door once a month--by joining as a Friend of PM Press. Here are your options:

- **$25 a month:** Get all books and pamphlets plus 50% discount on all webstore purchases
- **$25 a month:** Get all CDs and DVDs plus 50% discount on all webstore purchases
- **$40 a month:** Get all PM Press releases plus 50% discount on all webstore purchases
- **$100 a month:** Sustainer - Everything plus PM merchandise, free downloads, and 50% discount on all webstore purchases

Your Visa or Mastercard will be billed once a month, until you tell us to stop. Or until our efforts succeed in bringing the revolution around. Or the financial meltdown of Capital makes plastic redundant. Whichever comes first.

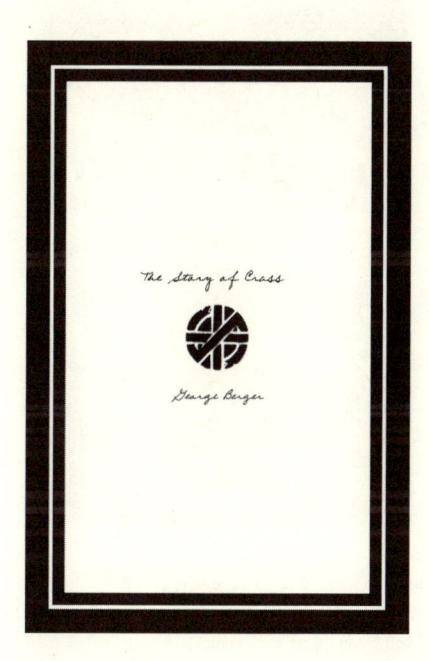

The Story of Crass

Crass was the anarcho-punk face of a revolutionary movement founded by radical thinkers and artists Penny Rimbaud, Gee Vaucher and Steve Ignorant. When punk ruled the waves, Crass waived the rules and took it further, putting out their own records, films and magazines and setting up a series of situationist pranks that were dutifully covered by the world's press. Not just another iconoclastic band, Crass was a musical, social and political phenomenon.

Commune dwellers who were rarely photographed and remained contemptuous of conventional pop stardom; their members explored and finally exhausted the possibilities of punk-led anarchy. They have at last collaborated on telling the whole Crass story, giving access to many never-before seen photos and interviews.

Reviews:

Lucid in recounting their dealings with freaks, coppers, and punks the band's voices predominate, and that's for the best. — **The Guardian UK**

Thoroughly researched...chockful of fascinating revelations...it is, surprisingly, the first real history of the pioneers of anarcho-punk. — **Classic Rock**

They (Crass) sowed the ground for the return of serious anarchism in the early eighties. — **Jon Savage, England's Dreaming**

About the Author:

George Berger has written for *Sounds*, *Melody Maker* and Amnesty International amongst others. His previous book was a biography of the Levellers: State Education/No University.

Product Details:

Authors: George Berger
Publisher: PM Press
Published: Sept. 2009
ISBN: 978-1-60486-037-5
Format: Paperback
Page Count: 304
Dimensions: 8 by 5
Subjects: Punk Rock, Anarchism

Vegan Freak: Being Vegan in a Non-Vegan World

Going vegan is easy, and even easier if you have the tools at hand to make it work right. In the second edition of this informative and practical guide, two seasoned vegans help you learn to love your inner vegan freak. Loaded with tips, advice, and stories, this book is the key to helping you thrive as a happy, healthy, and sane vegan in a decidedly non-vegan world that doesn't always get what you're about.

In this sometimes funny, sometimes irreverent, and sometimes serious guide that's not afraid to tell it like it is, you will:

- find out how to go vegan in three weeks or less with our "cold tofu method"
- discover and understand the arguments for ethical, abolitionist veganism
- learn how to convince family, friends, and others that you haven't joined a vegetable cult by going vegan
- get some advice on dealing with people in your life without creating havoc or hurt feelings
- learn to survive restaurants, grocery stores, and meals with omnivores
- find advice on how to respond when people ask you if you "like, live on apples and twigs."

In a revised and rewritten second edition, *Vegan Freak: Being Vegan in a Non-Vegan World* is your guide to embracing vegan freakdom. Come on, get your freak on!

Reviews:

Going vegan is the single most important thing you can do to live nonviolence and the abolition of animal exploitation in your everyday life. In this down-to-earth and entertaining guide, Bob and Jenna Torres not only convince you that you have to go vegan today, they also give you what you need to live as a healthy and happy vegan for the rest of your life. — **Gary L. Francione, Distinguished Professor of Law, Rutgers University**

Vegan Freak *is a witty, helpful, wall to wall look at going vegan. A must read for anyone who's felt like the only vegan-freak in the room.* — **Sarah Kramer, author of** *How It All Vegan*

About the Authors:

A recovering academic, Bob Torres holds a Ph.D. in Development Sociology from Cornell University. Co-host of Vegan Freak Radio, Bob has been quoted extensively in media pieces on veganism and animal rights. He maintains a web presence at www.bobtorres.net.

Jenna Torres has a BA in Spanish and a BS in Plant Science from Penn State University, and received her PhD from Cornell University in Spanish linguistics. She currently works at a small liberal arts university in upstate New York, and co-hosts Vegan Freak Radio, a podcast about life as a vegan in a very non-vegan world.

Product Details:

Authors: Bob and Jenna Torres
Publisher: PM Press/Tofu Hound Press
Published: Dec. 2009
ISBN: 978-1-60486-015-3

Format: Paperback
Page Count: 248
Dimensions: 8.5 by 5.5
Subjects: Vegetarianism, Activism